Global Poverty, Democracy and North-South Change

Global Poverty, Democracy and North-South Change

Steven Langdon

Garamond Press

Garamond Press,
67 Mowat Ave., Suite 144,
Toronto, Ontario M6K 3E3

garamond@web.net
www.garamond.ca/garamond/

Cover photographs courtesy International Development Research Centre, Ottawa

Editor:	Robert Clarke
Cover:	Robin Brass Studio
Typesetting:	True to Type

Canadian Cataloguing in Publication Data

Langdon, Steven
   Global Poverty, democracy and North-South change

Includes bibliographical references and index
ISBN 1-55193-016-1

1. Poverty - Developing countries. 2. Developing countries - Economic conditions. 3. Developing countries - Economic policy. 4. Developing countries - Politics and government. 5. Democracy - Developing countries.
I. Title.

HC59.7.L3185 1999   330.9172'4   C98-930993-2

The publishers gratefully acknowledge the financial support of the Canadian Studies Bureau, Department of Canadian Heritage, in the publication of this book.

Contents

Tables, Diagrams and Graphs

Preface

This book is dedicated to Sarah Jingyi, a baby girl left alone in a railway station in southern China when she was a few months old. For millions of children like her, the poverty shaping so many young lives is not a question of theory or history or abstract analysis. It is the real world, although it need not be.

In Africa, Latin America, Canada, and elsewhere, I have worked with people trying to change that reality and I have learned from them. This book is written to share that experience and in hopes that it will be helpful to the future of children like Sarah Jingyi. This is also my tribute to democracy — that fundamentally subversive belief that people are so essentially equal that they should all have a say in decisions.

Perhaps it is too idealistic and hopeful these days to work for a fairer world. Rich and powerful minorities often seem to dominate policy in their own interests. But research and experience convince me that different directions could be chosen. This potential for fairer choice does not mean it will come to pass —that takes people working together for change. But widening the policy agenda on particularly economic and social issues, as this book does, helps make social justice a viable and rational goal, not just a sentimental dream.

Our new daughter, Sarah Jingyi, is now in Canada and has found a new world. Her joy in it is a challenge to shape a fair world for all children.

* * * *

Writing a book is always a collaboration between past and future, between learning and advocacy, between initiative and co-operation. So an individual author incurs a collective obligation to all who have helped. The strengths of the book reflect these debts; its weaknesses the author must carry alone.

My thanks to my teachers and friends for their long-term support and insight, to my Southern colleagues for their determination and bravery, and to my students for helping with some of these ideas. The men and women with whom I worked at the International Development Research Centre, especially when I represented IDRC in Eastern and Southern Africa, were the finest of partners. The parliamentarians with whom I now work, from Ghana, Ethiopia, Mozambique, South Africa, Tanzania, Uganda, and Mexico, are committed, caring, intelligent — and energized by their societies. The institutions I work with — the Parliamentary Centre, Trent University, the Economic Development Institute of the World Bank, CIDA, Jackson & Associates — are represented by people with heart and with integrity.

Then there are the civil society leaders I have been so fortunate to have known, both South and North, women and men working in communities, movements, institutes, and unions for greater social and political justice. But most of all I thank those men and women in many countries of the world who have shared their hard experiences of reality with me — the fishing families on Lake Kafue in Zambia who loaned us a reed house in which to spend the night, the Swahili trader in Mombasa who showed me the documents from the Kenya mining project stolen away from him by government-multinational collusion, the farmer in Tanzania who explained to me the difference fast-growing sorghum had made to family food security, the northern Ghanaian woman near Walewale who outlined how a new well she had helped build and supervise was transforming life dramatically for female villagers.

This book has also been helped greatly by the late Bill Graf's probing comments and critique, and by the work of editor Robert Clarke. A grant from the Canadian Studies Bureau of the Department of Canadian Heritage greatly contributed to its production. My last acknowledgement is my most profound. Shirley Seward has sustained and improved this work with her intellectual contribution on every page, just as she transforms and enriches my life on every day.

S.L. 1998

PART I

The Basis of Global Poverty

CHAPTER 1

The North-South Divide

Elmina Castle stands by the beach and amidst the palm trees of Ghana's coast, its damp dungeons quiet. Now only tourists slip down through the narrow slits in its massive walls, tracing the footsteps of the eleven million slaves taken from western Africa between 1450 and 1870. Elmina's brooding presence, with its grim cannons and its strong defences, is an enduring reminder of how European traders and American plantation owners made millions from the suffering of African men and women.

Today, near Elmina, Ghanaian fishing boats set out in brightly coloured profusion. Women sell a wide variety of foodstuffs in the local market, and drivers head their trucks north to the thriving small-scale enterprises of Kumasi or out along the coast to pick up imports in fast-growing Accra. Ghana is seen as one of the success stories of Africa, with average real incomes per person growing some 2 per cent per year for most of the 1990s — a rate of yearly per capita income increase higher than Canada's.

Yet one-third of Ghana's families live in poverty. This is deep and serious poverty, conveyed by local-level studies such as that conducted in 1993 in parts of the Northern Region of the country. A joint Canadian-Ghanaian social survey found that some 70 per cent of households had run out of stored food before the end of the lean season (when no food crops are growing); more than 90 per cent of adults were illiterate; over 70 per cent did not have access to safe water; at least 50 per cent of children had not been immunized; and only 13 per cent of households were within one hour of a health clinic.[1]

Severe poverty marks many parts of what has come to be called "the South" — those countries in the world economy that are not part of the richer, industrialized grouping of the OECD (Organization for Economic Co-operation and Development), such as the United States, Japan, Germany, the United Kingdom, France, and Canada.

In Mexico, for example, the rate of extreme poverty in rural areas of the south is more than three times the national average. Some two-thirds of the

3

two million producers in seven south and central states (Chiapas, Guer-
rero, Hidalgo, Michoacan, Oaxaca, Puebla, and Veracruz) have five or less
hectares of cultivable land, most of it producing very low yields of maize.
The conditions of road infrastructure and access to drinking water are
extremely poor in these states. A 1995 study concluded that 36 per cent of
the rural population there are without access to unpolluted water and noted
that recent factors "have reduced margins in subsistence agriculture to the
point where farmers can no longer invest in their farms, and are increasingly obliged to adopt unsustainable farming practices just to survive."[2]

"The overall scenario that is emerging," writes Rajni Kothari of his
native India, "is one of a growing divide in the human community between
high consumption elite classes and the poor."[3] According to Kothari,
"There is one India which is rapidly progressing towards the twenty-first
century, with access to technology, information and resources. This India is
comprised of the urban and rural elite, the big farmers, the industrialists,
the bureaucrats, the executives and professionals, and the intelligentsia.
Though a small percentage of the population, they consume a large bulk of
its resources and own, control and allocate the remaining according to their
priorities and interests."

Kothari adds, "Then there are those who belong to the other India,
impoverished, malnutritioned, toiling day and night for survival. They pop-
ulate much of the country and are an overwhelming majority 'serving' the
first India through daily toil and drudgery (as do the slum-dwellers in the
cities and the landless in the villages), but have little say in the manner in
which their country, their resources and even their lives are governed."[4]

Widening inequalities are evident in many places. In China, for instance,
despite a past growth that is relatively broadly based, one township (Hong
Miao) in Shanghai averaged real industrial growth of 40.6 per cent per year
over five recent years,[5] while the Office of Poverty Alleviation of the State
Science and Technology Commission notes that there are now eighteen
designated "poor areas" in China in which environmental problems,
climate, and population distribution result in high levels of poverty.[6]

This growing global poverty is the subject of this book. What are its
dimensions, what are its characteristics and its roots, how can development
theories help respond to it? What social and political forces matter in
understanding poverty, and what policy priorities will help counter it? The
book is also about democracy — centring on the belief that empowerment
of the poor is at the heart of democracy, and that such empowerment is a
crucial step in overcoming global poverty.

My basic argument can be sharply put. This first chapter shows the continuing extensive growth of human poverty throughout the world. The
reasons for this reality rest in the historical impact of European-based
expansionism (chapter 2), in broad failures in past development theory

(chapter 3), and in mistaken policies followed in the South in the rural sector (chapter 4), as well as in urban industry (chapter 5) and macroeconomic strategy (chapter 6). In most Southern countries this combination of factors has shaped state systems that have served narrow minorities, worsened gender and other inequalities, and led in many cases to economic and social collapse (chapter 7). Policies to spread impersonal market forces throughout the world have not been able to overcome this social distress.

New community-based movements in various countries, though, are now finding new "empowerment-oriented" policy approaches to pursue in newly democratizing governance settings, policies that provide hope of seriously countering the prevalence of poverty (chapter 8). The book's conclusion is that most Canadians will also see a better world for themselves and their communities in this countervision (chapter 9).

1: The Dimensions of Global Poverty

International poverty can be thought of as a mosaic of social elements. Any comprehensive analysis must stress, as a core concern, gender inequalities: the unequal access to assets, opportunities, and status that women experience, compared to men, in most of the world, and particularly in many Southern countries. This wide-ranging differentiation interacts with severe social disparities in many rural parts of the South, where most households live. Small minorities in many countries control huge shares of productive land, with hundreds of millions of people squeezed onto small plots or left landless. Environmental pressures, often driven by external forces of economic expansionism, commonly undercut the potential of even these small rural land and other resource bases that remain for the poor. In the cities, privileged economic opportunities based on superior educational access or regulated favouritism accentuate the inequalities, shaping a small class that benefits from enriching urban assets while millions of the poor crowd into bleakly makeshift slums.

In recent years broad statistics have begun to capture these dimensions of extreme social division. Under the prodding of United Nations agencies, simple income measures have been given more depth and have been combined with health and educational measures, anthropometric review of the height and weight of children to detect malnutrition, analysis of economic activity opportunities, and some consideration of assets owned.[7]

What the use of such careful measures shows is a dramatic and stark contrast in the world. Some countries, such as Norway, Sweden, or the Netherlands in Western Europe, have extensive programs aimed at equity for women and children (such as in Sweden), for outlying regions (especially in Norway), and for workers displaced by trade changes (such as in the Netherlands), conditions that have made poverty a rare characteristic. There are even Southern countries that have implemented approaches that have made a difference. In South Korea, for instance, a social mobilization effort called the Saemaul Undong Movement (or "new village movement") has brought in a rural land reform and human resource development that have helped to achieve "both fast and equitable growth."[8]

But many of the largest Southern countries have seen levels of poverty increase in recent years — as we have seen in the experiences of India and Mexico (two of these larger countries). Brazil, the largest Latin American country, with its 160 million people, also shows growing poverty. "Measures of poverty," a 1995 analysis of Brazil concluded, "encompass many dimensions including low income, hunger, and poor health, just to name a few." The study stressed that while mechanisms had been at work to reduce poverty in Brazil in the 1960-80 period, this process had been reversed in the 1980s and the number of poor rose by 1 million to about 24 million Brazilians.[9]

These sorts of trends led the relatively conservative analysts of the World Bank — using a wide range of expenditure, health, nutrition, educational, and access-to-opportunity measures — to their 1991 assessment that well over a billion people in the Southern countries had to be considered to be living in real poverty: 800 million of them in Asia, 180 million in Africa, and the rest in Latin America.[10]

Most of the poor were in rural areas, like the Embu families in Kenya (mostly led by women) who had been pushed out to "marginal" farming areas by growing land concentration and population expansion in an environment with limited rainfall,[11] or the peasant producers in Zimbabwe's Gokwe region, with its poor infrastructure and uncertain climate.[12] But many were in urban settings, like the children working to learn crafts in the old towns in Nepal, or the families crowding into slums on the steep slopes of the hills in Rio de Janeiro, or the new migrants streaming into the exploding slums of Johannesburg.

Today's global poor have many faces, and they fight the battle to survive in many different circumstances.

2: A Profile of Poverty

A broad profile of poverty and where it is concentrated can begin with some simple measures of absolute deprivation and of extreme inequality. Table 1 provides an outline of varied national situations, showing percentages of populations in extreme poverty (living in households in which consumption equivalents per day are below what $1 per person could buy in the United States), shares of national income for the lowest 40 per cent of

Table 1:1: Poverty & Inequality Measures in Southern Countries, 1990-97

Country	Extreme Poverty % (under$1/day)*	Lower 40% share#	Highest 10% share	Gini Index	per capita $GNP-PPP*
AFRICA					
Nigeria	31.1	12.9 (1993)	31.4	45.0	$ 880
Ethiopia	33.8	. . . (1996)	. . .	44.2	510
South Africa	23.7	9.1 (1993)	47.3	58.4	7490
Tanzania	10.5	17.8 (1993)	30.2	38.1	640
Kenya	50.2	10.1 (1992)	47.7	57.5	1110
Uganda	50.0	17.1 (92/3)	33.4	40.8	1050
Ghana	. . .	19.9 (1992)	27.3	33.9	1790
Ivory Coast	17.7	. . . (1995)	. . .	38.0	1640
Zimbabwe	41.0	10.3 (1990)	46.9	56.8	2280
Zambia	84.6	. . . (1996)	. . .	52.4	880
Niger	61.5	19.3 (1992)	29.3	36.1	920
Senegal	54.0	10.5 (1991)	42.8	54.1	1670
ASIA					
China	22.2	15.3 (1995)	30.9	41.5	3570
India	52.5	22.2 (1994)	25.0	29.7	1650
Indonesia	11.8	20.4 (1995)	28.3	34.2	3450
Pakistan	11.6	21.3 (1991)	25.2	31.2	1590
Philippines	28.6	15.5 (1994)	33.5	42.9	3670
Nepal	50.3	19.1 (95/6)	29.8	36.7	1090
Malaysia	5.6	12.9 (1989)	37.9	48.4	10920
THE AMERICAS					
Brazil	23.6	8.2 (1995)	47.9	60.1	6240
Mexico	14.9	11.9 (1992)	39.2	50.3	8120
Colombia	7.4	9.9 (1995)	46.9	57.2	6720
Peru	49.4	14.1 (1994)	34.3	44.9	4390
Ecuador	30.4	14.3 (1994)	37.6	46.6	4820
Costa Rica	18.9	12.8 (1996)	34.7	47.0	6410
Honduras	46.9	10.5 (1996)	42.1	53.7	2200
Guatemala	53.3	7.9 (1989)	46.6	59.6	3840
OECD					
Canada	. . .	20.4 (1994)	23.8	31.5	21860
Great Britain	. . .	20.3 (1991)	. . .	32.4	20520
United States	. . .	15.3 (1994)	28.5	40.1	28740

Source: World Bank, *World Development Report, 1997*, Washington, 1997, tables 1, 5 in World Development Indicators, pp. 214-15, 222-23. Supplemented by 1997 updating from World Bank Web Site, using revised Deininger and Squire data set, and from *World Development Report, 1998*.
* These are "purchasing power parity" measures of average per capita GNP in U.S. dollars, and of poverty-level living standards. They diverge significantly from usual GNP per capita measures and give a better indication of relative living standards (on average) across countries.
# The date indicates when the detailed survey was completed for these next three columns.

Diagram 1:1: Gini Index Concept

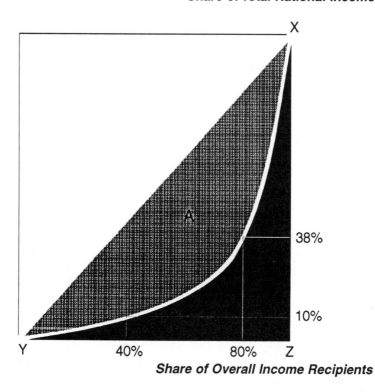

Share of Total National Income

Share of Overall Income Recipients

Gini index is the percentage "A" represents of the triangle, XYZ. "A" is the area within the curve, XY, which represents the share of national income received by a given percentage of income recipients. Eg., point "d" on the curve shows the lowest 40% of income recipients received 10% of the country's overall national income; point "e" shows the bottom 80% received 38% of national income. This distribution is quite close to the pattern in Kenya, giving a Gini Index of 57.5. That is, the area "A" makes up 57.5% of the total triangle area XYZ.

the population compared to the highest 10 per cent of the population, Gini index numbers of relative equality (where 100 represents complete inequality and 0 represents complete equality), and "purchasing power parity" (PPP) measures of average per capita GNP.[13] This table covers the largest Southern countries for which data are available.

The table shows the impact of high inequality. It is true that lower average incomes in most Sub-Saharan African countries lead to high proportions of people in poverty in that region, but particularly great inequalities lead to especially high poverty levels in countries such as Kenya, Zambia, and Senegal. Very low average incomes also lead to high poverty levels in Asia (India and Nepal), but higher inequalities, as in the Philippines also shape higher poverty than in lower-income Pakistan. Extremely wide income disparities in Latin America also lead to much more incidence of poverty in countries with higher average incomes (like Brazil, Peru, and Guatemala) than in poorer African countries like Tanzania.

Taking as signs of major poverty and living-standard inequality, one of a) extreme poverty levels over 25 per cent, b) a Gini index over 50, c) an income share below 10 per cent for the bottom 40 per cent, or d) an income share above 40 per cent for the top 10 per cent — then 9 of 12 African, 3 of 7 Asian, and 7 of 8 Latin American cases show such signs. These cases include the three largest African cases in Table 1, one of the two largest Asian cases, and the three largest Latin American cases. Altogether, these seven countries include over 1.6 billion people.

The probing of poverty should also focus on the young, because it is among small children that some of the clearest indicators emerge of the physical and social consequences of being poor; and the economic consequences of child poverty are particularly obvious. As Partha Dasgupta, professor of economics at Cambridge University in the United Kingdom, has noted, "Much detailed evidence has been amassed in recent years to the effect that increases in nutrition and health status are associated with increases in productivity. Similarly, primary education has repeatedly been shown to be one of the most productive investments that a poor nation can make."[14]

Thus it is that UNICEF, the UN agency that concentrates its attention on the well-being of children, has developed a package of four basic indicators to permit ongoing monitoring of poverty among children and their mothers. The first focus is on early childhood mortality, measured in terms of the death rate of children per 1,000 live births in the first five years of life. The second indicator is the percentage of children under five who are suffering from malnutrition (using weight and height measures matched to age for children throughout the world). Thirdly, UNICEF assesses the percentage of children enrolled in primary school, and finally it presents the maternal death rate per 100,000 live births.

The UNICEF indicators provide basic data for a broad profile of global poverty. Table 1:2 reports the statistics on these four key poverty measures and fills out the dramatic and extensive inequalities that mark the globe. Taking several OECD countries (including Canada) as a base, analysis shows that in those countries childhood death has become rare (below 1 per cent of births), basic education is near-universal, child malnutrition has faded, and maternal mortality rates are low. But in most of the Southern countries the absolute conditions of life for most people are very different,

Table 1:2: Child-Related Poverty Data by Country, 1995

Country	Mortality rate under 5	% under-5 underweight	% in primary school	Maternal mortality rate (1990)
AFRICA				
Nigeria	191 of 1000	36	59	1000 of 100,000
Ethiopia	195	48	21	1400
Congo (Zaire)	207	34	56	870
South Africa	67	9	96	230
Tanzania	160	29	64	770
Kenya	90	23	84	610
Ghana	130	27	70	740
Ivory Coast	150	24	48	810
Zimbabwe	74	16	91	570
Zambia	203	28	77	940
Niger	320	36	27	1200
Senegal	130	22	45	1200
OECD COUNTRIES				
Sweden	5	—	99	6
Canada	8	—	97	6
U.S.	10	–	100	12
ASIA				
China	47	16	95	95
India	115	53	68	570
Bangladesh	115	67	82	850
Indonesia	75	35	91	650
Pakistan	137	38	66	340
Nepal	114	46	69	1500
Philippines	53	30	90	280
South Korea	9	—	93	130
THE AMERICAS				
Brazil	53	6	91	220
Mexico	32	14	98	110
Ecuador	40	17	94	150
Costa Rica	16	2	87	55
Guatemala	60	27	70	200
Bolivia	105	16	89	650
Nicaragua	60	12	79	160
Haiti	124	28	26	1000

Source: UNICEF, *The Progress of Nations*, 1997, Statistical Profiles.

right from childhood. Perhaps the most staggering impact of poverty as revealed by the data is that all three major Southern regions have countries in which well over 10 per cent of the children die before they are five years old. The level is as high as 32 per cent in Niger in the African Sahel, 19 per cent in oil-endowed Nigeria, and over 20 per cent in Zambia, with its extreme inequalities. In Pakistan almost 14 per cent of young children die despite average incomes higher than in Bangladesh, India, or Nepal (where child mortality rates are lower — though still close to 12 per cent). The near-13 per cent levels in Haiti and 10.5 per cent in Bolivia show that child-hood death is still prevalent in parts of the Americas.

With respect to these measures, average national income levels clearly do matter. More young children survive, and escape malnutrition, in countries that have achieved higher average incomes — as comparison of lower-income Ethiopia shows in Africa against the mortality and malnutrition data from higher-income Zimbabwe. The same reality is apparent when we compare lower-income Bangladesh and Nepal in Asia against the higher-income Philippines — and contrast Ecuador and Guatemala in Latin America against higher-income Mexico. But the child poverty data can also lead to other insights, revealing a grimmer picture than the broad outline in Table 1. First, in absolute terms, it is tragic to see that in the 1990s over one-third of children under the age of five suffer from malnutrition, in the three largest African countries (Nigeria, Congo-Zaire, and Ethiopia), and in four of the five largest Asian countries (Bangladesh, India, Indonesia, and Pakistan). Some six million youngsters under five died in these seven countries in 1995.

Second, it is striking and depressing that some Southern countries, despite major advances in average per capita incomes, show child poverty indicators that are clearly higher than other significantly lower-income countries. South Africa, for instance, with per person PPP equivalents of $5,030, has childhood mortality rates (67 per 1,000) that exceed those of the Philippines (53), China (47), and Ecuador (40) — all of which have lower income levels. This situation reflects South Africa's massive racial inequalities which have left whites with "personal incomes per capita of about 9.5 times those of Africans."[15] The poorer performance of Mexico and Brazil, on childhood and maternal mortality and on malnourishment, compared to Costa Rica (across roughly similar income levels per capita) points out the poorer poverty record of the two largest Latin American countries too, based on the very low percentage of income going to the lowest 40 per cent of the population (some 7 and 9 per cent respectively). The same point can even be made in the context of the OECD countries, where U.S. child mortality rates are double those in Sweden, and maternal mortality rates are significantly higher, despite a greater U.S. average income per capita.

A third point that deserves emphasis is that some countries in a variety of income categories have clearly paid greater attention to poverty concerns, which has resulted in better measures of child poverty performance. In Asia, China's record stands out with lower childhood mortality (47 per 1,000), less malnutrition (16 per cent), and low levels of maternal mortality (95 per 100,000) — all measures that not only exceed higher-income countries such as Indonesia and the Philippines but also show that China outperformed Brazil in Latin America on two of three indicators (despite much higher average Brazilian income levels). The levels for Zimbabwe are better, too, than for the economies of the Ivory Coast and Senegal at the same general level of per capita income.

One of the most striking revelations of the general poverty profile is the remarkable extent of childhood malnutrition in the Asian context, a condition that calls for further probing of the contours of global poverty. Bangladesh, India, and Nepal show half of their children under age five suffering significant malnutrition, with high mortality rates. The same holds even more true for Pakistan. UNICEF's data show below-average performance on childhood malnutrition for many other Asian countries, including Malaysia, Thailand, the Philippines, and Indonesia. As UNICEF analysts conclude, "Almost as surprising as these figures is the fact that they are so little investigated."[16]

Comparing the Asian indicators with the African, we can see that the reasons for the much higher Asian measures do not seem to lie in better agricultural performance in Africa (if anything, the contrary has been true); nor are there fewer income inequalities in Africa (again the evidence suggests the opposite). Rather, three key dividing points appear to be evident in child development in Asia compared to Africa:

a) Low birth weights are much more common in Asia (affecting one-third to one-half of babies born in India and Bangladesh, compared to one-sixth in Africa) — in large part because most women in South Asia gain only half the weight during pregnancy of their African counterparts.

b) Frequency of disease in young children is also greater in Asia, because of poorer conditions of hygiene (related to population densities of 230 per square kilometre, 10 times the African level, reflecting overcrowded Asian urban slums);

c) Faltering of Asian infant growth rates shows up strongly around the fourth month when, despite continued breast-feeding, Asian women appear not to be receiving sufficient nutrition to rely exclusively on breast-feeding and at the same time they are not able to shift to complementary foods early enough. "In other words, many children in South Asia may need complementary food earlier but receive it later."[17]

These points take our discussion back to the central and overriding issue of gender inequality — the core element of the poverty mosaic. The conclusion of the UNICEF analysts is blunt, and absolutely crucial to any new policy thrust against poverty. They stress that "the exceptionally high rates of malnutrition in South Asia are rooted deep in the soil of inequality between men and women." In general, "The women of sub-Saharan Africa, and particularly poor women, have greater opportunities and freedoms than the women of South Asia ... a difference captured not so much in the statistics of literacy or age at first marriage, as in the evidently greater opportunities for social interaction and independent behaviors."

Noting that some 50 per cent of African women are involved in economic activity outside the home, compared to 25 per cent in South Asia, the analysts conclude "This lack of freedom for women in many of the poor communities of South Asia ... restricts transmission of new knowledge about health matters and child care, damages the self-esteem of women, and induces a kind of crushed dependency on the husband.... And the quality of child care suffers along with the quality of women's own lives."[18] Women favour the role of providing food for their husbands, even during their own pregnancies. They therefore suffer heavily from iron-deficiency anaemia; and they do not provide food equitably for themselves even to maintain the quality of breast-feeding.

Poverty, considered in this multifaceted way, then, is all too heavily common in almost all the larger countries of South Asia (especially India, Bangladesh, and Pakistan) and Africa (Nigeria, Zaire, and Ethiopia,) and has also been growing in the larger countries of Latin America (Mexico and Brazil). In Asia, this large-scale poverty has been associated with the particularly dominated position that has constrained the lives and options of women; and this has also been an important factor stressed in the context of Mexico, where women have been described as being "extremely subordinated to male authority."[19]

What this means is that countering poverty is, above all, about empowerment for women, about empowerment for children, and about overcoming the gender inequalities that have crippled the potential of so many lives for far too long. National inequality extremes are important factors, and so too are differences in average income levels, but the impact of gender inequality is particularly crucial within this complex mosaic.

3: Themes in the Analysis of Poverty

The inequality of women thus represents a fundamental and central theme to be stressed in probing the causes, contours, and counters to global poverty. This cross-cutting inequality interacts with rural and urban social inequalities. It is rooted in deep divisions in access to assets and status in rural areas, and in harsh impediments for many that block urban opportunities for education and incomes. As well, environmental pressures, often driven by external forces of economic expansionism, commonly undercut the potential of even the limited resource and income options that remain for the poor.

The classic symptoms of class divisions, shaped by history and socioeconomic structures, show up especially in the character of much rural Southern poverty. A great percentage of the poor in Africa live in rural areas (80 per cent in Ghana, 92 per cent in Madagascar, 96 per cent in Ivory Coast, 99 per cent in Malawi).[20] The same is also true in many parts of Asia. These rural poor are sometimes landless labourers and small-plot tenant or share-crop farmers, people whose lack of land leaves them much worse off than other farmers, even when high-yielding seeds become available, because they are less able to afford the fertilizer inputs that often complement the new seed technology. Sometimes they are peasants in areas of low and irregular rainfall, like the Embu women near Mount Kenya, relying on food crops grown mainly for their own subsistence. Or they are pastoralists in remote areas such as the African Sahel, people who rely on their herds in places where drought has been a recurring phenomenon. They may even be export cash-crop producers, facing circumstances of long-term falling prices, state tax or marketing board levies, or the development of cheaper substitute products that markedly reduce revenues.

These rural roots of poverty can be strongly reinforced by environmental factors. In Honduras in Latin America, for instance, Stonich traces how in the south of the country the environmental consequences of cattle and shrimp-based development strategies (driven by U.S. demand factors and enterprises) have concentrated landholdings, leaving 34 per cent of area families landless and another 21 per cent on farms of less than one hectare. Meanwhile eight large shrimp concessions took the rights to 69 per cent of coastal areas, where they cleared mangrove swamps and displaced local artisanal fishing families.[21] Similar environmental pressures have reduced rural living standards and generated poverty in particular cases in India, Thailand, Guatemala, Costa Rica, Malaysia, Pakistan, and Madagascar.[22]

African women, despite their fuller participation in economic activities, have seen environmental inequality with men restrict their abilities to make ecology-related decisions important to maintaining longer-term sustainability of viable peasant farming systems. Women have, for instance, been restricted from valuable tree-planting in the Embu area of Kenya because of female land-rights limitations;[23] and they have also been restricted from selling cattle in timely response to changing environmental conditions in cattle-grazing areas of Zimbabwe, because their migrant husbands control all cattle sales.[24] In both cases the failure to adopt sustainable environmental practices increased poverty for the household.

Often, regional imbalances have added to this rural and/or environmentally based poverty. Thus northern Ghana has been much less advantaged than the more prosperous south. More mountainous areas of China have been the more remote and difficult areas for farming improvements. And the northeast of Brazil became the source from which many of the poor migrants sought out the harsh slums of Rio de Janeiro.

The poor have not just stayed in rural areas. Rural pressures have pushed many to the rapidly expanding cities of the South, leading to visible urban inequalities. Formal employment has expanded slowly in Southern cities, and many people have had to seek opportunities in the "informal sector" — in the "jua kali" (or "hot sun"), as Macharia calls it in Nairobi — the unregulated sector, with skills learned on the job, often undercapitalized, with little machinery and a wide variety of roles, from retail hawking to producing simple cooking stoves. Macharia shows the serious economic losses that can be imposed on these vulnerable people when those in power try to restrict them for political or economic reasons. There has been a tendency in the literature to stress the potential and role of the informal sector, but Macharia shows that there is also a dramatic vulnerability there when the state acts against the sector.[25]

That continuing vulnerability is the crux of the poverty reality for many people of the South. While levels of poverty are dramatic enough, it is also the case that many people live on the edge of being poor. A slim harvest, illness, or loss of an economic opportunity can quickly drop a household into poverty. A careful examination of household panels in the Ivory Coast over three years by Grootaert and Kanbur shows this dramatically. Their review reveals marked increases in both poverty and the seriousness of poverty in the Ivory Coast in the second half of the 1980s, but perhaps the most interesting finding from their panel analysis is the fluidity of poverty lines for households. While some households did shift upwards in 1988 (6.3 per cent of total households) and in 1987 (8.4 per cent), their analysis shows that a much larger percentage of households experienced downward mobility into the low-income levels of the poor and the very poor (24.5 per cent of total households in 1988, and 18.6 per cent in 1987).[26] Some one-third of poor households became very poor in 1988, and fully one-quarter of non-poor households became poor.

The key message here is uncertain vulnerability among people, given that so large a proportion of non-poor households can so easily drop into that condition of poverty. It is not just poverty, but the risk of poverty, that marks life for the majority in most Southern countries.

4: Conclusion

From India to Mexico, from Nigeria to Indonesia, from northern Ghana to southern Honduras, babies die young, children suffer from malnutrition, and overcrowded slums make conditions of hygiene and health worse than ever. Despite high average individual incomes and extensive facilities in countries such as Canada, the United States, and Britain, most of the world lives a much harsher and more restricted existence. The rest of this book will analyse the roots of this reality, the forces that perpetuate it, and the ways to counter such poverty.

At one level this global poverty represents a profound moral crisis for new generations that for the first time are growing up with spaceship pictures of the one globe we all inhabit. How can a "one-world" view ever justify the gross social differences that exist in our integrated global system?

At another level, our political and economic connections internationally may mean that many see global poverty as a fundamental threat. Whether it is nightmare scenarios of incurable viruses sweeping out of overcrowded slums, or visions of desperate terrorists armed with rogue nuclear weapons, the injustices of mass poverty, some may fear, will contribute to future political and social instability.

But at the most important level, global poverty imposes an impetus towards global social justice. The worldwide drive towards greater democracy and empowerment for the poor — increasingly led by Southern movements for change — is bound to challenge and transform our world in the years ahead. As the documented profile of poverty suggests, that drive towards justice will have widespread, diverse, and strongly based roots. The movement for gender equity will be at its core and will ultimately challenge the entrenched privileges of the small, rich minorities who now own and control so much of the international economy. As diversity, opportunity, and participation replace elite controls, privileges, and restrictions, people have the potential to bring about a creative transformation of the entire world.

Notes

1 See Jackson and Associates and G.A.S. Development Associates, "Norrip II Baseline Study," February 1993, pp.5-7.

2 See World Bank, "Mexico-Agricultural Development and Rural Poverty Project, Project ID MXPA7711," July 28, 1995.

3 Rajni Kothari, *Poverty* (London: Zed Books, 1995), p.29.

4 Ibid., p.146.

5 See Peng Zhenwei, "Market Towns in Metropolitan Shanghai," in *Small Towns and Regional Development*, ed. You-tien Hsing, Centre for Human Settlements, University of British Columbia, Vancouver, 1992, p.94.

6 See State Science and Technology Commission of the People's Republic of China, "Proposal—System for Co-ordinating Development of Technology and Environment in China's Poor Areas," Bejing, 1992, pp.2-3.

7 See World Bank, *World Development Report, 1997*, Washington, 1997, pp.205-10.

8 Ponna Wignaraja, ed., *New Social Movements in the South* (London: Zed Books, 1993), p.14.

9 World Bank, "Brazil—Poverty Assessment," report no. 14323, June 27, 1995.

10 Ibid.

11 See Susan Joekes et al., "Gender, Environment and Population," in *Development and Environment*, ed. Dharam Ghai (Oxford: Blackwell Publishers, 1994), pp.148-49.

12 See E.D. Breslin, "U.S. AID, the State, and Food Insecurity in Rural Zimbabwe: The Case of Gokwe," *Journal of Modern African Studies*, vol. 32, no.1 (1994), pp.95-96.

13 There are differences in what given amounts of money can purchase in different countries in terms of similar-type goods and services. Calculation of "purchasing power parities" (PPP) for average per capita GNP measures attempt to take these differences into cross-country comparisons of living standards. For a discussion of some of the complexities involved in doing this, see World Bank, *World Development Report, 1997*, pp.251, 254.

14 Partha Dasgupta, "Commentary: National Performance Gaps," in UNICEF, *The Progress of Nations* (New York: United Nations, 1996).

15 See Peter Fallon and L.A. Pereira de Silva, "South Africa: Economic Performance and Policies," discussion paper no. 7, Southern African Department, World Bank, Washington, 1994.

16 See Vulmiri Ramalingaswami, Urban Jonsson, and Jon Rohde, "Commentary: The Asian Enigma," in UNICEF, *Progress of Nations*.

17 Ibid.

18 Ibid.

19 Joekes et al., "Gender, Environment and Population," p.155.

20 World Bank, *Adjustment in Africa: Reforms, Results, and the Road Ahead* (New York: Oxford University Press, 1994), p.166.

21 See S. Stonich, "Struggling with Honduran Poverty: The Environmental Consequences of Natural Resource-Based Development and Rural Transformations," *World Development*, vol. 20, no. 3 (1992), pp.385-99.

22 See articles by Colchester, Gadgil and Guha, Ghimire, and Utting in *Development and Environment*, ed. Ghai.

23 See Joekes et al., "Gender, Environment and Population," pp.153-54.

24 Jessica Vivian, "NGOs and Sustainable Development in Zimbabwe," in *Development and Environment*, ed. Ghai, pp.179-80.

25 Kinuthia Macharia, "Slum Clearance and the Informal Sector in Nairobi," *Journal of Modern African Studies*, vol. 30, no.2 (1992), pp.221-36.

26 C. Grootaert and R. Kanbur, "The Lucky Few amidst Economic Decline: Distributional Change in Cote d'Ivoire," *Journal of Development Studies*, vol. 31, no. 4 (1995), pp.603-19.

CHAPTER 2

Political Economy, Colonialism and Poverty

There is, says Rajni Kothari, "a growing amnesia towards the poor everywhere."[1] Clearly, the widespread dimensions of human poverty do not justify this neglect. Yet Kothari may be right about the decreased attention given in recent years to analysis of the development concerns of poorer people in Southern countries.

A lament that may help explain why this is so comes from Michael Edwards, of Save the Children Fund: "Why is so much that is said, written and spent on development having so little effect on the problems it seeks to address?" His answer: "Practitioners do not write, and theoreticians remain in the abstraction of their theories."[2]

Building on that challenge from Kothari and Edwards, then, this chapter sets out a broad political economy framework for examining the poverty mosaic — and attempts to use that framework to understand the historical European-based expansionist processes that have contributed to the deep inequalities in many Southern countries. Chapter Three reviews development theories, with poverty analysis a central focus.

1: A Political Economy Approach

"Political economy is one of the most complex and contested concepts in social science."[3] This means it provides a broad and well-debated framework within which much useful analysis can be undertaken in development studies. Drawing on the work of Karl Polanyi, with his emphasis on how all economic processes of material want-satisfaction are ultimately imbedded in varying forms of social and political institutions,[4] the approach stresses how economic, social, and political aspects of analysis must be integrated through a careful understanding of the differing historical institutions within a given country, and how these institutions become transformed over time.

Thus in the centralized authoritarian empire of the Dahomey Kingdom in West Africa in the eighteenth century, the historical institutions in place led to the redistribution of material goods by the king as the main means of economic allocation.[5] Among the Pokot in East Africa, reciprocal gift-giving dominated economic allocation of cattle as recently as 1960.[6] And "the great transformation" that Polanyi traced in 18th and 19th century Britain comprised the way in which the self-regulating market mechanism, depending on supply and demand, came to dominate economic allocation increasingly free of any social or political constraints. This was a broad pattern of change that ultimately spurred social movements and political regulations to put some controls on the unconstrained operation of the market (such as health regulations, child labour, and minimum wage laws).[7]

The political economy concept stresses the dynamics that shape and reshape these historical institutions. These dynamics emerge especially through the social partitioning associated with various political and economic institutional forms. "Political economy," as Cox puts it, "is concerned with the historically constituted frameworks or structures within which political and economic activity takes place. It stands back from the apparent fixity of the present to ask how the existing structures came into being and how they may be changing, or how they may be induced to change."[8] The question is: What social forces, economic pressures, and political conflicts are at work within the institutions of any given political economy, and how might they be expected to bring about change? In short, political economy starts from the assumption that conflicts or contradictions can emerge within the context of given historical institutions, given changing social partitioning, and can generate pressures for broader change.

Given these historical but potentially fluid conditions, global economic and political forces play a crucial role. These international pressures have been powerful historically (as Sandbrook, among many others, has noted in the African context).[9] And Cox, Rosenau, and Gill all stress responses to growing forces of globalization as likely to be at the heart of any change in political economy in the years ahead among Southern countries.[10]

In analysing political economies, we need also to focus on a further point — the key role in continuity of institutions (and in their eventual challenge) played by ideological-cultural factors. Antonio Gramsci emphasized the major significance of "the hegemony of a fundamental social group over a number of subordinate groups" — by which he meant that fundamental group's ability to "impose itself, to propagate itself throughout the whole social sphere, causing, in addition to singleness of economic and political purpose, an intellectual and moral unity as well."[11] Gill has suggested that Gramsci's view of countermovements against this broad hegemony of ideas

Diagram 2:1: A Political Economy Framework Sketch

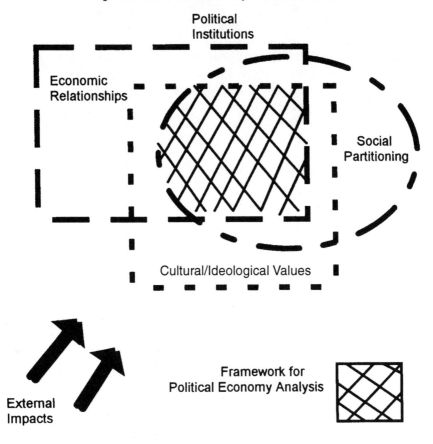

is a crucial part of the notion of dialectical reactions to the institutions imposed by the world system.[12]

Diagram 2:1 sketches this concept of overlapping social, economic, cultural, and political relationships, all interacting in a context of inherited historical traditions and changing external connections. The area of intersection in the diagram (marked) of the four dimensions of a political economy (the economic, political, social, and cultural) represents the historical-institutional setting within which dynamic forces interact in conjunction with external impacts to bring about broad changes.

Gill also suggests that the political economy approach appropriate in the 1990s should consider the political sphere to be wider than just the state and to include such elements of a "broader civil society" as women's groups, trade unions, churches, business enterprises, and political parties. Schuurman characterizes civil society institutions as increasingly including the rise of "new movements," seeing these as assertions often against global power and as important elements in building a democratic countermovement (in the case of Chile, for instance, playing a key role in the process there of reasserting democratic values against the authoritarian market-dominance that global forces had imposed via the Pinochet regime).[13] These civil society groups in many respects are reflections of more complex contemporary social partitioning.

Analysts like Booth stress that these new elements mean that recent political economy approaches, since they are concerned both with broad-level institutions and increasingly with these community-based groups, are more and more "amenable to a style of analysis that moves back and forth between the macro and the micro."[14] So that Diagram 1 needs also to be seen in multidimensional terms — over time, external-internal, and local-national, as well as social-political-economic-and-cultural in intersection.

Thus careful analysis of the institutions of the state and of the meaning and dynamics of civil society in any given country must be seen as preoccupying the new political economy approach. This is particularly the case in a context in which gender equity issues, and the role of micro- and macro-level women's movements, are crucial factors to encompass in an ongoing analysis of the political economy of countering poverty. (Chapter 7 returns to the dynamics of the state role, and the impact of civil society groups, particularly those representing women.)

2: Political Economy and the Canadian Example

One way to gain a better understanding of the political economy approach is to consider briefly the rapid emergence of Canada as a relatively developed area in the 19th and 20th centuries.

Celso Furtado provides the backdrop to this' Canadian development process, tracing the dimensions of Polanyi's "great transformation" in Britain: "The advent of an industrial nucleus in eighteenth century Europe disrupted the world economy of the time and eventually conditioned later economic development in almost every region of the world."[15] In particular, Furtado notes, this led to an emphasis in non-European parts of the world on "the creation of a flow of foreign trade . . . to get development under way without previous capital accumulation."[16] As Robert Baldwin discusses at a general level, variations in the production patterns associated with the different kinds of trade goods produced and exported back to that European nucleus shaped differential local demands for inputs to this export production — which in turn could shape different social structures, consumption demands, subsequent economic investments, and even widely variable political institutions in areas supplying these different export trade goods in different ways.

In one area, for instance — producing an export crop like sugar, best produced on labour-intensive plantations — sharp income differentials would emerge, as well as limited demand for either diversified infrastructure or basic domestic manufactured goods (since high-income plantation owners would import European luxury items and plantation labourers would barely have enough to feed themselves). Narrow, authoritarian political institutions would also be likely to emerge to suppress the mass of poor indentured labourers or slaves.

In another area — producing an export crop like wheat, best produced on widespread family farms — a much more even income distribution would emerge, as well as high demand for diversified infrastructure to get the wheat to market and for basic manufactured goods for many modest farms (a demand that could be met by local production.) More participatory political structures would be likely to emerge as well.[17]

Much of Canada's economic history has been understood in terms of these global trading pressures, shaped by European industrial expansionism, setting up demand for different "staple" products from Canada (fish, furs, timber, wheat) with these different staples shaping changing social, economic, and political institutions within Canada as the country shifted from reliance on one staple export to another.[18]

This perspective has some explanatory power. In Central Canada a political economy gradually emerged with reliance on family-operated farms, exporting wheat and other agricultural products, supplemented by some significant timber exports to Europe and lumber exports to the United States. But as McCalla stresses, the staple export product analysis is not fully satisfactory. Trade ties were not the only way the emerging North Atlantic economy shaped what was happening in Canada. "Other external influences included population movements, trends and fluctuations in prices and rates of exchange, flows of ideas and information (including technology), short- and long-term flows of credit and capital, and the policies of outside governments, including those from Britain, Lower Canada, the United States, and even individual states."[19]

The decentralized family-farm economy, with its limited but strategic wheat and potash exports bringing a wide cash base for basic consumer demand and for simple farm equipment, encouraged the growth of local industry and kept a wide number of small merchants viable in many Upper Canadian communities. This relatively egalitarian social structure in turn spurred a drive for democratic political systems, which interacted positively with British-based moves towards electoral reform at home, leading to elected, responsible governments in the Canadian colonies, as well as independent newspapers, farm protest movements, competing political parties, organized trade unions, women's groups, and other signs of "civil society" in much of colonial Canada.

Significantly, where the British crown instead granted privileged company monopolies, in cases such as the charter given the General Mining Association for coal-mining in Nova Scotia in the 1826-40 period, the result was significantly retarded economic expansion and more restricted industrialization.[20]

In terms of external forces and their impact on Canada, however, the major factor was unquestionably the extremely high rate of British capital investment in colonial railway-building, especially in Central Canada. At least $100 million was invested in railways in Canada between 1850 and 1860, some 70 per cent of it in Upper Canada (now Ontario.) In comparative terms, while three adjoining U.S. states (Ohio, Michigan, and Indiana) saw gross investment of $39 per capita in their railroads between 1851 and 1860, the Upper Canada figure was $50 per person. This led to a massive demand for wage labour and to much evidence by 1870 of "industrial development in the leading cities."[21]

Within the farm-based political economy, the local merchant classes of the various larger cities of the region had become the dominant political and ideological leaders — men like W.H. Merritt of St. Catherines and the "merchants of the St. Lawrence" who were all fighting for canal and railroad construction to expand their commercial hinterlands. But as farm-based consumer and simple machinery demand grew, and railroad-building and railway operation spurred even more manufacturing activity, a new "hegemony" gradually began to be established by industrialists in the changing political economy, and railroad and financial business interests increasingly identified with these industry leaders.[22] New institutions arose, such as the Association for the Promotion of Canadian Industry, which eventually became the Canadian Manufacturers' Association and had sufficient political strength and ideological power to bring the Conservative Party and most of the electorate to support a "National Policy" of high Canadian tariffs, aimed at building up Canadian-based manufacturing industries centred in Ontario and Quebec.[23] These changing social dynamics within the Canadian context, themselves interacting with increased trade union and working-class activity, were critical in shaping the development choices in the emerging Canadian political economy.

Despite the dominance of the free-market mechanism in Britain, therefore, and how the hegemony of that "laissez-faire" perspective was reflected in the British political economy of the second half of the 19th century (a period when the repeal of the Corn Laws represented the most dramatic evidence that free-trade views, and belief in unregulated markets, were paramount), the Canadian political economy structured its relations with the British-dominated North Atlantic economy in such a way as to resist that free-trade ideology. The contrast with other staples exporters that remained completely open to British manufacturing trade (from India to Argentina to Jamaica) was remarkable. The Canadian economy industrialized, diversified, and expanded much more dynamically.

A different political economy had emerged in Canada, not only based on the family-farm structure of the production system but also reflecting the emergence of different social forces, with different ideas, to the position where they were able to dominate the relatively democratic political system and initiate a strategy of nationalist industrial expansion.

This political economy would confront difficult conflicts in the future. The National Policy would make Ontario rich at the expense of regional imbalances in the Western and Atlantic provinces. Conflicts in civil society between business interests and labour and farm protest groups would accelerate. The political institutions appropriate for rapid economic expansionism would prove much less able to successfully confront pressures for gender equity, Aboriginal rights, or social, racial, and regional balances.

But these would represent the political struggles of a relatively prosperous country, despite Canada's colonial past. The political economy of colonialism in many Southern countries shaped much sharper social divisions — and the basis for contemporary global poverty.

3: The Political Economy of Colonialism in the South

The European expansionism of the last 500 years has been a complex process, with different phases, varying characteristics, and consequences that have been diverse and complicated in the variety of Southern areas affected by the commercial, financial, industrial, and political forces spurred outward from Europe throughout what became a global economy. When for analytical purposes we identify certain broad patterns and effects, we inevitably oversimplify matters. Still, it is nevertheless true that trade pressures have been a constant of the European expansionism, just as they have been in Canada. There have been specific targets of such trade, and how those targets were reached would shape the social and political institutions of the Southern areas.

One fundamental means of response, whether for sugar in the Caribbean and Northeast Brazil or cotton in the southern United States, was the plantation system — supplied by the millions of slaves sent as labour from West Africa. Beckford has traced the severe impoverishment that resulted for the great majority of people in the plantation colonies (even after emancipation), the starkly authoritarian government structures and extremely hierarchical social institutions that were shaped around race, and the limited linkage effects of this form of political economy for the Caribbean and Northeast Brazil economies.[24] Anthony Hopkins, writing of the impact of the slave trade on West Africa, makes the case that it also had very few long-term economic linkage benefits from an African perspective, even if certain African warrior states made some commercial gains.[25]

The East African slave trade accelerated later than that in West Africa and never came close to the millions of people sold into slavery from Elmina Castle south to Luanda in Angola, but by the early 19th century the Portuguese were sending over 10,000 slaves per year from Mozambique to Brazil. By mid-century the slave markets of Zanzibar were delivering from 50,000 to 70,000 slaves a year. The result was disruption of local agricultural production throughout many parts of East Africa, and the encouragement of war-like states with aggressive authoritarian structures within the African interior.[26]

Slave-based societies were only one of a number of non-market-based sociopolitical institutions that European expansionism relied on in the earlier years of the penetration of the Southern parts of a widening world economy. In the case of much of Latin America, for example, the Spanish and the Portuguese established an "encomienda" system of granting authority to notables from Europe, who gradually established a pattern based on large-scale landholdings or "latifundios," to which local indigenous peasant farmers came to relate in what were very much like tenant farmer ties in the context of a feudal system. Within this broad framework, a diverse but relatively limited amount of mineral production provided the major trade links to Europe.[27]

Meanwhile, within two other great centres of early European expansionism in Asia — the Indian subcontinent and the sprawling islands of Dutch Indonesia — the strength of European traders rested on two major mercantile institutions, the British East India Company and the Dutch East India Company. Both outfits were chartered by their European home countries to take control of trade, and they did so by also governing the country, so as to benefit their trade control. As a result, "British industry had been helped by British fiscal policy in India to destroy sooner, rather than later, the handcraft industries of India."[28] Belshaw notes that Dutch commercial monopoly and political control in Indonesia in the same way destroyed pre-existing Indonesian enterprise.[29]

In both India and Indonesia, in the isolated latifundios of Latin America, in the slave economies of the Caribbean and Brazil, and in the disrupted African subsistence economies pressured by slaving, these trends left the great bulk of the population blocked off from dynamic economic development, oriented to promoting or avoiding slave raids, or else enmeshed in the institution of slavery itself in the misery of harsh plantations.

But as slavery was gradually stamped out after the mid-19th century, the momentum of European economic expansionism accelerated rather than slowed, and it came to have a new character — driven more by free-trade ideology in Britain, resorting more to colonial control in Africa as competition among the European powers grew, and increasingly penetrating China too as the international economy became ever more global. Furtado has described the effects of this accelerated penetration of European industrial expansionism: "The result, however, was almost always to create hybrid structures, part tending to behave as a capitalistic system, part perpetuating the features of the previously existing system."[30]

Thus the colonial political economy in most Southern countries generally became fundamentally different from that in Canada. Rather than an integrated system, with most of the population fairly closely interconnected economically and politically, as in the Canadian case, and therefore subject to dynamics of interaction, concerned to build infrastructure for purposes of interconnection, and oriented to political actions and plans that cut across the whole society, the powerful trade pressures of the European economies tended to shape one minority sector of the Southern political economy into relationships that were segmented from much of the rest of the society.

A review of various African political economies — of their staple export products and how they were produced — demonstrates this key point clearly, showing the segmentation in the South as compared to the interconnected political economy integration of 19th-century Canada. This segmentation meant broad, internally based economic and social transformation was rare.

In Uganda, for instance, in what was a classic case of peasant cash-crop production, cotton became the key staple around which trade grew — with exports growing from some 48,000 bales (from 162,000 acres planted) in 1919 to 402,000 bales in 1937.[31] Using coercion to promote such cotton-growing, and restrictions at the same time to prevent Africans from moving into more profitable coffee production (which was kept largely for white-owned plantations until 1922), a minority of Ugandan Africans were drawn forcibly into the international economy very much on British terms. At the same time large parts of Uganda remote from the railroad were largely left out in the new segmented structure of political economy. Thus in 1919 the Northern and Western provinces contributed only 15 per cent of African cotton production, and by 1937 this share was down to 12.5 per cent, even though the two provinces made up 43 per cent of Uganda's population. Once coffee production did become encouraged among Africans, the Buganda area became the centre of production, producing over 90 per cent of African output of this more lucrative crop by 1938, 95 per cent by 1948, and 93 per cent in 1956 — despite containing only 26 per cent of the Ugandan population.[32]

The same segmentation, based on peasant cash-crop exports expanding in specific regions while other areas were neglected, could be seen in what is now Ghana (where cocoa output grew dramatically in the Ashanti region), in Nigeria (especially with cocoa production in the Western region around Ibadan), and in Senegal (where groundnut exports expanded while the southern Casamance region and the eastern Oriental region were ignored). The Ivory Coast showed the same processes from coffee and cocoa exports; the regional imbalances in this case showed up in 1950 cash crop revenues in the south that were 63 times greater than in the north, with per capita annual revenues in the southeast area three times higher than those in the south-central area.[33]

In Zambia copper exports became the major trade item, spurring an even more polarized political economy. A well-paid, increasingly unionized workforce in the Copperbelt made up the core of the perhaps 15 per cent of the African population employed, with the great majority of Zambians living as subsistence peasants largely disconnected from the mining enclave. A small number of white settlers supplied food to that enclave, and very few colonial resources were devoted to educational improvement for Africans outside the mining sector. Indeed, by independence Zambia had only 100 African university graduates, and 1,500 people with secondary education.[34] The skewing of the economy around copper (which proved to be a staple export dangerously vulnerable to massive price decreases and consequent national revenue collapses) meant the downplaying of opportunities for other basic African production in peasant agriculture and artisanal fisheries. Essentially the same kind of economic polarization and extreme social differentiation occurred in what is now Congo-Zaire (with the wealth concentrated in copper-producing Katanga), in Sierra Leone (around the alluvial diamond fields of that country), and in Gabon (around mining of manganese and extraction of petroleum.)

The most extreme African colonial dichotomies, however, clearly emerged in the white settler economies, such as Kenya, Zimbabwe, Mozambique, and South Africa. In Kenya, for instance, while some peasant production was encouraged in certain cases (as with cotton production by Africans around Lake Victoria), the general pattern was: a) to use colonial resources on agricultural research to find exportable products that settlers could grow (Wolff demonstrates how this led Kenyan colonial administrators, after much review, to focus on coffee as a settler crop);[35] b) to use the colonial authorities to ensure a low-paid African labour supply to the settlers by means of high hut taxes and continuing forms of forced labour;[36] and c) to constrain other African income opportunities by restrictions on the growing of crops such as coffee and tea and by use of a pass system to limit the search for urban or commercial options. As Carlsen concludes of this Kenyan settler-oriented strategy, "This had a totally damaging effect on the development of the productive forces in the African peasant economy. ... The African economy was *under*-developed during this period."[37]

This same coercive system, implemented with even more force, a wider set of restrictions, and a larger number of white settlers shaped even more polarized social differentiation on racial lines in Mozambique (where over 200,000 Portuguese left at independence in 1975), in what is now Zimbabwe (where a long guerrilla struggle preceded liberation), and in South Africa (with its current income differentials of 9.5 to 1 between whites and blacks).

Finally, several African political economies, including Tanzania, had been German colonies and after World War I became League of Nations mandates, consigned to an uncertain status that inhibited infrastructure investment, settler interest, or intensive commercial penetration or activity. As a result, Tanzania saw only limited plantation development, of a crop (sisal) doomed to serious replacement pressures and consequent price collapse soon after independence. Peasant cash-crop production, of coffee, cashews, and cotton, was also limited. Though Tanzania experienced some regional differentiation (spurring gains for the Chagga area around Mt. Kilimanjaro and the Arusha region around Mt. Meru), the main consequence of its limited colonial involvement in the international economy was a relatively egalitarian but very poor political economy.

On the whole, these African cases illustrate how the thrust of colonialism led to the dominance of staple production and export throughout the continent — and in turn to a structural segmentation of the political economies being shaped. The leading segments of the various colonies became organized around specific staple products (from cotton to copper to coffee), produced in the context of differing historical social and political structures (from the peasant cash-crop patterns of Uganda and the Ivory Coast and the well-paid enclaves of the mineral exporters to the coercive regimentation of the white settler preserves), while most Africans were restricted from making significant gains from new economic opportunities, although migrant labour options were often available to spread minor economic benefits. The general result was a growing social division between an increasingly rich minority and an increasingly poor majority.

The emerging forms of political economy did matter. The settler economies, for instance, spurred more infrastructure investment, more industrialization, and more local linkages to new economic activities — as well as much greater social polarization (including much landlessness) within societies. The enclave political economies tended to spur few local linkages, left African agriculture especially undeveloped, and concentrated infrastructure very narrowly — as well as generating the widest social and regional imbalances within the African population itself. The peasant cash-crop cases had more linkage effects than the enclave cases, but fewer than settler economies; they also had more rudimentary infrastructure improvements than the settler cases, but these were more widely spread than in the enclave economies — and they did share economic opportunities more widely among Africans than either of the other political economy forms. (See, for example, the more egalitarian Gini index numbers reported in Table 1, chapter 1, for African economies based on peasant cash-crops, such as Ghana and the Ivory Coast.)

But the peasant cash-crop political economies also saw indigenous peoples lose large amounts of surplus through cash-crop export taxes and stabilization levies that helped the colonial home countries with balance of payments constraints and limited the dynamism of peasant producers from achieving wider spread effects in their own countries.[38] In Uganda, for instance, after a decade of peasant producers receiving much less than the value of their output, by 1953 the total in such levies and export taxes on their cotton and coffee had reached some £82 million (41 per cent of the total export revenues generated from 1943 to 1953 for the two crops of some £200 million).[39] In Ghana peasant export producers also lost over 40 per cent of their potential gross incomes due to marketing board deductions between 1947 and 1961, while in Nigeria the average peasant loss was 27 per cent. As Hopkins concludes, "There would seem to be a case for supposing that had the funds accumulated by the Boards been left in the hands of the farmers, the market would have grown faster and expenditure on consumer goods would have given further impetus to import-substituting industries."[40]

Even in the relatively less polarized peasant cash-crop cases, therefore, the political economy of colonialism involved marked limitations on the economic opportunities of Africans. These limitations were usually reinforced by racist restrictions that affected all Africans. In West Africa, for instance, "As members of the coastal elite, African merchants suffered social humiliations as well as economic defeat. Educated, Christian Africans found themselves treated with less consideration after the expansion of colonial rule than they had been in the nineteenth century."[41]

Colonialism, then, involved more than just selective export production for the world economy. The political economy of external control involved both the promotion of a hegemony of cultural and ideological perspectives and a reliance on state and non-state forces to help in that promotion. Racist views were central to this culture of dominance, even though church and missionary efforts also promoted colonial values of a somewhat different sort. In Britain the missionary was seen as "an agent of humanitarianism: he might carry civilization and material advances more directly to colonial peoples than the administrator."[42] Thus missionaries took schooling into West and East Africa, stressed medical assistance, and expanded new forms of agricultural production. But, as Mutiso puts it in the context of Kenya, "Missionary activity was the most important influence in restructuring African society" and "must be seen in the context of the imposition of foreign power."[43] The missionaries essentially promoted pro-European values along with education and health improvements, says Mutiso, including notions of monogamy, regular wage labour, and acceptance of white superiority. Those Africans who conformed to this way of life, and lived on the African missions, became what Mutiso calls the "*asomi*" — favoured by the colonial authorities and provided with special economic privileges to cement their allegiance to the external connection; and (armed with educational credentials through missionary schools) they came to dominate the African levels of the colonial political bureaucracy. Meanwhile, those who became involved with the missions but ultimately rejected their white-oriented view, became what Mutiso calls the "dissociative *asomi*." They took the educational skills learned through the missions into political leadership of the great majority of Africans (the "non-*asomi*"), there challenging the racist character of colonialism in movements for national independence. Yet, even in opposition, they were significantly influenced by many of the ideological/cultural values absorbed in the missionary context.

Such cultural value considerations played a powerful role around the world. In India missionaries were also highly active, and the role of British-style education inculcated strong attachments to the imperial power. As Southgate writes of the 19th century, for example, "as early as the sixties and seventies Dadabhai Naoroji (1825-1917) lived in Britain for a decade with the aim of explaining the truth about discrimination and lack of opportunity for Indians in India, convinced that the truth, if known, would prevail."[44] In China, too, missionary activity was extensive. There, and in Latin America, Britain did not even rely on formal colonial control in order to reinforce its informal expansionist dominance. Gallagher and Robinson trace out how, via strategic moves such as transporting the Portuguese king to Brazil during the Napoleonic wars and signing trade treaties with Mexico, Colombia, and Argentina, Britain effectively made Latin America part of its informal political economic empire. Similar efforts were not as economically effective in China, where commercial pressures increasingly destabilized the declining Chinese Empire, but British political influence did become stronger as this happened.[45]

Both trade pressures and cultural/ideological factors were powerful in the process of informal dominance in Latin America. Coffee exports became crucial to Brazil, and to Colombia; petroleum became the key export commodity in Venezuela; nitrates, then copper, dominated Chile's trade; wheat and cattle were the main staples in Argentina; tin shaped the political economy of Bolivia; and cattle exports were central in Uruguay.

But capital investment flows, especially around railroad-building, also became powerful external factors in the Latin American case. By 1914 some 20 per cent of British overseas investment was in Latin America, about half of it in railway bonds, with the heaviest concentration in Argentina and Brazil. France and Germany also had fairly large bond investments, and the United States had a large amount of direct investment in the region. In general, by 1914 a total of about US$8.5 billion was invested in Latin America, some 44 per cent from Britain, 20 per cent from the United States, 14 per cent from France and 11 per cent from Germany. About one-third of this investment was in Argentina, and one-quarter in each of Brazil and Mexico.[46]

Unlike the Canadian experience, the concentrated railroad-building based on foreign investment did not create either a widespread internal infrastructure to back up a domestically oriented and broadly integrated local market, or industrial expansion to service railway operational demands, which would lead to the emergence of significant local manufacturers. Instead, as Ferns has stressed of Argentina, the historical structure in that country in the later 19th-century was "worked out by the Argentine landed and commercial interests. ... If, over a long span of time, Argentina has possessed a weak and narrowly based industrial structure compared with the United States or even with Canada, this has been due to the concentration of effort in Argentina upon agricultural and pastoral enterprise and upon the production of pastoral and agricultural commodities."[47] In contrast with Canada, too, the great majority of Latin American countries continued to rely on the latifundio system, concentrating control of land among large-scale owners and leading to the extreme polarization of economic opportunities (so much so that 5 per cent of households controlled some 30 per cent of income in all three of Brazil, Mexico, and Argentina)[48] — thereby blocking widely based consumer demand for products that could be produced locally, and encouraging luxury imports instead.

European expansionism, then, had powerful effects in shaping most Southern political economies. The trade pressures of the emerging world economy set in motion demands for particular staple products and led to devastating migrations of slave labour to serve the production of some of those staples. The same pressures shaped different kinds of hybrid structures in most Southern countries to supply staples to the European nucleus of the expanding international economy. Most Southern countries, as a result, came to have their economic conditions strongly tied to market-based changes in revenues for their export staples; and the social and political institutions of their political economies were shaped powerfully by how those staples were produced: reliance on ex-slave plantations, or former white-settler colonialism, or Latin American latifundios, or export enclaves, or cash-crop peasant production — with its mechanisms by which peasant dynamism was retarded. Each of these forms had varying specific effects;

but each also represented structures of segmentation, by which the majorities of people living in Southern political economies were restricted from socioeconomic opportunities to a greater or lesser extent.

Investment flows were also important factors, and so were direct political controls in many cases (from India and Indonesia, Nigeria, the Congo and Eastern Africa, to the Caribbean and Korea). Cultural/ideological hegemony was a consistent goal of external influence, often achieved; and local social, political, and economic structures were powerfully shaped in distinct ways, usually leading to marked social polarization within Southern countries.

4: Conclusion

Colonialism, then, played out its global course. In most cases new economic penetration took place; new opportunities were shaped for the South, but in restricted and segmented ways; infrastructure and health were improved, but with a focus on where exports were being produced; education was furthered, but especially for males and around a Euro-centred value system that left a distorted legacy for the postcolonial period. The general pattern that resulted in Southern countries contrasted significantly with the family-farm, decentralized, democratic, infrastructure-intensive, highly integrated political economy structure that had emerged in later 19th-century Canada, with its widespread domestic manufacturing, industrialist bent, and marked economic expansion.

Particularly striking was the difference between the social groupings that emerged powerfully in Central Canada (such as prominent industrialists, farm-oriented movements, trade unions, Women's Institutes, and community-based municipal councils that invested heavily in railroad building to seek local prosperity), and the colonial regimes in Africa and Asia (dominated by outside administrators, imperial trading companies, and missionaries oriented to values abroad), or the governments in Latin America (run by the descendants of notables who still identified with Europe, considered themselves distinct from local majority Indian populations, and saw commerce and staple export production as the keys to their prosperity). These differing social structures made for distinct state roles in Southern countries.

European expansionism shaped historical institutions in significant ways. The limitations imposed on opportunities for the majorities of most Southern populations — the male-centred assumptions of the colonial value systems, the antidemocratic bias of colonial administration, which discouraged community-based action by poorer people, the external orientation of most economies, which retarded emphasis on agricultural food production for domestic nutritional goals — were all factors that can be traced to the impact of external dominance. In crucial ways these factors shaped the contemporary prevalence of Southern poverty.

But a political economy approach must also recognize dynamics that bring about change, and the processes of colonial expansionism did ultimately generate change. Four broad forces, at both the global and colonial levels, helped to bring about decolonization after World War II.

First, important changes took place in international geopolitics and the related balance of economic strength among countries. This included the decisive emergence of the United States as the most powerful nation-state in the world. A country with few formal colonies (and an emphasis on informal economic expansionism that could produce disputes with countries that tried to maintain formal colonial controls), the United States had a growing dominance that undercut formal colonial structures in Asia, the Caribbean and Africa. The greater strength of the Soviet Union, and the potential for Cold War use of anticolonial movements to increase its influence, underlined the U.S. anticolonial stance. The weakened position of a number of European colonial powers after occupation in World War II (such as the Netherlands and France) added to this momentum, as did the destruction of Japanese colonialism (in Korea, for example).

Second, and also at the global level, the 1945-60 period saw a dramatic expansion in direct foreign investment in the international economy. U.S. enterprises in particular raised their direct foreign investment, from a U.S.$11 billion total in 1949 to $65 billion by 1968 — while the United Kingdom raised its total to almost $20 billion by the same year. Both countries raised their share going to Southern countries outside Latin America, and both stressed manufacturing investment as the largest proportion of such direct investment (50 per cent of the annual average flow for the United States over 1960-64).[49] This change in economic strategy not only reflected the new importance of technological knowledge in the production process (which could be most efficiently and profitably commercialized through the institution of the international firm), but also suggested the new capacity of more advanced industrial political economies to establish manufacturing facilities in Southern countries to take best advantage of markets and labour supplies there.

Third, World War II also had important effects on the cultural/ideological hegemony of the colonial system, especially in Asia, where the racist roots of colonial control had been contradicted by the Japanese period of success in the early part of the war. It was much harder for the French in Vietnam, the Dutch in Indonesia, and the British in Malaya and India to remain secure. Within a few years independence had been conceded almost everywhere in Asia. The capture of power by Communist parties in China, North Vietnam, and North Korea added to this momentum towards change.

Fourth, and finally, in Africa the processes of educational advance, peasant grievance around cash-crop taxation and levies, trade union opposition to high profits in export enclaves, and a generalized reaction against racist restrictions and inequalities all fed growing nationalist movements. Mutiso's model of the dissociative *asomi* leading the non-*asomi* may capture the dynamic at work in certain cases, while in other cases the move to independence was a more collaborative process by which leading Africans associated with the French (for example) took power to avoid more radical developments. Only in the strong settler political economies (such as Zimbabwe, Kenya, Mozambique, and South Africa) did armed confrontation take place before power transfer agreements were arranged.

But to what degree did the move to independence represent structural change in the historical institutions shaped by colonialism? The answer varied, depending on time and place, but it is fair to say that certain major realities were not substantially altered. Most Southern countries remained oriented to external trade pressures (although the nature of the trade sometimes changed, as in Nigeria's development of oil resources or Asian shifts towards labour-intensive manufacturing exports). The segmentation of political economies also persisted (although the structures could become somewhat more complex given the increased foreign direct manufacturing investment in many Southern economies). The orientation of the new leaderships to many colonial values and ideas often continued, too, thanks to the powerful impact of colonial education, the strength of colonially trained bureaucracies, and the role of new aid relationships with European-North American donors (although, again, the particular mix of European values and the new political leaders' ideas was often somewhat different than had characterized the colonial state in the immediate pre-independence period).

Perhaps the main difference that gradually emerged was that in many cases the postcolonial state was no longer a direct creature of external political forces. By and large, the political economy base of each new government began to be defined increasingly in local terms, with varying social and regional sources of support, differing relations with military authorities, and divergent strategies towards community-based popular movements at micro- and macro-levels. These differing governments began to look to varying strategies in the attempts to shape their political economies. In doing so they faced constraints and historical legacies from the colonial period; but they also faced choices in approaches to development.

Notes

1 See Kothari, *Poverty*, p.29.
2 Michael Edwards, "How Relevant Is Development Studies," in *Beyond the Impasse*, ed. F. Schuurman, (London: Zed Books 1993), p.77.

3 Bjorn Hettne, "Introduction: The Political Economy of Transformation," in *International Political Economy*, ed. B. Hettne (London: Zed Books, 1995), p.1.

4 Karl Polanyi, *The Great Transformation* (Boston: Beacon Press, 1957), especially chapter 21.

5 Karl Polanyi, "Redistribution: The State Sphere in Eighteenth Century Dahomey," in *Primitive, Archaic and Modern Economies*, ed. George Dalton (New York: Doubleday, 1968), pp.207-37.

6 C.S. Belshaw, *Traditional Exchange and Modern Markets* (Toronto: Prentice Hall, 1965), pp.29-34.

7 Polanyi, *The Great Transformation*, chapter 19.

8 Robert Cox, "International Political Economy," in *International Political Economy*, ed. Hettne, p.32.

9 Richard Sandbrook, *The Politics of Africa's Economic Recovery* (Cambridge: Cambridge University Press, 1993), pp.24-25.

10 See Cox, "International Political Economy," James Rosenau, "Distant Proximities: The Dynamics and Dialectics of Globalization," and Stephen Gill, "Theorizing the Interregnum: The Double Movement and Global Politics in the 1990s," in *International Political Economy*, ed. Hettne, pp.46-99.

11 Antonio Gramsci, *The Modern Prince and Other Writings* (New York: International Publishers, 1957), p.170.

12 Gill, "Theorizing the Interregnum: The Double Movement and Global Politics in the 1990s," p.67.

13 See Frans Schuurman, "Modernity, Post-Modernity and the New Social Movements," in *Beyond the Impasse*, ed. Schuurman, pp.187-206.

14 David Booth, "Development Research: From Impasse to a New Agenda," in Ibid., p.63.

15 Celso Furtado, *Development and Underdevelopment* (Berkeley: University of California Press, 1967), p.127.

16 *Ibid.*, p.64.

17 Robert Baldwin, "Patterns of Development in Newly-Settled Regions," *The Manchester School*, May 1956, pp.161-79.

18 For a description of this traditional view, and some questioning of it, see D. McCalla, *Planting the Province: The Economic History of Upper Canada, 1784-1870* (Toronto: University of Toronto Press, 1993), pp.4-5.

19 Ibid., p.5.

20 See Marilyn Gerriets, "The Impact of the General Mining Association on the Nova Scotia Coal Industry, 1826-1850," in *Farm, Factory and Fortune*, ed. K. Inwood (Fredericton: Acadiensis Press, 1993), pp.61-92.

21 McCalla, *Planting the Province*, pp.205-15.

22 Graham Taylor and Peter Baskerville discuss the complex interaction between industry on the one side, and railroad and financial business interests on the other side, in *A Concise History of Business in Canada* (Oxford: Oxford University Press, 1994), pp.239-44, 249-61.

23 See Michael Bliss, *A Living Profit* (Toronto: McClelland and Stewart, 1974), chapter 5.

24 George Beckford, *Persistent Poverty: Underdevelopment in Plantation Economies of the Third World* (New York: Oxford University Press, 1972), chapter 3.

25 A.G. Hopkins, *An Economic History of West Africa* (London: Longman Group, 1973), pp.119-23.
26 See E.A. Alpers, *The East African Slave Trade* (Nairobi: East African Publishing House, 1967).
27 See Celso Furtado, *Economic Development of Latin America* (London: Cambridge University Press, 1970), chapter 2.
28 Donald Southgate, "Imperial Britain," in *Britain Pre-Eminent: Studies in British World Influence in the Nineteenth Century*, ed. C.J. Bartlett (London: Macmillan, 1969), p.166.
29 Belshaw, *Traditional Exchange and Modern Markets*, p.97.
30 Furtado, *Development and Underdevelopment*, p.129.
31 C.C. Wrigley, *Crops and Wealth in Uganda* (Nairobi: Oxford University Press, 1970), pp.47, 59.
32 *Ibid.*, pp.6, 74.
33 Peter Anyang'Nyong'o, "The Development of Agrarian Capitalist Classes in the Ivory Coast, 1945-1975," in *The African Bourgeoisie*, ed. P.M. Lubeck (Boulder: Lynne Rienner Publishers, 1987), p.205.
34 See René Dumont, *False Start in Africa* (London: Sphere Books, 1968), p.232.
35 R.D. Wolff, *The Economics of Colonialism: Britain and Kenya, 1870-1930* (New Haven: Yale University Press, 1974), pp.73-79.
36 This controversial point regarding reliance on forced African labour in Kenya is documented at length in R.M.A. van Zwanenberg, *Colonial Capitalism and Labour in Kenya, 1919-1939* (Nairobi: East African Literature Bureau, 1975), chapters 4 and 5.
37 See John Carlsen, *Economic and Social Transformation in Rural Kenya* (Uppsala: Scandinavian Institute of African Studies, 1980), pp. 20-22.
38 "Spread effects" are a measure of the extent of economic linkages from a staple export.
39 See Wrigley, *Crops and Wealth in Uganda*, pp.68-74.
40 Hopkins, *An Economic History of West Africa*, pp. 286-88.
41 *Ibid.*, p.256.
42 Oliver Furley, "The Humanitarian Impact," in *Britain Pre-Eminent: Studies in British World Influence in the Nineteenth Century*, ed. Bartlett, p.147.
43 Gideon Mutiso, *Kenya: Politics, Policy and Society* (Nairobi: East African Literature Bureau, 1975), p.3.
44 Southgate, in *Britain Pre-Eminent: Studies in British World Influence in the Nineteenth Century*, ed. Bartlett, p. 169.
45 John Gallagher and Ronald Robinson, "The Imperialism of Free Trade," in *Great Britain and the Colonies, 1815-1865*, ed. A.G.L. Shaw (London: Methuen and Co., 1970), pp.152-56.
46 M.D. Bernstein, ed., *Foreign Investment in Latin America* (New York: A.A. Knopf, 1966), pp.37, 40-41.
47 H.S. Ferns, "Britain and Argentina: Laissez-Faire Imperialism?" in *Foreign Investment in Latin America*, ed. Bernstein, p.125.
48 Furtado, *Economic Development of Latin America*, pp.54-61.
49 M.B. Brown, *The Economics of Imperialism* (Harmondsworth: Penguin Books, 1974), pp.208-9.

CHAPTER 3

Global Poverty and
Development Theory

The libraries are full of books and journals that discuss and debate broad theories of development, all aimed at countering or at least addressing, the great material divisions between North and South. The malnourished children, so many dying so young, living in constricted rural households or in crowded unhealthy slums, may often lack schooling, but millions of words have been written on how best to tackle their countries' problems. Yet no broad consensus has ever been reached. As the year 2000 looms, bitter and fundamental disagreement continues over matters of "development."

On one side are those whom Kothari accuses of having forgotten about the immensity of human poverty in the world. These are the "neo-liberals," who stress the unregulated dominance of the free-market economy. They have pronounced the field of "development studies" to be dead and have simply applied the economics of the advanced industrial societies in the differing political economies of the South. This "neo-liberal" approach has become a powerful strand in policy analysis in many Southern countries.

At its core, the neo-liberal approach is straightforward: Simply let the market operate, get the state out of the way, privatize all the institutions you can, and leave everything to corporations and individuals interacting through the marketplace. In practice this approach has meant stressing macroeconomic policies that aim to eliminate budget deficits, massively reduce the size of the public sector, cut the rate of monetary expansion (in hopes of reducing inflation), move to completely free exchange rates and tariff-free trade regimes, deregulate financial regulations, and eliminate state subsidies and other interferences with the market mechanism. The tendency has been one approach fits all, and that approach says leave things to the market.

This view builds on the "modernization theories" of past development analysis, but it takes that approach to a fundamentally new extreme — seeing global reproduction of an idealized U.S.-style competitive capitalism as the means by which the whole world can best achieve a combination of dynamic economic growth and maximum individual freedom. This view also sees the work of policy analysis as essentially a process of meshing countries successfully into the global economy and overcoming local rigidities and structures that impede the smooth operation of international market forces.

The counterview to neo-liberalism comes from different traditions. As Manor points out, "The neo-liberals usually ignore elements of the political process."[1] The result, he says, is an extreme bias in the neo-liberal view: "They tend to react so sharply against the state that they lose sight of its creative potential." As a result, an exclusively "economic" analysis emerges, which runs against the thrust of more complex political economy approaches, leads to questions of poverty and inequality being ignored, and forgets the whole purpose of focusing on the special concerns of the poorer Southern countries.

New "empowerment" approaches have instead stressed a creative diversity of analysis and debate around gender and class and around specific middle-range policy questions such as agricultural emphases or technology strategy. Analysis has emphasized a micro-level diversity that implies room for social action and advance in rural development.[2] The approaches focus on action-research in a social context, too, stressing empirical findings and insights aimed at achieving change. This tendency has represented the heart of a new belief in community-based movements for change.

"Empowerment" as an approach can have various meanings. It can focus on a new restructuring of gender relations that shares powerfully between women and men at local, regional, and even national levels;[3] it can focus on local-level efforts to achieve a serious say in shaping development plans; it can involve the efforts of those harmed by environmental pressures to insist on a role in shaping the decisions that lie behind those pressures.[4] But above all, theories of empowerment are about challenging dominant local and national social forces — and that in turn often comes to involve challenges to international links and external socioeconomic forces of various kinds.

This "empowerment" approach is only now being defined in development theory, and it lacks the integrated coherence of the much narrower perspective of neo-liberal economics. But the approach rests on a strong counterreaction against the simplified abstractions of neo-liberal theory, which seem to leave out of consideration such profound social realities as the widespread human poverty so prevalent in most Southern countries. The new counterapproach rests on the view that the challenge to a dominant world economy that leaves out most of the poor must come in the end through shifts in power brought about by movements to empower themselves made up of those who are excluded. It also rests on the argument that the growing global divide itself requires such an approach. As Kothari puts it, "We are increasingly realizing that it is only by substantial empowerment of the people, individually and culturally, that poverty can ever be removed." Kothari goes on to stress that this requires significant decentralization of power, not only in the sense of shifting authority more to local levels closer to the majority of the people, but also in the sense of "a shift of power from State and government institutions to those of civil society."[5]

This empowerment approach in turn builds on the past perspectives of dependency theory and Marxian analysis, in shaping a counter to the neoliberal views that are pushed so fervently by privileged minorities.

The debate goes on, but its background is not always well understood. This chapter puts this argument into a longer-term context — and in the process suggests the need to move beyond theory and ideology and to probe more seriously and deeply the specific realities of Southern countries.

1: Broad Theories of "Modernization"

As the transition from formal colonialism moved ahead, various perspectives on development theory emerged and gradually matured around the growth and change experiences of Southeastern Europe, Puerto Rico, parts of the Caribbean, Latin America, and West Africa in the 1950s.

At the heart of what came to be called *modernization theory* was a vision of democratic, capitalist societies such as the United States, United Kingdom, and France. The usually implicit assumption was that economic development and growth involved a process of becoming like those societies and would be achieved essentially as those societies had achieved it: through economic change focused around industrialization, through social changes that would introduce Western institutions based on universalism and merit/achievement, and through political changes marked by secularization and the bureaucratic efficiency of the state. Max Weber, tracing the rise of what he called "the capitalist spirit" in Western Europe in the 19th century, stressed this dominance of "a rationalistic economic ethic," as well as the free labour market and an efficient state bureaucracy, as crucial to capitalist development.[6]

A) The Lewis Model. Arthur Lewis, a black Caribbean economist, dramatically summed up the process in talking about how development was a matter of creating patches of light in "a sea of darkness" and then of expanding those patches as rapidly as possible through labour transfer at fixed, low wages from a stagnant agriculture sector to the industrial sector.

In the model, industrialists would hire workers until the point L^*, where

Diagram 3:1: Surplus Labour View

Diagram 3:2: Growth & The Lewis Model

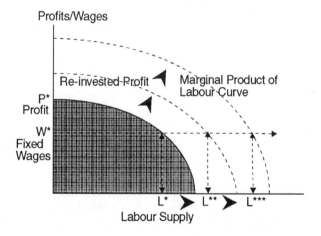

the fixed wage W* was equal to the extra output of the last worker hired at that level of capital being invested in industrial production. The profit being made by the industrialist at that point (P* - W*) — or the amount above the fixed wage line and below the marginal product of labour curve — would then (according to the model) be reinvested, thereby shifting the marginal product of labour curve outward (as in Diagram 3:2) and increasing the number of workers to be hired out of the subsistence agriculture sector at the low fixed wage (L* to L** to L*** — and so on, as further rounds of reinvestment took place in an ongoing process).

Lewis suggests, "The central problem in the theory of economic development is to understand the process by which a community which was previously saving and investing 4 or 5 per cent of its national income or less, converts itself into an economy where voluntary saving is running at about 12 to 15 per cent of national income or more." Extra saving would mean more investment and then more jobs and output from workers using that new invested capital in machines. This surplus labour model, says Lewis, explained how this would happen — entirely around a dramatic, continuing skewing in income distribution. The per capita income of the peasantry and the informal-sector wage would stay low and constant, the modern-sector wage would therefore also be relatively low and constant, and the dynamic increasing element would be profits — these would form a low percentage of overall national income at first, but as they expanded, given the constant returns to labour inputs, the share of profits (which in effect constituted the overwhelming share of savings) would also increase.[7]

This approach was extremely influential in Southern countries, as the new postcolonial governments shaped their development strategies, because it gave strong justification for an emphasis on industrial development as crucial to modernizing societies. Regardless of the short-term sacrifices of low wages and growing inequalities, Lewis and his theory recommended this approach as the way to accelerate economic expansion and ultimately achieve advanced-economy status.

Probing more deeply into this labour-transfer view, however, revealed some serious problems. As Lewis himself accepted, the approach had serious negative implications for the agricultural sector. "The fact that the wage level in the capitalist sector depends upon earnings in the subsistence sector is sometimes of immense political importance, since its effect is that capitalists have a direct interest in holding down the productivity of the subsistence workers." The countries following this approach would place little or no stress on improving agriculture; but at the same time, as the capitalist sector expanded, terms of trade could turn against that industrial sector unless there was also rising productivity in subsistence agriculture. So, despite the neglect of agriculture in the allocation of benefits, the ideal solution for industrial capitalist growth was a rising rural productivity, though it had to be combined with a minimal benefit to the peasantry to keep wages low in the modern sector, thus preventing rural-urban terms of trade from hurting industry and thereby maximizing profits to that modern sector and its expansion. In this sense, Lewis says, "It is true to say that it is agriculture which finances industrialization."

Thus the kind of development pattern envisioned was highly skewed,

industry-centred, coercive in keeping agricultural returns down and industrial wages fixed, and based on a relatively unexamined assumption that
the largest returns from investment could be achieved in the industrial sector.

In the end all of the key mechanisms of the Lewis model represented
major question marks waiting to be solved in most Southern countries.
Where would those crucial capitalists come from who would invest and
reinvest all their money at home in expanding local production? Where
would they get the first critical amounts of relatively large-scale capital to
turn on the "patches of light"? And what about the supposedly surplus
labour that Lewis was convinced would work for low wages, and at no real
sacrifice in production elsewhere in the society? Many of these were men
and women growing the basic foodstuffs on which the population
depended, and as later studies showed, their withdrawal from peasant production often meant that essential workers were absent at important bot-
tleneck periods of labour shortage in the food production pattern. Other
so-called surplus workers, according to Lewis, were women, and development studies has since learned a great deal about the manifold tasks carried
out by women in Southern countries — so much so that it is more common
now to describe women as working a "double day" (because of heavy
domestic responsibilities plus major crop-production roles, especially in the
food-growing segment of the economy), rather than suggesting that they
represent a part of the "surplus labour" force that rapid industrialization
can easily utilize.

The most recent reviews of time-allocation by gender in Southern countries confirm that women's workloads are 15-25 per cent higher, on
average, than those of men. This workload includes agricultural work and
wage employment, as well as extensive home-production activities such as
obtaining water and firewood, preparing meals, and child care.[8]

B) The "Stages of Growth" Approach. A second broad modernization
theory came from W.W. Rostow, who, concentrating heavily on historical
patterns of economic growth, claimed to see a broad pattern of similar
stages through which all countries moved in reaching prosperity.

Rostow's basic notion is that:

i)   almost every society has a brief period of 20 to 30 years that sets in
      place a self-perpetuating acceleration of economic growth and change
      that fundamentally transforms the society — the "take-off";
ii)   clearly identifiable preconditions for this takeoff can be understood
      universally and sought and achieved by policy-makers in any given
      society; and
iii) at the heart of the takeoff is an "industrial revolution" involving the

"rapid growth of one or more new manufacturing sectors (as) a powerful and essential engine of economic transformation."[9]

This is an extremely seductive way of seeing the world. You work at the
preconditions for takeoff (including encouraging the rise of new entrepreneurs, education, public health measures, new infrastructure capital, commercialization of agriculture, and reform of traditional institutions), you
await "a particular sharp stimulus," and, as a result, the "prior development
of the society and its economy result in a positive, sustained, and self-rein-
forcing response to it." During this take-off period there is a doubling of
capital investment, a key new push in manufacturing, and the impact of
dynamic institutional frameworks of social, political, and economic agencies able to build new production attitudes and technologies around this
impetus.

The theory is persuasive, but again its underlying analysis is weak.
Rostow has a serious problem with identifying a take-off point, because of
its broad, descriptive character as a concept. Indeed, he finds it easiest to
define the point by looking backwards, once it has been reached. Thus he
writes in the 1950s of Chile, India, and Mexico: "Whether the take-off
period will, in fact, be successful remains in most of these cases still to be
seen." If not, only then can one conclude that the preconditions for takeoff
were not in place. His stages thus become categories for classification purposes after the fact, rather than analytical guides to policy.[10]

Insofar as his model conveys a broad policy message, that thrust is
twofold. First, it places a heavy stress on industrialization. Although the
model includes a discussion of decentralized agriculture, it does not see
that sector as crucial to the take-off process. Second, the implication is that
development is a universal process, through which each society moves in its
own time, in response mainly to internal factors. But as Dudley Seers later
wrote, the development of the advanced industrial economies from which
Rostow derived his base model should instead be "recognized as a highly
special case."[11] The impact of the world economy as a whole clearly shaped
the processes of change in ways that Rostow underplayed far too much in
the Southern countries he examined.

And then there are distributional questions. Stages of growth, like the
labour surplus model, stressed urban, industrial sectors at the expense of
rural development and regional and gender balance. But even as the
emphasis on modernization continued, theories of development began to
react to these widening disparities.

C) Rising Distributional Concerns.
The Lewis-type and Rostow-type
models plus their offshoots stressed industrialization as being at the heart
of development. This was not an isolated emphasis. Other mainstream

development analysts, from Rosenstein-Rodan and Nurkse to Albert Hirschman in the Latin American context, saw the development of industrial production as essential to widening productivity growth, increasing higher-wage employment, and improving techniques of production.[12]

There is no question that this theoretical perspective was powerful, not least because it conformed to certain international economic trends (such as the growth in direct foreign manufacturing investment) and because it responded to the dominant East-West polarized worldview that shaped much intellectual-elite thought in the North Atlantic economies (this was particularly true of Rostow's work, which saw itself as a "Non-Communist Manifesto"). Modernization approaches were also a fundamentally optimistic and relatively straightforward approach that both supported Western-bloc intervention in Southern countries via aid and buttressed dominant governing groups in those countries — groups that could be seen to be seeking in benign ways the best for their peoples by bringing in foreign projects, multinational corporations, and links with Western societies. But, in practice, the perspective also had serious problems.

a)   One problem was intrinsic to the view itself. By stressing the advance of a relatively small minority, especially in the absence of rapid growth rates, the inequalities already shaped by colonialism grew dramatically in many Southern countries. This was especially so in Latin America, where the top 20 per cent of the population received 61.5 per cent of Brazil's national income, 64 per cent of Mexico's and 73.5 per cent of Ecuador's; but it was also true in Kenya, where the top 20 per cent received 68 per cent, in the Ivory Coast (57.1 per cent), and the Philippines (53.8 per cent) — compared to an income share of around 40 per cent for the top 20 per cent in OECD industrial countries such as Canada and the United Kingdom).[13]

b)   The lack of attention paid to small-scale agriculture tended to worsen this trend. Michael Lipton concluded that this approach to development had a strong "urban bias," which not only made small farmers poorer, but also hurt India (for example) economically, because the return from investment in low-cost improvements in peasant agriculture would have had a much higher payoff than industrial investments.[14]

c)   The problems with industrial-sector expansion tended to be especially great in places where new factories had been put up to serve the local market through import-substituting industrialization. In many cases, the factories established operated at average costs of production per unit from 118 per cent (Brazil in 1966) to 271 per cent (Pakistan in 1964) higher than the usual world costs for that manufacturing process.[15]

d) Finally, the approach had a significant impact on social structure and the state. In many cases the state became the intermediary between Western interests pursuing modernization goals and the domestic political economy, a tendency that opened up widespread opportunities for self-enrichment on the part of state and political personnel and made the state much less of an independent developmental agent for change.

Various development analysts probed the meaning of this approach for poorer people in Southern countries. The strategists included a team based around Hollis Chenery at the World Bank in Washington and Richard Jolly at the Institute of Development Studies at the University of Sussex.[16] Irma Adelman also traced the results of the modernization approach on distribution with a careful statistical analysis of Southern countries, showing that the stress on industrialization in most countries was worsening income distribution. What was most striking, Adelman found, was the massive inequalities of Brazil, Mexico, Kenya, the Philippines, and other countries following the policies advocated by modernization theorists using the labour-transfer approach. "A major reorientation of development strategies," she concluded, "is required to achieve equity-oriented growth. Marginal adjustments to current strategies simply will not work."[17]

The cases of South Korea, Singapore, and Taiwan, she said, showed that equitable growth strategies were possible, using human capital-intensive resource strategies aimed at massive educational improvements as well as early stage redistribution of assets (primarily land). The last stage in policy reorientation, following the other key points, had been export-oriented industrial incentives, built on shifting from earlier import-substituting strategies.

From her work, Adelman also stressed the wide variety of country situations evident, and the careful mix of policy measures that might be needed (and differ) in any given country. But Adelman was cautious in her conclusions. She recognized only to a limited degree the international forces at work and she ignored the role of gender.

Perhaps most problematic, however, was the question of how such new equity-oriented strategies were to be initiated. What social forces explained new directions? What economic imperatives were at work? Was the new equity and growth project just to be the ethical choice of a national elite? If so, why? And how did that political basis for change shape the serious asset redistribution and resource allocation shifts that seemed required to achieve equity and growth?

In general, the broad modernization theories did not succeed as viable approaches to development, either in intellectual terms or as serious long-term policy guides. The labour-surplus models collided with the realities of capitalists who were most interested in sending their capital abroad, not in reinvesting it — while food production and women's work had far less surplus labour to contribute than Lewis assumed. The stages of growth theories held out the notion of "take-off" like the Holy Grail, but could not analyse how to shape national policy in the context of world economic forces so as to achieve that point of takeoff. "Modernization" became the short-sighted justification for stressing industrialization, usually relying on inefficient import-oriented foreign direct investment, and the inequalities of the colonial period were generally widened at the expense of women and agriculture. Some analysts recognized the inequalities and saw that growth and equity could go together, but they were unable to analyse the dynamics of political economy that could take most Southern countries in that direction.

In the end a case could be made that modernization theory contributed to growing inequality and, through the discrimination against small-scale rural producers and women, was responsible for a significant share of the growing Southern poverty that became so devastating a social reality towards the end of the 20th century. In that sense, modernization theories in the Southern context became a crucial part of the problem, rather than an intellectual contribution to achieving balanced and fair socioeconomic development.

In the face of this failure, theoretical reactions grew, and counterpositions gathered force. Of these, the Marxian approach was to be especially powerful.

2: The Marxian Approach

In development studies the work of Marx can be considered from at least three angles:

a) Marx as social analyst — Marx helps in responding to the question of how social groupings in Southern countries could emerge and challenge the growing inequality there, and carry societies in the direction of more egalitarian social institutions associated with better growth records.

b) Marx as political economist — with a detailed and somewhat complicated series of categories, Marx analysed capital accumulation and economic change in industrial capitalist societies, including the dynamics that he said would radically reshape such societies.

c) Marx as analyst of the world economy — his approach considered the role of today's poorer Southern countries in that international context.

A) Marx as Social Analyst. On a broad level, Marx was reacting against the idealist philosophers of the 18th and early 19th centuries, thinkers who saw ideas as the force that really shaped the world. As Marx put it in *The German Ideology*, "In direct contrast to German philosophy, which descends from heaven to earth, here we ascend from earth to heaven. That is to say ... life is not determined by consciousness, but consciousness by life." This emphasis on historical materialism was the centrepiece of the Marxian view of history and change.

Within each epoch of differing production — such as feudalism or capitalism — the nature of the material conditions, Marx said, shapes the social groupings that exist in society — and those social groupings develop views of their material situation that reflect their relations of production, given the particular technological forces of production that predominate. But Marx took the analysis one step further. He saw inherent tensions developing between the relations and the forces of production in any given material situation, and he showed how these inherent tensions or contradictions bring about social and economic transformation, in a process of dialectical materialism that moved the society ahead.

That is the broad framework, but the actual social analysis to which it led Marx could be complex. For example, in *The Eighteenth Brumaire* Marx analysed the various social forces playing key roles in the coup d'état of Louis Napoleon in France in 1852 and pointed out that the underdeveloped nature of the productive forces of industrial capitalism in France, reflected in a very weak emerging bourgeoisie (and weak working class), left the French peasantry relatively strong compared to England, and created a situation in which a powerful state, virtually independent of different social forces, could dominate French society. "The state seem(ed) to have made itself completely independent," Marx said, with "industry and trade" brought "to prosper in hothouse fashion under the strong government."

This perception of the state, as autonomous from controlling social forces — just one example of the valuable insights provided by Marx as social analyst — has since been used in an important way to help understand the political economy of many contemporary Southern countries.

B) Marx and Economics. To examine the economics of Marx, however, is to dig more deeply into his analysis of the 19th-century capitalist mode of production, making more specific not only the contradictions that he saw within that mode of production but also the dialectic between relations and forces of production that he saw pushing society beyond the capitalist mode. The question is whether this analytical framework can also be useful in understanding Southern political economies.

Marx started from the notion that the production process was able to create value only when labour-power was added to the machinery and raw

Table 3:1 The Marxian Economic Relationships

$$\text{Rate of Profit} = \frac{s}{(c + v)} = \frac{s/v}{c/v + 1}$$

$$\text{Rate of Profit} = \frac{\text{Rate of Exploitation}}{\text{Organic Composition of Capital} + 1}$$

1) Thus if the Organic Composition of Capital rises and the Rate of Exploitation stays the same, the Rate of Profit falls.
2) If the Rate of Exploitation falls because wages increase, the Rate of Profit falls.
3) If the Rate of Profit is to stay steady, and the Organic Composition of Capital rises, the Rate of Exploitation must rise.

materials that made up the constant capital of the enterprise. What that labour-power received for its work was wages, making up a wages bill, which Marx called the variable capital of the production process. In addition, a surplus or profit would be created, which was the excess over the costs of the constant capital and the variable capital within a given period. What we have in effect is a total value of production, comprising the sum of the cost of the constant capital, and of the variable capital, plus the surplus or profit, within a given period. This total production can be expressed in shorthand terms as $c + v + s$.

Marx worked with these terms to derive ratios that played an important role in his notion of the dynamics of capitalism:

a) rate of profit = $s/(c + v)$
b) rate of exploitation = s/v
c) organic composition of capital = c/v

Some simple mathematics point out the dynamics that Marx saw at work under capitalism, given these relationships. The technique was to divide both the numerator and the denominator of the fraction in expression (a) by "v" (which does not change the value of the ratio in the fraction) to achieve the results shown in Table 3:1.

What Marx argued from these relationships, was that:

i)   the rate of profit will fall (all other considerations being equal) when there is technical progress, which is what he believed was reflected in an increase in the organic composition of capital;
ii) given such an increase in the organic composition of capital (to be expected as capital accumulation increases), the rate of profit can be maintained only if there is an increase in the rate of exploitation;

iii) if there is resistance to an increase in the rate of exploitation, the rate of profit will fall, creating a crisis of accumulation — because capitalists will not continue investing if the rate of profit is falling — which will lead to increases in unemployment — and consequent pressures to decrease wages so as to increase the rate of exploitation and thereby restore profit rates.

Marx saw these realities as "contradictions" — tendencies inherent in the way the system operated that either undercut the capacity to accumulate of the system (which was its central goal), or generated periodic crises that undercut the social viability of the system (since workers lost their jobs). Marx also saw inherent tendencies for the system to create and accelerate conflicts between the relations and the forces of production — what he called dialectical patterns that would lead to the system being increasingly challenged and ultimately supplanted. In particular, he saw the inherent drive that improved the technological capacity of production (and raised the organic composition of capital) just as inevitably driving capitalists to increase the rate of exploitation — or else undercutting accumulation in the system, as reinvestment slowed down in response to falling profits, and workers lost jobs. Thus conflicts in the social relations of production (based around private ownership that forced workers and capitalists to battle over the rate of exploitation) increasingly held back expansion of the forces of production that were following the logic of increased capital being used to improve technology (and raise the organic composition of capital). Marx saw those experiencing the increasing exploitation directly (industrial workers) challenging the owners of the forces of production (whose concern for high profit rates also led periodically to reduced investment, lower accumulation, and increased unemployment). Out of this growing challenge by workers, Marx argued, would come the transition to a socialist economy, where accumulation and technological progress would no longer be undercut by such periodic crises.

C) Marx and the South. Leaving aside Marxian social analysis, this broad economic perspective leads to two differing perspectives on Southern countries.

First, there is the question of how capital accumulation began in Western Europe, which leads to Marx's answer of "primitive accumulation." In volume 1 of *Capital* Marx provides a vivid description of the dispossession of peasant producers in Europe, an occurrence that would later have even bloodier and more ruthless equivalents in many Southern countries. The slave trade, the use of slaves to accumulate huge fortunes in the Caribbean, the destruction of societies and the looting of Indian empires in Mexico and Peru, the devastation of the opium trade in China — all this played a part in the early accumulation process that launched European industrial capitalism, according to Marx. This could be seen as a devastating and destructive intervention experienced by people in the South.

But what were the long-term consequences? Here Marx showed a certain ambivalence. He recognized the damage to people in the South. But one element of the dynamics of European capitalist accumulation that Marx discussed was that another way to maintain profit rates, given pressures for higher wages that would reduce the rate of exploitation, was to export capital to poorer countries for investment in activities with a lower organic composition of capital, thereby improving the profit rate by lowering the average organic composition of capital in the system. This could take capitalist penetration further into Southern societies, and analysts such as Bill Warren, writing in *New Left Review*, have argued that this export of capital could lead to accelerated accumulation, advancing the forces of production in many cases and often transforming relations of production in Southern countries from precapitalist to more productive capitalist relations much faster than would otherwise have happened. Capitalism coming to Southern economies, Warren says, in broad historical terms has been a progressive and positive development.[18] Other Marxists, including Paul Baran, concentrating on the surplus capital taken out of Southern countries by primitive accumulation and by later forms of monopoly capitalism imposed by the world economy in areas of the South, have seen capitalist penetration from abroad as a process that has damaged Southern economies.[19]

D) An Evaluation of Marx. So where does all this lead in considering the Marxian framework of analysis?

Marx's social analysis emerges as subtle and useful in analysing many countries, as a good starting point. The emphasis on material conditions was a helpful corrective in the 19th century, but there is not much doubt that gender considerations, ethnic/communal relations, language differentiation, race, and a variety of other points of social differentiation also have to be taken seriously in modern analysis. Nor can one simply assume that consciousness of one's social relations, based on the structure of production, will be automatic; much careful and complicated work has been done on consciousness, elite manipulation, and mechanisms of social control in recent years — not least by modern Marxists.

There is also a problem with Marx, just as with Rostow: Marx was less crude in the "stages of growth" he used, but the flavour of unidirectional, similar paths for diverse societies was nevertheless there (as Dudley Seers stressed when he applied his famous attack on the "economics of the special case" to Marxian analysis as well).[20]

Marxian economic categories do reflect a conflictual economic system, subject to periodic crises and battles over income shares. But the categories are quite abstract, are set at a very broad level, and are therefore difficult to define effectively for the purposes of policy analysis. Other economic analysis, in a structuralist and Keynesian tradition, seems somewhat more insightful on many specific points and uses clearer concepts that have precise meaning for policy applications. In a development context, the Marxian view also retains not only a strong emphasis on industrial development that is questionable for many countries but also a lack of emphasis on the complexities of trade, technology transfer, macroeconomic management, and the role of multinational corporations on the world economy level. Nor did Marx himself provide much insight on the reality of political economy in most Southern countries, leading to the contradictory views of different Marxists such as Baran and Warren.

That is what pushed many development analysts in somewhat different directions, including dependency and structuralist analysis. This was a perspective influenced by Marxian social analysis, but which took up a broader political economy framework recognizing the diversity of differing country experiences.

3: Structuralism and Dependency Analysis

In reaction to what became seen as the failure of the modernization approach and the limitations of the Marxian alternative, a "structuralist" emphasis emerged that stressed the historic sociopolitical institutions and built-in economic constraints shaped partly by the past interaction of Southern countries with the international economy (and with colonialism), and partly by ongoing imbalances in the domestic and international economies. Furtado and other structuralists stressed how past ties shaped a feudal-style society in much of Latin America and how more recent capitalist penetration from abroad did not broadly transform this configuration. The result was a structural segmentation in Southern societies that prevented an internal development dynamic that would take change to all parts of society and see that development benefits were broadly shared.

From these structuralist bases, analysts in Latin America (such as Sunkel, Villamil, and the Valenzuelas), in the Caribbean (Brewster, Girvan, and Farrell), and in Africa (Oculi, Amin) articulated a "dependency" view, stressing how powerful pressures from the expanding world economy continued to shape the institutions and processes of the internal political economies of most Southern countries in unbalanced, unequal ways.[21]

Much discussion of dependency theory stressed how powerful industrialized countries dominated the world economy, and how asymmetrical the links were between such countries and poorer Southern countries, as well as the size and flexibility of multinational corporations. This led some analysts to try to "test" dependency theory by measuring the extent of external linkage (for example, levels of foreign ownership of industry, or the amount of economic activity accounted for by primary product exports, or levels of technology payments abroad) and relating these indicators to measures of material well-being in Southern countries.[22] But as one Latin American dependency analysis insisted, "The point of dependency analysis is not the relative mix at one point in time of certain identifiable factors, but the evolution over time of structural relations which are intimately related and which help to explain the very different question as to why some forms of capitalism were more successful than others. ... Dependence in any given society is a complex set of associations in which the external dimensions are determinative in varying degrees of the internal ones and, indeed, internal variables may very well reinforce the pattern of external linkages."[23]

A) Sunkel and the Transnational System. Sunkel suggests how this complexity was increased by the rapid expansion of the global economy, and the spread of highly integrated transnational institutions (like the multinational enterprise) with very sophisticated internal communication and planning mechanisms operating worldwide. The dominant minorities in most Southern countries, Sunkel said, have been integrated into what has become a transnational society with increasingly shared tastes and values, while the majorities of national economies have experienced disintegration of their societies as their patterns of life have become increasingly separated from those in the transnational community. A key point in Sunkel's view was the emergence of global capitalism as a much more integrated and interconnected system, including the great majority in Northern countries (with a small minority excluded) and a minority in the South (see diagram 3:3).

The crucial point, according to Sunkel, was that incorporation of some people in the system in Southern nations cut across (and therefore complicated) classic social partitioning categories, with many elite and middle-class people in many Southern countries, and even a minority of better-paid workers with higher technology positions in certain multinational subsidiaries, being incorporated into the transnational system and gaining a share of benefits.

This process had two powerful effects. First, it meant that there were strong social forces (in terms of their strategic positions if not their numbers) who reinforced the integration of Southern countries into the global economy, despite the way in which the many more marginalized people were subjected to increasing polarization and inequality through the national disintegration that accompanied the incorporation of the minority

Diagram 3:3 The Sunkel Model of Transnational Integration

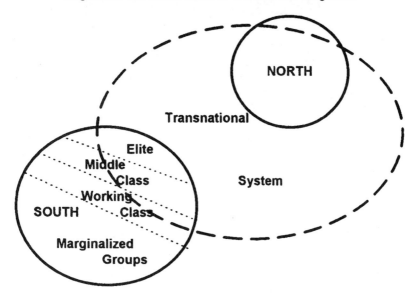

segment internationally. The political economy of large-scale poverty could be seen to have a political economy logic to it, given this dependency model, despite its wide human costs.

B) Brewster and "Internal Policy Capacity." Brewster stressed the second implication of this integrated–non-integrated structure. In a Northern economy, such as Canada, the various parts of the economy, such as employment levels, wage rates, exports, output, consumption, prices and investment, were closely related to each other. What we might expect to happen in Canada if, for example, investment increased significantly, would be increases in employment, followed by some wage increases, consumption increases, and output gains. These "functional interrelationships," as Brewster called them, would lead to high positive correlations over time among the statistics measuring these economic data.

But after examining 20 years of such statistics from Trinidad-Tobago, Brewster found no such pattern. The correlation coefficient between changes in investment and in employment, for instance, was only a very low .379. Wages and consumption levels seemed to have no real connection (the figure was .019), and investment did not seem to be associated with higher output (the figure was again low, at .226.) Brewster's conclusion was blunt. He said that employment is "the most important area of economic policy," yet any effort to deal with the jobs question "is premised on economic relationships which seem to be non-existent but which are nonetheless supposed to be administered through a standard range of institutions — the Plan, the Planning Department, the Central Bank ..."[24]

For Brewster, then, dependence was this "lack of capacity to manipulate the operative elements of an economic system," and it was "characterized by an absence of interdependence between the economic functions of a system." Based on the powerful impact of external economic forces, dependence was thus also a crucial resulting weakness to be able to act effectively internally, because of the structure of the domestic economy, in order to shape new policies to initiate new directions.

C) An Assessment. As a framework, dependency analysis had certain broad theoretical strengths. It recognized the significance of the world economy and stressed careful understanding of the dynamics and institutions of that international economy; and it emphasized the impact of external factors on internal structures so that the interconnection would always be understood. That is a key analytical point, but also an important policy point: The roots of a problem might lie in external factors, but dealing with the problems required action on the internal structural discontinuities, segmentation, and imbalances that existed in the domestic context.

But following that approach was often difficult, given Brewster's points about many domestic economic policy relationships. The approach could lead to a sense of paralysis — and no clarity on what sociopolitical forces would or could generate change. There was no broad notion of dialectics explicit in the dependency framework.

In similar terms, unlike modernization theory, the dependency approach identified no lengthy set of policy conclusions that cut across most situations — though there might be several broad common points to stress. (Breaking down the segmentation that had been shaped in many Southern countries was one goal, along with policy efforts to counter marginalization.)

Yet dependency analysis in the end continued to be an "approach" and was "far from being consciously considered a 'theory' of development."[25] That was its strength as well as its weakness. It pointed out the difficulties faced by Southern countries seeking social justice in an unequal global economy, without providing a detailed set of policies that could confront those difficulties successfully. This failure could lead to pessimism and even paralysis amongst those seeking changes to benefit poor majorities in the South. But the approach also stressed the diversity that existed among Southern countries, and the potential for effective specific strategies in particular circumstances.

By stressing that no grand theory existed to solve Southern problems, that external constraints were simply too powerful for that to be true, dependency analysis might have significantly helped others to push towards effective responses to specific concerns in individual Southern countries, regions, or communities — where locally based policies could respond to the diversity that gives individual areas differing historical institutions of political economy, structured by varied experiences of interaction with the world economy. In that sense, the broad critiques of the dependency theorists helped define the more community-based and diverse approaches of the new empowerment approaches.

4: The New Theoretical Divide

For some analysts dealing with Southern countries, including many in the World Bank and the International Monetary Fund, the failures of modernization theories, the weakness of the Marxian economic categories, and the policy limitations of structuralism/dependency led to an easy conclusion. They pronounced the field of "development studies" to be dead and simply applied neo-liberal economics to the differing political economies of the South. Yet the insights of all the past perspectives on development, from Marx to Lewis to Adelman to Brewster, have emphasized the distinctive structural differences in social, political, and economic interrelationships in Southern countries.

The result of ignoring these political economy insights has been serious failures in the application of neo-liberal solutions, so much so that the World Bank, for example, has now reassessed its views and once more started to stress the importance of an effective state, and of good governance systems, in achieving broad development goals, including marked poverty reduction.[26]

As Manor has pointed out, the neo-liberal stance has at least three basic weaknesses: a) it assumes "too much cultural, social, historical and political homogeneity among the less-developed countries"; b) it underestimates the powerful significance of the global economy on individual countries; and c) "the neo-liberals usually ignore elements of the political process."[27] There is also, says Manor, an extreme bias in the neo-liberal view: "They tend to react so sharply against the state that they lose sight of its creative potential." As a result, an exclusively "economic" analysis emerges, which ironically calls for major changes in state policies and institutions, without having done any analysis on the capacity of the particular state involved to be able to do what makes economic sense.

Yet the weaknesses in practice of neo-liberal approaches have not led to their complete rejection, in large part because some economists within the international financial institutions have used the political leverage of lending essential money to help with high debt burdens and have continued to try to impose neo-liberal policy conditions on Southern governments.

But the empowerment approach that has also emerged, building on both the social analysis of Marx and the political economy perspectives of structuralism and dependency, has been gaining momentum at two levels in the debate with neo-liberalism.

One key part of this new empowerment approach has been an emphasis on diversity, as David Booth underlines. There was, he says, a notion of policy "impasse" that emerged in dependency analysis and in the failures of broad modernization theories. But new approaches have stressed creative diversity of strategic and policy intervention around gender and poverty concerns, and also around specific middle-range policy questions such as agricultural emphases or technology strategy. There is now widely seen to be a micro-level diversity that implies room for social action and advance in rural development.[28] There has been a focus on action-research in a social context, too, stressing empirical findings and insights aimed at achieving change. This has represented the heart of one new emphasis on empowerment.

In the push for local-level action-research in development studies, as Wignaraja suggests, "People who are impoverished and marginalized by current growth processes are seen as ... the prime movers of history in the future."[29] NGOs in both Southern and Northern countries have become potential partners in this empowerment process — but only once these organizations enter into real dialogue with and support for Southern poverty groups.[30] An increasing number of Southern NGOs make such partnerships easier to carry forward in ongoing ways.

Overall, then, certain approaches are stressing the importance of global poverty, and emphasizing empowerment of the poor as the heart of new theoretical analyses aimed at fundamental change. Much of the detailed work on which the new approach is based emerges from micro-level local cases,[31] from the experiences of the women's movement in many areas,[32] and from the actions of local people in defence of their environmental future.[33] To be effective in a powerful way, however, the approach will ultimately have to move from the local to a second focus — to national levels of empowerment for the marginalized.

That shift presents a difficult challenge, as Stiefel and Wolfe point out. After exploring a wide range of "popular participation" experiences, they suggest that "the capacity of economic and political changes in wider spheres to obliterate even the most firmly established gains have become all too evident." In global terms, they conclude, "Exclusion seems to be gaining over incorporation."[34]

Still, the increasing spread of democracy and democratic institutions throughout the world represents the broad trend that challenges that pessimistic conclusion. The increasing focus in development thinking on questions of governance represents the same underlying reaction against the neo-liberal assumptions of free-market dominance. From the overthrow of authoritarian regimes in Brazil and the Southern Cone of Latin America to the spread of popular elections to South Africa, Mozambique, and Ghana to the democratization of governments in the Philippines and South Korea, participation in government through democratic means has been spreading dramatically. The emphasis on improved governance in terms of greater participation by people, more transparent and open performance by governments, and enforced democratic accountability to ensure state integrity is a further powerful sign of new empowerment currents flowing in many Southern countries.

After working personally with some of these new parliaments and seeing the effects of greater democratic input on thinking about policy choices, I am convinced that empowerment of the poor and democratization go together in Southern countries. The new approaches to development theory are starting to focus on global poverty; and the emerging democratic institutions across Southern countries give this new empowerment framework a significant potential to spur changes that will benefit poor majorities.

Notes

1 James Manor, "Politics and the Neo-liberals," in *States or Markets*, eds. C. Colclough and J. Manor (Oxford: Clarendon Press, 1991), pp.307-8.

2 See David Booth, "Development Research: From Impasse to a New Agenda," in *Beyond the Impasse*, ed. Schuurman, pp.49-69.

3 See Janet Townsend, "Gender Studies: Whose Agenda?" in *Beyond the Impasse*, ed. Schuurman, pp. 169-86.

4 For a number of examples, see Ghai, *Development and Environment*.

5 Kothari, *Poverty*, pp.73, 159 (his emphasis).

6 See Max Weber, *General Economic History* (New York: Collier Books, 1961), chapters 29 and 30.

7 See W.A. Lewis, "Economic Development with Unlimited Supplies of Labour," *The Manchester School*, May 1954.

8 See L. Haddad, L.R. Brown, A. Richter and L. Smith, "The Gender Dimensions of Economic Adjustment Policies," *World Development*, vol. 23, no. 6 (1995), pp.886-87.

9 See W.W. Rostow, "The Take-off into Self-Sustained Growth," *Economic Journal*, March 1956.

10 See the critique on this point in H. Myint, *The Economics of the Developing Countries* (London: Hutchinson University Library, 1974), pp.11-14.

11 See Dudley Seers, "The Limitations of the Special Case," *Bulletin of the Oxford Institute of Economics and Statistics*, May 1963.

12 See P.N. Rosenstein-Rodan, "Problems of Industrialization of Eastern and South-Eastern Europe," *Economic Journal*, 1943; R. Nurkse, *Patterns of World Trade and Development*, Wicksell Lectures 1959, Stockholm, 1959; A.O. Hirschman, *The Strategy of Economic Development*, New Haven, 1958.

13 M.S. Ahluwalia, "Income Inequality: Some Dimensions of the Problem," in *Redistribution with Growth*, ed. H. Chenery et al. (London: Oxford University Press, 1974), pp.8-9. The data is generally for the 1969-1971 period.

14 See Michael Lipton, *Why Poor People Stay Poor: Urban Bias in World Development* (London: Temple Smith, 1977), pp.49-52.

15 See G.K. Helleiner, *International Trade and Economic Development* (London: Penguin, 1973), p.131.

16 See Chenery et al., eds., *Redistribution with Growth*.

17 See Irma Adelman, "Growth, Income-Distribution and Equity-Oriented Development Strategies," *World Development*, vol. 3, no. 2/3 (1975), pp.312-23.

18 See Bill Warren, "Imperialism and Capitalist Industrialization," *New Left Review*, 81 (1973).

19 See Paul Baran, "On the Political Economy of Backwardness," *The Manchester School*, 1956.

20 Seers, "The Limitations of the Special Case."

21 Among other examples of this literature see O. Sunkel, "Transnational Capitalism and National Disintegration in Latin America," *Social and Economic Studies*, March 1973; J.S. Valenzuela and A. Valenzuela, "Modernization and Dependence: Alternative Perspectives in the Study of Latin American Underdevelopment," in *Transnational Capitalism and National Development: New Perspectives on Dependence*, ed. J.J. Villamil (Sussex: Harvester Press, 1979), pp.31-65; T. Dos Santos, "The Crisis of Development Theory and the Problem of Dependence in Latin America," in *Underdevelopment and Development*, ed. H. Bernstein (Harmondsworth: Penguin, 1976), pp.57-80; Norman Girvan, *Technology Policies for Small Developing Countries* (Mona: University of West Indies, 1983); Havelock Brewster, "Economic Dependence: A Quantitative Interpretation," *Social and Economic Studies*, vol. 22, no. 1 (1973), pp.90-95; T.A. Farrell, "A Tale of Two Issues: Nationalization, The Transfer of Technology and the Petroleum Multinationals in Trinidad-Tobago," *Social and Economic Studies*, vol. 28 (1979), pp.234-81; Okello Oculi, "Green Capitalism in Nigeria," in *The African Bourgeoisie*, ed. P.M. Lubeck (Boulder: Lynne Rienner Publishers, 1987), pp.167-83; Samir Amin, *Neo-Colonialism in West Africa* (Harmondsworth: Penguin, 1973).

22 See, for example, R.R. Kaufman, S.G. Daniel and H.I. Chernotsky, "A Preliminary Test of the Theory of Dependency," *Comparative Politics*, vol. 7 (1975).

23 See J.S. Valenzuela and A. Valenzuela, "Modernization and Dependence: Alternative Perspectives in the Study of Latin American Underdevelopment," pp.44, 46, 57.

24 See Brewster, "Economic Dependence: A Quantitative Interpretation," p.93.

25 See Valenzuela and Valenzuela, "Modernization and Dependence: Alternative Perspectives in the Study of Latin American Development," p.51.

26 See World Bank, *World Development Report, 1997*, chapters 1 and 2.

27 James Manor, "Politics and the Neo-liberals," in *States or Markets*, ed. C. Colclough and J. Manor (Oxford: Clarendon Press, 1991), pp.307-8.

28 See David Booth, "Development Research: From Impasse to a New Agenda," in Schuurman, *Beyond the Impasse*, ed. Schuurman, pp.49-69.

29 Wignaraja, ed., *New Social Movements in the South*, p.32.

30 See Jessica Vivian, "NGOs and Sustainable Development in Zimbabwe," in *Development and Environment*, ed. Ghai, pp.183-84; see also C. Malena, "Relations between Northern and Southern Non-Governmental Development Organizations," *Canadian Journal of Development Studies*, vol. XVI, no. 1 (1995), pp.7-30.

31 See, for example, Orlando Fals Bordo, "Countervailing Power in Nicaragua, Mexico and Colombia," in *New Social Movements in the South*, ed. Wignaraja, pp.201-13.

32 See, for example, T. Turner and M.O. Oshare, "Women's Uprising against the Nigerian Oil Industry in the 1980s," *Canadian Journal of Development Studies*, vol. XIV, no. 3 (1993), pp.311-57.

33 See Kojo Amanor, "Ecological Knowledge and the Regional Economy: Environmental Management in the Asesewa District of Ghana," in *Development and Environment*, ed. Ghai, pp.41-68.

34 See M. Stiefel and M. Wolfe, *A Voice for the Excluded* (London: Zed Books, 1994), p.241.

PART II

A Political Economy of Southern Poverty

CHAPTER 4

The Rural World

To reach the fertile rice fields of remote Ulanga district in central Tanzania meant crossing several large rivers by means of hand-pulled ferries. In a period of food-supply problems in other parts of the country, the fields stretched lush and well-tended in Ulanga, with women and children working with the men in the paddy fields to complete the harvest. From a typical hectare, close to 4,300 kilos of paddy rice were being produced, at a cash cost of some 2,750 Tanzanian shillings and an official price-value of about 14,000 shillings.

But growers were refusing to sell rice to the Tanzanian marketing authorities at this official price (3.25 shillings per kilo) and were diverting some rice into beer production, which could be sold in unregulated markets. They were still also holding a substantial amount of rice in the fields for sale to "parallel market" buyers — who, however, found it very hard to get in via the poor roads and rudimentary ferries to this outlying area of peasant productivity.[1]

Meanwhile, a thousand miles to the south, in the Sebungwe region of Zimbabwe, over 300,000 people were crowding into a dry-land cropping zone, with quite limited soil potential, much rainfall variability, and very little transport or services infrastructure. Here they were relying on maize and sorghum for food crops and on low-priced cotton as a cash crop. Widespread rural poverty and limited economic opportunities for most families were the result — leading to considerable migration to urban centres of people seeking better options. A major factor in the continuing deprivation in Sebungwe was the concentration of most policy benefits for agriculture and most infrastructure development among the 6,500 large-scale (white) settlers who occupied about half the good agricultural land in Zimbabwe.[2]

In the rural south of Honduras in Central America, different dynamics were at work. The expansion of commercial cattle production, in particular, led to increasing concentration of landholdings, leaving 34 per cent of rural families landless by 1974 and 21 per cent with farms less than 1

65

hectare in size. Food-crop production was squeezed by cattle-grazing, and data collected in 1982-83 in nine communities showed that 65 per cent of children under age five were stunted and undernourished — with most of them coming from landless households. The introduction of shrimp farming, eventually dominated by eight large mainly-foreign enterprises, caused further environmental damage to local food sources of fish and in the end came to benefit unskilled labour from the city rather than local landless households.[3]

In the state of Maharashtra in India, like many parts of rural Asia, a village near Satara had also experienced rapid agricultural change in the 1976-87 period, but in this case it was due to expanded irrigation and the introduction of new sugar cultivation. Households with irrigated land increased from 19 per cent to 43 per cent, and living standards improved significantly. Rather than leading to increased participation in community and economic life for women, however, the result was to weaken the personal autonomy and control over resources of women in the village. The attitudes of women appeared to have become less assertive and more dependent, even as their material positions had improved.[4]

At another extreme, some 300 kilometres south and west of Lusaka in Zambia, in the remote, wind-swept flats near the extreme end of Lake Kafue, shifting households of fishing people moved their sparse reed homes in response to changing water levels and fish stocks. With almost no cash, and no schools or health facilities for their children, households in Swilili lived in extreme poverty, drying the fish they caught to exchange for maize-meal and sugar on the occasional visits of passing traders. Their biggest danger was the gradual expansion of fishing at the other end of the lake, closer to Lusaka, and the ultimate decline this would bring to the fish stocks in the common property resource they depended on. Such environmental pressure would deepen their poverty.[5]

What do these snapshots of the Southern rural world suggest? Most obviously, there is an extremely widespread variation in the situations and conditions of rural life in Southern countries. Rural households represent a majority of the population in the South, and poverty problems are most extensive in rural areas, but crucial differences shape the rural reality in different settings. No overall generalizations are possible. Nevertheless, these snapshots point towards certain key themes that need to be explored in analysing the rural context in order to find ways of reducing poverty and broadening social and economic opportunities.

For one thing, these particular cases highlight the prevalence of "peasant agriculture" in most Southern countries — the production of both food and cash crops by households, on relatively small plots of land, using mainly family labour. As the Ulanga example suggests, this form of rural production can often be dynamic and expansionary, but it depends in major ways on external agricultural and infrastructure policy conditions that can discourage or encourage peasant farm activity. As in Sebungwe, however, peasant farming can also provide far fewer opportunities in different, harsher environmental conditions.

The Maharashtra example from India underlines both the complexity and the importance of drawing gender questions into consideration of the rural context. It cannot be automatically assumed that agricultural improvements in themselves will lead to improvements in the lives of women. As we have also seen as regards incorporating gender analysis into understanding the greater prevalence of child malnutrition and higher infant mortality in Asia (chapter 1), specific attention must be given to the role of women in the rural environment. As the Maharashtra example also suggests, the intervention of new technological inputs (in this case irrigation) can have marked effects on peasant agricultural communities. The major area of such technological innovation in recent years has been the package of new high-yielding seed varieties and associated fertilizer increases loosely termed the "Green Revolution." This phenomenon has been concentrated in Asia, but has also had an impact in Africa, and it deserves careful analysis.

As the major land inequalities in Zimbabwe illustrate, it is essential to consider land reform as a part of improving agricultural output and broadening economic opportunities. The growing number of landless families in southern Honduras and the child malnutrition associated with that trend underline the need to consider land redistribution (and associated broadening of credit access) as central in reducing rural poverty.

The environmental degradation caused by the great spread in cattle-grazing and shrimp farming in Honduras demonstrates the importance of understanding environmental pressures and conflicts in analysing the rural context. Kojo Amanor has shown in the Asesewa district of Ghana how peasant households have utilized their own environmental knowledge to develop low-cost methods of land regeneration, and such concerns are becoming fundamental in analysing many rural settings in Southern countries.[6]

The Lake Kafue case emphasizes how rural households include more than peasant farmers. An important poverty component consists of people far less settled than that — whether they are nomadic fishing communities, reliant on a communal water resource, or households often called "tribals" in India and elsewhere, dependent on communal forest or grazing resources. Environmental factors can clearly spur adverse changes for such households, too.

Finally, factors like the urban migration in Sebungwe in Zimbabwe and increased Lusaka fish demand in Zambia point to yet another theme. While the dynamics of the rural household are important in understanding poverty, including its causes and its alleviation, the rural economy does not operate in isolation from the rest of Southern societies.

1: The "Ins" and "Outs" of Peasant Agriculture

There was a time in the early penetration of European colonialism into Africa and Asia when peasant agriculture was seen as largely unchanging, undynamic, non-innovative, and unresponsive to opportunities. The general thrust of colonial policy was to coerce indigenous people to work on European plantations and settler farms, and the colonial authorities self-justified this policy by claiming that Africans, for instance, would "only stagnate under a regime of universal peasant proprietorship."[7]

This view could not, however, be sustained in the face of rapid peasant agriculture responses to economic opportunities when these did emerge. In West Africa, for instance, cocoa production expanded dramatically via household production in both the French and British colonies. Differential prices for higher quality cocoa, palm oil, groundnuts, and cotton over the 1950-62 period also led to marked peasant agriculture responses that raised quality grades consistently and quickly.[8] Dramatic expansions in peasant coffee and tea production in Kenya, after the end of colonial bans on African growers, followed the same pattern.

Based on such cases, some analysts began to argue that peasant producers simply responded to economic incentives like anyone else. Looking at the case of India, for instance, where great expansions in agricultural production made the country self-sufficient in food (and even a net exporter), T.W. Schultz pointed out that the key factor in that success had been a reliance on the responsive and efficient "economic behavior of farm families, especially as they opt for improvements in education and wealth."[9]

This recognition of peasant rationality and responsiveness was a useful corrective to patronizing colonial views that perpetuated myths of the "backward," traditional peasant household, unwilling to consider change. But still, important aspects of the reality of peasant agriculture and rural life in the South were missed by the simple perspective of peasant as "economic man."

The most crucial reality is the high risks faced by many peasants, in a context in which accumulated assets to offset those risks are limited. Some of the risks are the result of rainfall variability that is much greater than in temperate areas of the globe;[10] and these risks are heightened when peasants move towards more reliance on high fertilizer inputs — which will lead to much better output levels if the rains are good, but a virtual wipe-out of the crop if rains fail. Crop failures that come when peasants have few assets to fall back on can mean the loss of the small landholdings that peasant households rely on for their food survival — or they can mean a move into tenant farming relations with larger-scale farmers/moneylenders, resulting in a high and permanent squeeze on incomes that means long-term poverty.

Add imperfect market conditions to this in many real-life situations, with monopolistic buyers able to force down prices considerably if crops are good, and it is clear that many peasant households will have to stress a different strategy. Rather than profit-maximization, they follow survival strategies that emphasize minimizing risk as the key priority.[11]

The few peasant households with access to more land, better soil, more regular rainfall, and assets based outside of farming (such as public-sector incomes or shops) could take a more high-rise approach. The result was almost always growing social and economic inequality in peasant agriculture areas. In parts of Sebungwe in Zimbabwe, for instance, studies by 1992 within Gokwe showed that 2 per cent of households were seen as "wealthy," another 15 per cent seen as "middle class," and 68 per cent seen as "poor" or "extremely poor."[12] Similar analysis in Kenya saw increased shares of income going to an emerging stratum of richer households who were buying land and expanding their other holdings, while poorer households received a decreasing share and had to sell some of their land.[13] Stronich found the same pattern, in accelerated form, in southern Honduras.

On one level, this emergence of leading peasant households — the "ins" we might call them — represents an important, dynamic social segment in many rural areas. But on another level, the most crucial point about this differentiation process is that the great majority of peasant households are being left "out" of many opportunities because the risks of participating are just too high. Countering those risks so that wider rural gains can be shared emerges as a key concern in reducing poverty.

Government agricultural policies also appear to be major factors in shaping rural social polarization and differentiation. For instance, in her research in the southern part of Volta Region in Ghana Jette Bukh shows how 85 per cent of Agricultural Bank loans there went to absentee farmers (such as top bureaucrats and professionals), and these loans permitted investment in maize and cassava production that led to high profits. Larger-scale peasants in the village studied (about 6 per cent of households, who grew 37 per cent of the cocoa) had larger cocoa holdings (over 10 acres each on average), hired labour, and had returns high enough to invest in other rural activities. Middle peasants (another 48 per cent of households, growing 63 per cent of the cocoa in the area, on an average of 2.3 acre plots) could survive fairly independently on their cash-crop and food-crop production. But poorer peasants (46 per cent of the total households, with no cocoa holdings) had to combine for survival both food-crop production and wage labour for the absentee farmers.[14]

Other research has noted similar effects of government extension poli-cies in Tanzania, where the focus was on better-off, more innovative peasant households.[15] In Kenya, the Carlsen studies of four diverse micro-districts showed the same importance as in Ghana of public-sector salaries and bureaucratic access in shaping the growing social dominance of richer and larger landholding households.[16] In Zimbabwe government credit has also been crucial in creating lucrative agricultural income gains for some small-holders, but only 3 per cent of peasant households now receive such credit.[17]

To some degree the ongoing communal linkages and obligations exist-ing in many peasant-based societies offset increasing inequalities in peasant agriculture. Wolf has stressed the importance of what he calls a "ceremonial fund" that peasants must maintain, to take account of the mutual social relations that tie peasant communities together, from marriages to births to various kinship obligations.[18] This suggests a degree of informal, internal redistribution within rural peasant societies that income and asset distrib-ution data do not capture.

Widening social differentiation *within* given peasant communities also interacts with major distinctions in income and wealth *among* different agri-cultural regions in many Southern countries. Thus, looking at Kenya, Carlsen suggests that yearly agricultural income for average households in the richest tea-growing district of Kisii was 2.7 times higher than in the sugar-reliant Kisumu district, and twice as high as in the vegetable-pro-ducing Taita Hills and maize-cassava growing Kwale districts on the Indian Ocean coast.[19] These regional disparities often reflect the differential colo-nial trade strategies (noted in Chapter 2), which drew certain areas into extensive international production (from the peanut districts of Senegal to coffee-growing Buganda in Uganda), while leaving out other areas (from Northern Ghana to central Tanzania).

But the regional opportunity differences of peasants also point to other factors, which reflect the ongoing dynamics of international and national economic forces on peasant households.

At a national level, broader government economic strategies often strongly influence the options available to and constraints facing peasant agriculture. In Tanzania, for instance, the highly regulated marketing systems for rice (and other key agricultural commodities), combined with low official prices and severe foreign exchange limitations that cut back on available fertilizers and consumer goods, all worked strongly against Ulanga peasant rice producers. In Zambia, too, the National Agricultural Marketing Board paid farmers only Kwacha4, 30 per 90 kilo bag of maize, while the export price peasants could have received was at least Kwacha6,44 — some 50 per cent higher.[20] The situation for peasant export tree crops was often even harsher. In Ghana, for instance, the percentage of the export price of cocoa received by peasant producers (after state export taxes and state-run marketing overheads) varied in recent years from 27 per cent in 1985-87, up to 49 per cent in 1991-92, and down again to 30 per cent in 1993-94.[21] These pressures in national policy could have major effects on rural poverty. Detailed studies among peasant export crop producers in the Ivory Coast, for instance, showed that coffee and cocoa peasants there experienced much greater increases in poverty levels between 1985 and 1991 than any other social grouping in the country as a result of high export taxes and overvalued exchange rates that kept the real incomes of producers low and falling.[22]

These external pressures on peasant communities were partly the consequence of the changing dynamics of international commodity price shifts for cash crops produced. The world coffee price escalation of the late 1970s, for instance, led to rapid economic growth in Central Province in Kenya, in the Mt. Kilimanjaro region of Tanzania, in highland Costa Rica, and in central Colombia. The fall in world cocoa prices over the 1979-90 period hurt south-eastern Ivory Coast, the Ashanti region of Ghana, and western Nigeria. Overall, Southern countries experience continuing instability in the prices of non-oil commodity exports, ranging from an average annual price deviation from trend lines for food exports of 21 per cent between 1980-91, to 16.4 per cent for vegetable oilseeds, to 14 per cent for tropical beverages.[23] This adds to the risk factor facing many less-affluent peasant households as they make production decisions.

Even more powerful in its impact on peasant communities (and a major factor in growing export-crop peasant poverty in the Ivory Coast, for instance), has been the longer-term world price trend. Over 1980-91, the annual average change in real prices was a fall of 5.4 per cent for Southern food exports, a fall of 7.4 per cent for oilseeds, and a fall of 8.9 per cent for tropical vegetables. Combining these export price declines with the trends in unit values of manufactured imports provides a measure of the changes in terms of trade on the world level between Southern commodities exported and manufactured goods imported, which shows a decline by an annual average of 4.3 per cent over 1980-91 (compared to virtually no change over 1970-80). This finding shows a loss in terms of trade over 1980-91 for non-oil exporters in Africa of 25 per cent of their 1980 Gross Domestic Product, with a 14 per cent loss over the same period for Latin America and a 12 per cent loss for Asia.[24]

These price pressures reflect world demand and supply conditions for many peasant export commodities. It is typical to see low price elasticities of demand at the international level for products such as cocoa, coffee, and tea, which mean that (for instance) a 1 per cent decrease in price will lead to much less than a 1 per cent increase in quantity demanded. It is also typical to see a low-income elasticity of demand at the world level, which suggests that for a 1 per cent increase in world income there will be much less than a 1 per cent increase in demand for tropical beverages or food. The price elasticity of supply in Southern countries, in response to world price changes, is also often quite low, because tree crops such as cocoa, tea, and coffee take years from the time when they are first planted to when they first produce output.

A typical pattern, then, would be some shortfall in world coffee supply, caused (perhaps) by a frost in Brazil, leading to a slight decrease in world coffee supply — which in turn brings on large world price increases because of how small supply shifts make prices rise or fall significantly when world demand is inelastic. There is little short-run potential to increase supply, given very low price elasticity of supply — but peasant producers are encouraged over the longer run by the higher prices to plant new trees. When these trees mature in a number of years, the world coffee supply increases significantly — and given inelastic demand-responses to price changes, a very considerable price decrease will be needed to bring this higher world supply into equilibrium with demand. As a result of several years of better prices because of the Brazil frost, then, there will have been a long-term increase in coffee supply that will depress prices for a significant period and may under certain conditions mean that peasant farmers are receiving less net revenue for their crops than before they invested in new trees.

These elasticity conditions do lend themselves to supply-management efforts to restrict supplies to the international commodity market, and countries producing coffee and cocoa have undertaken limited moves in that direction. But these moves usually work to increase national marketing structure controls on peasant producers, and they can lead to increased shares of export-crop revenue going to others outside the peasant community (usually the state and/or marketing officials). They can also prevent further peasant entry into these relatively lucrative production sectors, and thereby increase continuing social differentiation and inequality in peasant areas. These may be seen as social costs less significant than the social gains to be achieved in given circumstances. But there does remain a difficult administrative question in many Southern countries of whether low-cost and effective operation of domestic supply management is even possible, given infrastructure limitations, cross-border smuggling options, and the increased reliance on small-scale marketing enterprises in many countries.

These international commodity-price factors are not the only sources of pressures on peasant communities. Some areas can escape export-crop concerns by concentrating on food-crop production for self-consumption and wider domestic market sale. The questions of national agricultural policy and infrastructure provision so clearly evident in the Ulanga and Sebungwe cases, can impinge on these efforts. Peasant producers may not be able to obtain the inputs they require if foreign exchange constraints are operative. Price controls may keep returns very low for peasant households in order to ensure stable prices for politically active urban populations, and national credit institutions are often unresponsive to peasant financing needs, except for export crops. In many peasant communities, too, the road system necessary to marketing food crops and providing consumer goods may be rudimentary, so that middlemen in the trading networks (even if they exist) take high shares of exchange prices.

But other dynamics also emerge within some peasant communities. Community-based initiatives have begun to deal with isolation and inadequate infrastructure through self-help organizations. Sometimes, as in various cases documented in India, this drive for local change has had an environmental focus. The Chipko movement in Himalayan peasant villages, for instance, not only resisted commercial takeover of communal forest land, but also included work that has since stressed the afforestation of other village lands.[25] Other initiatives, like the "Harambee" movement in Kenya, have stressed the local construction of schools and health clinics. In Northern Ghana, successful community development efforts have taken place to establish locally based water supply development boards that have drawn broad segments of the community into participation, raised considerable sums from poor villages, and set in place mechanisms to supply sustainable, clean sources of water for many communities in the area.[26] Such locally rooted community movements appear to be expanding rapidly in Ghana and elsewhere.

In general, then, peasant agriculture is subject to major pressures and internal dynamics of change in many Southern countries. Far from being stagnant and "traditional" sectors of stability, peasant communities are being reshaped by growing social polarization and external shifts. Some households (the "ins" with access to better land, favourable infrastructure, and state or other outside resources), have had new opportunities to respond to, especially as urban populations expand, low-cost rural labour becomes more available, and changing state macroeconomic strategies improve domestic rural-urban terms of trade. For most households, though, risks have remained high because of rainfall variability and limited assets. And for many households poverty has increased as world commodity prices have run strongly against peasant export crops, and national economic policies have squeezed peasant export returns and minimized new rural infrastructure.

For many peasant households, landholding has given way to land tenancy, access to communal "commons" lands has often been lost, and the combination of risks and lower export prices has made for increased reliance on low-paid work as rural labour.

For some peasants, community-based local organizing has represented a means for some to improve community life through self-help initiatives. But the fundamental conclusion remains. As a consequence of the high risks of rain-fed agriculture on small plots of land in variable climates, subject to adverse world price pressures, and hit by government policies that benefit a small minority, most peasant households remain at the core of Southern poverty. The gender dimensions of this rural poverty are a central reality that make for even greater complexities in analysis, especially in combination with environmental realities that confront many of the rural poor.

2: The Complexities of Rural Poverty: Gender and Environment

"In the earlier days," said an older peasant woman in the Volta region of Ghana in 1977, "men and women tilled the soil together. The plots they farmed were very small, because the soil was very fertile . . . and the yam was sufficient for the whole year."

But in contemporary Ghana, "If you are a woman farmer," a younger woman says, "life after being divorced is easier, because when you are married you will have to cook for the husband on top of all your work."[27]

As Bukh shows, the introduction of cash-crop cocoa production in this region took many men away from food-crop production, forced women to take much greater responsibility for growing food crops, and therefore led to a shift from higher nutrition yams (which require heavy, joint labour) to lower nutrition cassava (often grown on less fertile lands not needed for cocoa). This change placed heavier demands on land fertility and reduced environmental sustainability, and it also placed greater labour burden on the women of the community. This trend towards "double-day" responsibilities for rural women has been recognized as a general shift in Southern countries.

Formal time-allocation studies show, on average, that women spend increasing hours in agricultural and wage-generating activity and continue to devote far more hours than men to home-production needs from child care to obtaining water to preparing meals. Detailed studies suggest that women tend to spend some 20 hours per week in household work compared to 5 hours for men, and 42 hours on outside income-earning compared to 47 hours for men.[28] In part this phenomenon reflects colonial and postcolonial views on land tenure that not only aimed extension work on cash crops almost exclusively at male farmers, but also often ignored customary female land rights in formalizing titles to land; in part, it reflects in some cases appropriation of land by the state to transfer it to other activities.[29] In part, too, it must be seen as reflecting what Janet Townsend has called the "invisibility of women" in development studies.[30]

Townsend stresses how both development theory and development projects neglected to listen to the articulated concerns and priorities of women. Not surprisingly, this neglect made for an extra dimension of powerlessness that could deepen the deprivations of rural poverty. Recent poverty analyses carried out by the World Bank on a country-by-country basis during 1995 found that 11 of 19 cases of Southern countries reviewed were characterized by special poverty concerns related to women. In Argentina, rural women were a particularly hard-hit group; in Brazil, and in Cameroon, young women were leaving school at far higher rates than men because of poverty pressures; in Colombia, low educational levels among rural women were contributing to poverty; in the Dominican Republic, rural female-headed households were a special poverty target; in Ghana, poverty was greatest among rural women in the North; in both Honduras and Kenya, a lack of access to land was hitting rural women-headed households especially hard; in Mauritania, female-headed households also experienced higher poverty levels; in Senegal, analysis stressed the need for literacy among rural women to help counter poverty; and in Zambia, rural female-headed households were the group most damaged by very deep poverty levels.[31]

At the same time, certain dynamics at work in peasant farming systems make gender analysis complicated. We have seen this in how the better-off women of Maharashtra in India took the gains from irrigation in the form of increased leisure and reduced social autonomy, as a way of emulating higher-caste women. Opposite dimensions are suggested by the changing views of women in the Manya Krobo district of Ghana, where cocoa production is now declining — over one-third of women now felt they could plant and own trees, something denied to them in their past agricultural practice.[32]

These complexities emerge with special force in the context of rural environmental threats. In some cases gender inequalities have been heightened by environmental pressures, making rural responses to ecological concerns more difficult — and in other cases gender considerations seem to contribute to more effective counters against dangers faced by rural environments.

For instance, in Zimbabwe during the drought of 1992, enormous numbers of cattle died of starvation because of environmental deprivations, leading to massive economic losses for pastoralists, especially in the south of the country. This was a case in which selling at least some cattle could have saved other cattle from death and helped to maintain household wealth in monetary form until the drought conditions passed. Yet this was not just a badly managed natural disaster — it was a consequence of gender inequalities. The men owned the cattle, and about half of the men had migrated to the city. The women left caring for the cattle could not make the necessary environmental and economic decisions to sell the livestock without male permission. Informed by letters, the men in Harare could not be convinced to give that permission until it was too late. Similarly, Zimbabwean women were unable to take independent decisions to plant trees for purposes of environmental improvement.[33]

A 1991 study of Limbang district in Sarawak, Malaysia, showed few of the initial rural gender inequalities of Zimbabwe. Both men and women had ownership and use rights over land, and assets brought into a marriage remained under the control of the spouse who had originally possessed them. Women had major input into all decisions in the agricultural-fishing community, and there was little segregation of labour roles. In this case, though, environmental pressures were added to the existing context by the entry of extensive commercial logging near the community, which dramatically changed the situation. The logging hurt both genders by decreasing water quality in the river, reducing fish stocks, and increasing water pollution. But while the women directly experienced this new external pressure in negative terms, the men received some benefits — some 40 per cent of husbands were now away doing logging for the company for wages. This situation in turn increased the burden on rural women to undertake food-crop production and had the potential of decreasing the communitys long-fallow approach to agriculture, because the men needed for the heavier land clearance under that approach were now less available. Increased wage-remissions came from the male lumber employment to households, but overall the new environmental pressure damaged established and viable production patterns and produced gender inequality in opportunities and direct income benefits, a condition that had not previously been significant.[34]

But the dynamics of environmental stress could also move gender relations somewhat away from unequal conditions. In Embu in central Kenya, women historically had experienced few property rights, leaving men controlling all the assets and making the main decisions. There were clear labour-role divisions: men took little responsibility for food crops, yet also left women with all the main household responsibilities. Women, as in Zimbabwe, could not plant trees for environmental gains, unless males gave their permission, even though large numbers of the males had migrated to Nairobi. The dynamic features in Embu, however, included increasing subdivision of small plots of land, high rates of population increase, and the consequent movement of many households onto more marginal, lower-rainfall land more distant from Mt. Kenyas fertile areas. Clearly women were disadvantaged more than men in the context of the increasing poverty and environmental stress that this dynamic was producing in many parts of Embu. But the extent of environmental pressure and consequent economic difficulty was also producing an increasing fluidity in the sharing of tasks within households. There is now little absolute segregation of tasks, and in these more difficult conditions men are beginning to assist women in a substantial way in gathering firewood and water.[35]

All three of these cases — of Zimbabwe, Malaysia, and Kenya — stand in vivid contrast to the role played by women in communal fishing villages in the Solomon Islands. A 1991 study of the island of Marovo found that women appeared to be the leading environmental guardians of their community. This society is based around customary marine-tenure systems, in which both men and women have tenure rights (women somewhat closer to shore, men somewhat further out). Decision-making is described as shared, and women describe the men as "helpful" in doing household tasks. Yet as external commercial fishing fleets move more closely into the sea around Marovo, it is women (who play more of a role in cleaning fish) who have detected shifts in species being caught and have had enough power within the community to push everyone into concerted group action to reorder the terms on which commercial fishing is tolerated. This movement has significantly limited external environmental threats. The women have been especially prominent in this fight because the main impact of the commercial fleets has been on taking bait in inshore areas — where the womens fishing rights for inshore mollusc are concentrated.[36]

What do these complexities indicate? Again, the examples highlight the diversity of rural situations and dynamics within Southern countries. But two powerful overall conclusions clearly emerge.

First, environmental concerns do matter a great deal in analysing the roots of rural poverty in the South. U.S. economist Lester Thurow has claimed that "environmentalism is an interest of the upper middle class. Poor countries and poor individuals simply aren't interested." Yet as Bartelmus shows, people in most Southern countries have a deep concern about how environmental pressures undercut their rural resource base — through soil damage, drought, deforestation, loss of "commons" land, and water pollution.[37]

Writing of India, Agarwal and Narain point out that government takeover of the commons there has led to its neglect by villagers, with the result that planted trees do not grow and environmental degradation of village land accelerates, in part because the commons cannot be used and grazing must be concentrated elsewhere.[38] Ethiopia has also seen environmental problems grow, as peasant villages have turned to unrestricted cutting of hilltop forests, increasing water run-off, and erosion. In Costa Rica, Thailand, and Madagascar, conflicts have emerged between peasant households and national parks established without peasant involvement in planning and parks supervision.[39] Prawn-farm development in countries such as Thailand has had serious negative effects on small-scale local fishing communities, whose fishing areas have been damaged by pollution from the prawn-growing.[40]

In other places, peasant communities trying to shape cash-crop transitions have faced environmental tensions. In Western Ghana, for example, shifting cocoa production — seeking new frontier areas for more fertile soils — has brought peasant households into much more fragile forest environments, which is leading to significant deforestation, thereby having a rapid negative impact on environmental conditions in that part of the country. At the same time conflicts are being played out in former frontier areas, such as Manya Krobo district, as cocoa growing shifts elsewhere and peasant households promote locally developed tree species to help regenerate land fertility, while official Ghana government initiatives push for planting of imported trees that many peasants feel are unsuitable for local conditions.[41] In Zimbabwe, competition for land has generated environmental conflict, as those seeking new access to land have bought out what have been held as communal commons in peasant agriculture parts of the country, costing peasants the use of land resources from which they have gained in the past.[42]

Second, the cases outlined again emphasize the importance of gender analysis in understanding rural poverty. The degree of difficulty in countering poverty can only be understood by considering the micro-level discrimination against many Southern women so far as their control over resource improvements is concerned. The dynamics by which external threats to viable environments can also undercut gender equity (as in the Sarawak case above) reinforce this point.

This final perspective deserves emphasis not just as a negative blockage to overcome, but as a positive factor in community empowerment efforts. Gender inequality can prevent or limit environment-based responses to external resource threats (as with Zimbabwe women unable to sell cattle in the face of severe drought — or with Kenyan women prevented from planting trees to help improve farmland conditions). But involving women fully in community-based development efforts, with an environmental focus, can contribute strongly to the success of those efforts.

In Northern Ghana, for instance, local district assemblies have not been able to draw women into local-government institutions for development improvements (only 5-10 per cent of district assembly members are women in all three regions in the north), and the assemblies have generally been ineffective in promoting local development initiatives. But analysis at the community level found that 45 per cent of community organizations were women-only groups, 37 per cent were mixed, and 18 per cent were all-male.[43] The much more successful community initiatives through water supply development boards in the area assured that 36 per cent of board members across the 14 selected communities were women — Canadian-based aid support made extra efforts to draw in an even higher share of women for the future — and community-funded and managed initiatives are now supplying water to eight of the communities.[44] The much stronger involvement of women and womens groups made a crucial contribution to this community development success.

Thus gender inequalities are central factors in the continuing poverty for many of the rural poor. Indeed, many rural women are caught in an ongoing poverty cycle, with deprivation for mothers perpetuated via unequal options for daughters. That is why a recent, broad-based 1996 poverty review concludes that one of the most important priorities for reducing global poverty is to massively increase education support for rural girls, so that the deep education inequalities that help keep their mothers poor can be overcome through equal female-male education gains in Southern countries in the future.[45] This same study underlined how "increasing numbers of poor people live in areas that . . . are environmentally fragile."

3: Poverty, Distribution, and the Green Revolution

The changing of gender inequities, then, represents one dynamic element in improving rural living standards. What about new technological innovations as a significant anti-poverty factor?

Less than 25 years ago, a senior economist at the University of Singapore could write of the "food crisis of 1972-73" in Southeast Asia, and how it "put an end" to "unwarranted confidence in the Green Revolution."[46] In 1995 analyses from IFPRI (International Food Policy Research Institute) stated, "The world should be able to provide enough food to feed 8 billion people in the year 2020, with the main food crops selling at even lower prices than today." Southeast Asia should be able to keep its food production ahead of its population growth — so long as agricultural research budgets are maintained and expected advances on new high-yielding rice varieties continue.[47]

Problems have emerged in the context of some applications of the new technology package, but the Green Revolution has clearly had an overall positive impact on food supply.

Southern countries have centred out various food crops for major attention. One of these has been wheat, and new varieties have been developed by two international agricultural research centres, CIMMYT (International Maize and Wheat Improvement Centre) and ICARDA (International Centre for Agricultural Research in Dry Areas). A report from Egypt suggests the impact of this work:

In 1987, almost the whole wheat area in Upper Egypt was sown to aging wheat varieties like Giza 155 — although newer heat-tolerant varieties, bred by Egyptian scientists in collaboration with ICARDA and its sister center, CIMMYT, had been available for some years. In 1992/93 a team from ICARDA/NVRP [Nile Valley Regional Program] and Egypt's Agricultural Research Center (ARC) carried out a survey to see how widely these new packages had been adopted, and to try to quantify the real benefits to farmers. The results were encouraging; 64% of the farmers surveyed in Sohag and Qena had adopted the new varieties, 73% the new planting date, and 77% the recommended irrigation interval.

Average wheat yields in Egypt increased from 3.6 tonnes per hectare to 5.4 tonnes per hectare between 1981/83 and 1990/93 as a result, with total national wheat production up from 2 million to 4.5 million tonnes per year.[48]

Wheat production in India during the earlier years of the Green Revolution showed the same basic pattern of dramatic production increases. Between 1964-65 and 1968-69, wheat acreage in India increased by 19 per cent and wheat production by 52 per cent. The transformation was particularly remarkable in Punjab state, where innovative farmers in those few years planted 80 per cent of the land with new high-yielding varieties, increased the number of tube-wells for irrigation from 7,000 to 120,000, tripled the consumption of fertilizer, and consequently doubled wheat yields per hectare.[49]

In rice production, important output gains were made from the combination of new hybrid seeds and increased inputs of fertilizer, especially in Asia, but also in some Latin American countries, such as Colombia. The first successful cross-breeding to obtain semi-dwarf, high-yielding varieties of rice took place in China, with release in 1959; by 1965, a year before the first breakthrough variety released from the International Rice Research Institute (IRRI), some 3.3 million hectares of high-yield rice were already planted in four southern Chinese provinces.[50] From that period in the 1960s, work by IRRI and Chinese researchers pushed research ahead rapidly to improve yields and build in better resistance in new seeds to various diseases, along with dealing with other production problems. By the 1980s, the results could be seen in the elimination of rice imports into India, in the 133 per cent gain in Indonesian rice production between 1968 and 1981, and in high percentages of the total rice area in Asia planted with new varieties (ranging from 20 per cent in Bangladesh and 44 per cent in India, up to some 60 per cent in Korea and Indonesia and 75 per cent in the Philippines).[51]

In the case of Sub-Saharan Africa, Green Revolution production increases were less widespread. But important increases were evident in that area, too, in the case of maize. Eicher has traced the particularly significant case of Zimbabwe, where local maize-breeding efforts successfully produced the SR-52 seed for release in 1960, leading to maize yield increases of 46 per cent per hectare. From this success, the program moved on to production of short-season maize for drier land areas, which proved highly beneficial to smallholder African producers in the period after 1980. In the six years 1980-86, peasant households doubled their maize production, and in Zimbabwe they moved to a position in which virtually 100 per cent of maize production now uses the new hybrid varieties.[52] Ghana has also shown success in the development of improved maize varieties and production technologies. The Crops Research Institute there says those improvements increased national maize output from 0.5 metric tonnes per hectare to 2 tonnes per hectare over the 1970-95 period.[53] Kenya and Zambia have also experienced increased hybrid maize reliance.

Increased output has not always been the sole objective of Green Revolution research. In Ghana, for example, the national Crops Research Institute, working with CIMMYT and the International Institute for Tropical Agriculture (and financial support from the Canadian International Development Agency—CIDA), has developed a Quality Protein Maize called "Obatanpa" with twice the nutritional value of normal maize varieties; as of 1994, this was being used in food supplement programs in 800 schools in poorer parts of Ghana.[54] In Tanzania, crop research at the agricultural university at Morogoro developed sorghum varieties that could be grown in much shorter time periods than normal, which helped to counter drought conditions. In China, the Shanghai Academy of Agricultural Science worked with ICARDA in the Yangtze basin in the early 1990s to successfully develop a new barley seed variety, "Gobernadora," resistant to "scab" (a disease generating, in seeds, toxins harmful to human and animal health).[55]

In general, then, the evidence suggests that Green Revolution innovations have helped improve food supply considerably in the context of peasant agriculture in many Southern countries. This success is an important reality, in situations where basic food shortages have loomed. But any analysis of the effects of the Green Revolution on poverty must go further. How have the benefits of technological change been divided? Have production gains been balanced among regions and different producers? And what are the long-term dynamics of Green Revolution agriculture in shaping peasant social and economic interaction with the rest of Southern societies?

The evidence on these questions is less clear-cut.

For example, examination in the 1960s of the impact of new wheat innovations in the Punjab in India found that high financing requirements for essential irrigation (via tube-wells) and for required fertilizer inputs meant that larger farmers were quick to take advantage of the new opportunities, and to benefit from the higher prices for wheat being paid, while smaller farmers were unable to participate.[56] The same study found that mecha-

Table 4:1: Use of High-Yield Rice by Farm Size, India, 1976

State	Percentage of area in high-yield varieties on farms			
	below 1 hec.	1-2 hec.	4-10 hec.	over 10 hec.
West Bengal	18	13	15	50
Bihar	34	33	24	16
Orissa	28	30	35	38
Uttar Pradesh	34	34	31	21
Madhya Pradesh	0	0	0	1
Andhra Pradesh	34	42	54	49
Tamil Nadu	70	60	67	19
Assam	1	1	0	0
Maharashtra	4	6	12	0

Source: R. Barker et al., *The Rice Economy of Asia* (Washington: Resources for the Future, 1985), p. 149.

nization seemed to be required to benefit most effectively from the wheat innovation package. Moreover, the early adoption pattern associated with Green Revolution rice also seemed to be skewed towards better-off households.[57] This was also true of the first Green Revolution maize in Zimbabwe — not surprisingly, given that it was originally developed under a white-run government by settler-dominated commercial farmer organizations, who continued to enjoy the great bulk of credit used to support the innovations even once African peasants began to participate after 1980.[58] In Mexico, too, a dramatic increase in wheat yields occurred between 1948 and 1965 (from 880 to 2550 kilos per hectare), but was concentrated in newly settled and irrigated areas, not in the Indian peasant ejidos sector.[59]

The distribution patterns within communities often began to change quickly after 1970, once the high benefits of Green Revolution innovation became clear to small-scale producers, too. In Zimbabwe, for instance, peasants in high rainfall areas quickly adopted the new maize varieties, which were effective when good water was available. Some 70 per cent of smallholder maize sales to the Grain Marketing Board came from three provinces with such conditions.[60] In India, in the case of rice, by 1976 the adoption of high-yield varieties showed little difference by farm size (see Table 4:1).

In the nine most significant rice-producing states in that country, smallholders were more active in adopting high-yield varieties in four of the states, large landowners adopted higher percentage levels in three states, and no significant adoption took place in two states. The pattern in Bangladesh was tilted slightly towards smaller peasant households. Research in the 1980 season showed irrigated rice production with 86 per cent of farm area under 0.4 hectares planted in high-yield varieties, compared to 52 per cent for farms of over 3 hectares. Large farms used high-yield varieties somewhat more in dryland rice production (31 per cent of rice area vs. 24 per cent), with smallholders using more in deepwater rice cultivation (31 per cent of rice area vs. 23 per cent).[61] A relative balance between smaller and larger-scale landholders seemed to hold across much of Southern Asia, even when fertilizer use and labour inputs were included to provide a fuller measure of yield results from new varieties by land size. Studies in 18 locations in four countries, from 1969 to 1982, showed the average yield for smaller land-holders as 3.1 metric tonnes per hectare — exactly the same as the level for the largest landholders. Taking the five 1980 comparative studies in that total, smallholders achieved higher yields in three of five cases.[62]

The issue of rural hired labourers makes the question of the distribution of benefits from new technological innovations more complex. In the case of wheat, the concentrated gains of some larger landowners (given the invest-ment required in tube-wells) also led to more mechanization and therefore threatened to decrease demand for hired labour.[63] But this does not seem to have been the case with respect to rice, in part because new varieties permit-ted increased double-cropping in many areas. A detailed Indonesian study, for instance, followed two villages over a ten-year period. One of them uni-versally adopted high-yield rice varieties between 1968 and 1979, and the other had a low adoption rate of 14 per cent. The new-varieties village increased its yields by 38 per cent, while the less changed village increased its yields by only 14 per cent. But what is especially striking was that the high-yield village saw income gains to hired labour of 29 per cent and to family labour of 15 per cent, while the less-changed village saw gains to hired labour of only 4 per cent, and to family labour of 3 per cent. (Studies in India and the Philippines noted similar gains for hired labour in rice production cases.) At the same time, another large share of gains went out of the high-yield village in the form of purchases of new seeds and fertilizers.[64]

This chemical bias of the Green Revolution represented one problem in analysing the long-term socioeconomic impact of the new technology package, especially given how petroleum-based fertilizers and pesticides increased in price after the oil price shocks of 1973-74 and 1979-80.[65] The most serious effect of this bias may well have been in how some Southern gov-ernments, hard-pressed to reduce public expenditures and achieve macroeco-nomic balance despite major terms-of-trade shifts against them, aimed to cut agricultural price supports for fertilizer inputs after 1990. With peasant house-holds moving into higher yield seed reliance and counting on fertilizer inputs to achieve promised targets, these cuts have sometimes subverted the viability of Green Revolution innovations, especially for small-scale peasants. Eicher has stressed this point as a mistake made by World Bank/IMF adjustment strategies in Africa, noting IFPRI studies of how Indonesia's annual 5 per cent growth in rice production over 1970-88 depended on such subsidies.[66] This point stands out vividly in Ghana, where the rapid increases in fertilizer costs in the early 1990s, as subsidies were phased out, undercut efforts to transfer high-yielding maize to Ghanaian producers.[67]

Nor has the plan simply to develop new packages of agricultural varieties and associated inputs turned out to be a sufficient response to rural poverty. Sometimes the packages have experienced explosive problems with unforeseen insect pests or diseases, leading to major crop losses before scientists have been able to develop new, resistant seed.[68] Sometimes the Green Revolution approach has led to waterlogging and nutrient imbalances.[69] Beyond these signs of environmental pressure, sometimes major marketing problems have been associated with the significant output increases produced by peasants. In Zimbabwe, for instance, the success of the smallholder maize Green Revolution led to a national crop of three million tons in 1985, enough supply for three years of domestic demand. The high cost of financing such large surpluses and the storage complications involved led to a decision to reduce maize prices and credit dramatically — with damaging effects on long-term peasant livelihoods. In Ghana, too, after considerable success in taking the maize Green Revolution to 150,000 peasant households, the country experienced marked production increases as a result — and then huge price reductions and storage problems that discredited much of the work that Sasakawa-Global 2000 had been doing there (in conjunction with the Crops Research Institute). As a result Sasakawa began to concentrate on new forms of peasant crop storage by 1995, rather than increased Green Revolution promotion.[70]

Even in the case of rice, where considerable evidence points to balanced distribution effects of the Green Revolution technology within given settings, questions remain about the overall importance of these changes for significant poverty reduction. One estimate, for instance, suggested that the high-yield variety/fertilizer package added 7.7 million metric tons of additional rice to total Asian production in 1972-73 — but that was a fairly modest 4.9 per cent of the overall Asian total.[71] This level reflected how many parts of Asia were less suited to the new package, because of the very wide variety of differing climatic and cultivation conditions experienced in the region. In many respects, that wide variation of conditions is the most crucial point to stress in any consideration of the effects and use of Green Revolution technology. A key issue seems to be the ability to control water with a reasonable degree of certainty. On a regional basis within South Asia, the mainland delta areas where irrigation is limited were largely left out (in settings such as Bangladesh, Burma, Thailand, and Eastern India), the irrigated insular countries (such as Indonesia, Malaysia, Sri Lanka, and the Philippines) — plus irrigated mainland areas of India in the north and south, an irrigated mainland areas in China — saw concentrated high-yield adoption, and consequent gains.[72]

But even in Indonesia, the Philippines, and mainland areas of India, where adoption in rice areas was extensive, and small and large landholders benefited in a balanced way, the consequence of the rice-based Green Revolution was not to banish rural poverty conditions. The original inequalities were so large that they could not be significantly reduced. Thus a 1968-74 study of six Indonesian villages that all completely adopted high-yield varieties found that income distribution became less unequal — but this meant the lowest 20 per cent of households raised their share from 1.1 to 2.7 per cent of total income, while the highest 20 per cent decreased their share from 66.3 to 61.8 per cent of the total.[73] Continuing rural poverty in these countries is reflected in the 1995 child malnutrition rates of 53 per cent in India, 35 per cent in Indonesia, and 30 per cent in the Philippines. Some of the overall gain from improved production has gone to urban consumers in the form of lower prices, with a smaller or larger share staying with rural producers depending on what share of extra output is sold and whether world commodity prices are already dominant in internal urban food-pricing.[74] As Barker and his colleagues concluded in closely examining the work of IRRI, "The effect of resource ownership on the distribution of earnings is so great that any effect caused by technological change is marginal.... One cannot expect technological innovations introduced over a period of five years to modify a pattern of resource ownership derived from hundreds of years of history."[75] This was particularly true, given that the international agricultural research thrust has not touched many crops and regions, and that useful interaction with peasant farmers and their complex mixed farming-systems was often absent from the approaches used by the international research institutions.[76]

The Green Revolution, then, can improve the conditions shaping rural poverty — and particularly so when international researchers work closely with national researchers, and when both interact effectively and attentively with Southern rural producers themselves at the local village and farm level. But serious rural change aiming to overcome rural poverty also has to focus on resource distribution. "The Green Revolution may have provided a major breakthrough," Rajni Kothari says. But tackling poverty, he adds, also "calls for the other package of measures known as land reforms, so that the benefits of the Green Revolution are widely dispersed."[77]

4: Land Reform and Rural Poverty

In South Africa, the battle over land reform has become tough and angry. Some 10 per cent of the population (mainly white) owns 87 per cent of the best agricultural land, and the new ANC-led government adopted a plan of redistributing 30 per cent of arable land to black rural households over a period of five years. White farmers say, "all [the minister] is doing is spreading rural poverty from where it exists to the new land that is being made available for settlement."[78] But World Bank analysis stresses that South Africa's "massive inequalities . . . in land ownership" must be redressed to safeguard the country's economic future.[79]

This immediate case raises the three fundamental questions that have traditionally surrounded the land reform issue. How important a social priority is land reform in responding to rural poverty and inequality? Are there net economic costs or benefits of redistributing land from large landholders to smallholders? And what associated measures can help make land reform more or less of an economic success?

In the classic Sussex-World Bank analysis of "Redistribution with Growth," analysts stressed that land redistribution seemed most crucial as an antipoverty mechanism in the case of Latin America, but was also an important part of a significant attack on rural poverty in Asia.[80] In Latin America they saw the representative country-by-country land distribution at that time as leaving about 3 per cent of the rural population with landholdings of around 205 hectares per household and 47 per cent of rural land — compared to 48 per cent of the population on holdings of some 0.7 hectares per household (too little to maintain even marginal existence, and a total of just 3 per cent of overall rural land). Bell and Duloy noted that this distribution "is so skewed that an adjustment downwards of the mean size of the top 3% of large holdings from 205 to about 130 hectares is sufficient to bring up the mean land holding of the lowest 48 percent of households (including the landless) from 0.7 hectares to 5.0 hectares."[81] In short, they said, it seemed clear from the evidence that land reform could make a very big difference to the rural poor. Land inequalities, they suggested, were worst in rural Chile (where 6.9 per cent controlled 81.3 per cent of rural land), rural Brazil (4.7 per cent controlled 59.5 per cent), rural Ecuador (2.1 per cent controlled 64.4 per cent), rural Colombia (5.8 per cent controlled 72.8 per cent), rural Guatemala (2.1 per cent controlled 72.3 per cent), and rural Peru (3.5 per cent controlled 88.1 per cent).

"Redistribution with Growth" also examined the Asian setting as of the 1973-74 period, concluding that a strong case existed for redistribution in many South Asian countries. Again, Bell and Duloy set out what they believed was a "representative land distribution" case for South Asia — 50 per cent of rural landowners on submarginal plots of less than 2.5 hectares, comprising 7 per cent of total rural land — while about 15 per cent were on plots of 10 hectares or more, comprising 60 per cent of rural land; a more modest land reform, in which 22 per cent of the larger landholdings were redistributed (so as to enforce a 10 hectare ceiling), would reduce the submarginal percentage to 34 per cent and raise the number of small farmers (with 2.5 and less than 5 hectares) from 18 per cent to 31 per cent of the population total.[82] Although this step would have an impact, they stressed, it would be less dramatic in its effects on rural poverty than in the Latin American projection examined.

So land reform *could* make a difference, it seemed. But did it? Evaluations in the case of the major land reforms favouring peasant smallholders in Latin America have been cautious. An assessment in 1995 suggested that both the 1920-40 Mexican and the post-1952 Bolivian land redistributions "did not achieve much reduction in poverty."[83] But other evidence is more positive, noting that "detailed production data collected in Chile in the period 1965-70, on land reform settlements formed from expropriated land as well as on portions retained by landowners, showed significant increases in output per hectare."[84]

It is possible to examine the two important cases that have stayed in place for considerable periods. By 1910 in Mexico, over 8,000 haciendas had come to preside over rural life, dominating the great majority of villages in the great majority of states, and increasingly absorbing Indian-cultivated lands for their own export-crop purposes — in the end leading to a decade of revolution, led by Zapata and Villa, that began the process of land reform in the country. By 1934, 17 million acres of land had been redistributed; then Cardenas came to power, initiated a serious attack on hacienda political power, and raised that total in six years to 41 million acres, mainly in the communal *ejidos* forms of tenure that guaranteed Indian village-based control of peasant agriculture for the future.[85] Until at least 1960, the intensity with which peasants farmed these lands remained virtually comparable in productivity with large-scale private holdings that had not been affected by the land reform. Thus the initial stages of the redistribution process seemed to have been an economic and social success.[86]

But increasingly the Mexican government began to direct resources more to large-scale, privately owned farm households, especially for irrigation, and these became increasingly more dynamic than the *ejidos* sector, widening income inequalities and rural poverty problems.[87] This was particularly true of the wheat-based Green Revolution in Mexico, which produced large yield increases concentrated in newly settled, non-*ejidos* areas. The result of such skewing of policy was increasing rural poverty in seven south and central region states, resulting from very low maize yields, poor infrastructure, and very small landholdings on which peasants came to depend (see chapter 1).[88] The new political revolts of the "Zapatistas" in these southern Indian communities underline the continuance of Mexican rural poverty despite the earlier land reform changes.

The second major Latin American land reform was in Bolivia after the 1952 revolution by the urban and tin-miner based Movimiento Nacionalista Revolucionario (MNR). The haciendas redistributed in Bolivia were less comprehensively entrenched than in Mexico, but the degree of rural land inequality was the highest in Latin America, with 4 per cent of landowners owning 82 per cent of settled land; half of this was redistributed to the peasantry in just two years, mainly by changing tenant holdings into peasant-owned household plots.[89] The other major differences with Mexico, besides the speed of reform, were that major gains went to the peasantry in terms of increased food consumption for themselves, and via marked expansion of rural schools for their children (these schools had been prohibited on the large estates).[90] These differences suggest the social gains from land reform in this case, but that there were also economic gains in some areas is suggested by a detailed study of one village over the 1952-66 period: Average family consumption rose by three times; of 200 families, half had come to own radios (compared to one before), 120 had sewing machines (compared to 7), and 80 had bicycles (compared to 1).[91]

Nevertheless, Bolivia had not resolved its rural poverty problems for good. By the 1980s, 80 per cent of Bolivia's 700,000 farm households were crowded into plots in the highlands area that were usually one to three hectares in size. The land these households relied on was dropping in yields (the major national food crop of potatoes, for instance, produced 834,000 tons of output on 127,680 hectares in 1975, but only 700,000 tons on 190,000 hectares by 1988). And large numbers of landless labourers were becoming an important new rural poverty group in the newly settled eastern agricultural areas around Santa Cruz.[92] It is difficult to analyse clearly what happened in the rural areas of Bolivia, because of the massive expansion of coca production in the country in the 1980s (farm output of the crop grew by as much as 27 times in ten years, making illegal coca exports larger than all other national exports), but the UNICEF data, showing 1995 childhood mortality rates of 105 per thousand births (see chapter 1), document continuing serious poverty. Explanations for this result, despite major land reform, have been suggested in analyses of the significant fall in potato yields among peasants: "The lack of new seed varieties, chemical fertilizers, and irrigation systems, together with the continued exhaustion of the highland soils, was responsible for the low yields. In the late 1980s, the lack of financial credit at planting time represented the greatest impediment facing potato growers."[93] In contrast to this minimal state attention to the bulk of peasant producers, the great majority of new state infrastructure, credit, and other rural financial support went to the newly settled large-scale commercial farmers producing export crops and cattle in the eastern and northern lowlands.

If these Latin American cases are ambiguous over the longer run, a range of far-reaching land reforms in Asia seems to have had more markedly positive social and economic consequences. Perhaps the most dramatic was in South Korea, where post-1945 independence from Japan found the country with 75 per cent of its population in agriculture. Some two-thirds of these farm families were full-time tenants, with the rest mostly part-time tenants; extreme rural poverty resulted from rents paid to landlords of 50 per cent to 90 per cent of crops produced.[94] By 1950 two stages of land reform had eliminated landlords and established small but essentially equal landholdings as the norm, leaving almost all farmers with some land, and some 70 per cent owning all their land. Then the Saemaul Undong Movement worked to improve the quality of Korean rural life through new education facilities, rural co-operative marketing, and rural credit institutions.[95] This set of changes provided a much broader consumer base for Korean industrialization as it moved ahead — and provided the basis for the highly educated workforce that analysts see as crucial in explaining Korea's rapid industrial growth in the 1980s. The savings generated from increased production in Korean agriculture also helped to raise the national savings rate from 3.3 per cent of domestic incomes in 1962 to 21.5 per cent of such incomes by 1982.

The economic benefits in the rural economy itself, and the contribution of land reform to redressing rural poverty, are indicated by the rapid responsiveness of South Korean agriculture to high-yielding new rice varieties. First introduced in the 1971-72 season, the new varieties covered 75.5 per cent of total rice area by 1978-79. Korean researchers also showed an independent capacity to breed varieties directed specifically at the more temperate climate of their country. In 1976, as a result, the national rice yield average for South Korea reached six metric tonnes per hectare, higher for the first time than average Japanese rice yields. That these gains were shared widely in rural areas is suggested by the index of real wages for agricultural labour in South Korea, which rose from 100 in 1965 to 377 in 1980 (compared to an increase from 100 to 197 in Japan, 100 to 119 in Malaysia, 100 to 112 in Bangladesh, 100 to 107 in Punjab in India — and a fall from 100 to 84 in the Philippines).[96]

Taiwan was another area that experienced extensive land redistribution in favour of peasant households. When the Kuomintang fled from the mainland of China, they set a ceiling on landholdings and redistributed land to the poorest farmers.[97] Good land-tenure data in Taiwan made this possible, an outside bureaucracy could impose it, and the program (as in Korea) essentially transferred landlord rights to tenants who were already running farm operations.[98] The social result was to increase the percentage of owner-cultivators from 33 per cent in 1948 to 59 per cent in 1959 and to decrease the percentage of rural tenants and landless labourers from 43 per cent down to 19 per cent. This shift, in turn, reduced the share of net farm income going to landlords and moneylenders from 25 per cent of the total in 1936-40 down to 6 per cent in 1956-60 — while cultivators themselves increased their income share from 67 per cent to 81 per cent.[99]

The economic impact, again as in Korea, was assisted immensely by extensive agricultural research and extension efforts, excellent infrastructure networks, and widely available credit facilities. (As of 1960, Taiwan had 79 agricultural research workers per 100,000 farmers, more than the level of 60 in Japan and 1.2 in India.)[100] As a result, Taiwan was one of the areas in which new semi-dwarf rice varieties were first developed; and the impact of the new varieties on rice yields is shown by comparison of the 1957 average (3.2 metric tonnes per hectare) and the 1978 average (4.3 metric tonnes, or a 34 per cent increase). That is for just one crop, too, in a context in which double-cropping has now become the norm.[101] Again, the breadth of these rural income gains (as in Korea) is suggested by the farm wage of hired labour in Taiwan, which had increased to U.S.$7.60 per day by 1979, compared to $4.94 in Korea, $19.02 in Japan, $1.07 in India, $0.85 in the Philippines, and $0.65 in India.[102]

Finally, in the Asian context, there is China. It is not easy to trace the various shifts in land-tenure policy in China over the 1949-96 period; certainly some periods have made food supply conditions for Chinese peasants more precarious, while others have improved rural life. But the Chinese land reform outweighs any redistribution of rural assets that has taken place since World War II. It must therefore be analysed, and it does demonstrate certain points clearly.

First, the Chinese experience shows that fundamental land reform on a large scale can be successfully implemented. Some 80 per cent of the Chinese population was involved in agriculture, fewer than 10 per cent of that population owned 70 per cent of the land, and achieving serious progress against rural poverty clearly required major changes in this pattern. That change is what took place in 1949-52, with over 300 million peasants benefiting from reforms that took most land from landlords and some from rich peasants to establish a wide base of peasant cultivators with their own land.[103] After various forms of communal tenure, that direct peasant control over their own land reasserted itself after 1978.

Second, with rice the most important product in Chinese agriculture (44 per cent of grain output — providing 70-80 per cent of calories consumed in China in 1986),[104] the development of rice cultivation is a good indicator of the economic viability of this land reform, and the evidence has been positive. This includes increases in the multiple cropping index from 167 to 187 in the South China rice areas between 1952 and 1957 (more of a gain than in Taiwan), and it includes rapid take-up of Green Revolution technology, slightly ahead of the rest of Asia. By 1977 some 80 per cent of all rice areas were using high-yield varieties, and chemical fertilizer usage was growing by 17 per cent per year. As a result rice yields in southern areas increased between 1957 and 1978 by 52 per cent, more than the 34 per cent increase in Taiwan, and in more temperate areas the equivalent increase was 27 per cent. For China as a whole, rice yields grew from 2.7 metric tonnes per hectare in 1957 to 4 metric tonnes per hectare as of 1978.

Third, much of this improvement in rural food supply and incomes suggested by the rice data clearly came from infrastructure improvements, especially in the form of irrigation. In the 1965-80 period, rice production in eight Asian countries increased by over 117 million metric tonnes, with some 50.5 million of that coming in China, far more than in any other country (India was second with 35 million tons). Some 32 per cent of that increase in China was the result of irrigation improvements, 26 per cent from new seed varieties, and 23 per cent from increased fertilizer — compared to an average for all countries of over 24 per cent coming from fertilizers, 23 per cent from new varieties, and less than 29 per cent from irrigation improvements.[105]

Fourth, over time the combination of land reforms, Green Revolution technology, and rural infrastructure improvements markedly reduced rural poverty. According to the World Bank, one-third of the population lived below the absolute poverty line in 1978, but this figure of 270 million fell to 100 million, one-tenth of the population, by 1985.[106] The remaining areas of concentrated rural poverty have environmental problems such as serious soil erosion, difficult mountainous terrain, and combinations of drought and flooding that can only be countered by new technology and environment-based initiatives.[107] The much lower 1995 infant mortality and under-five malnutrition rates in China (47 per 1,000 and 16 per cent, compared to 115 per 1,000 and 53 per cent for India, or 75 per 1,000 and 35 per cent for Indonesia) indicate a significant reduction in rural poverty.

In Africa, land redistribution to smallholder peasants is now on the agenda in South Africa and Zimbabwe, but there is little significant evidence to draw on from Sub-Saharan Africa itself. Major initiatives were taken in the direction of land reform in Ethiopia, after the overthrow of the imperial regime there in 1974. But, in many respects, this was not a shift of land to peasant agriculturalists, but to new communal institutions that did not really take root in the complex, drought-afflicted, war-torn turmoil of Ethiopia under the Derg.[108] More relevant is the experience of Africans in Kenya, where some million acres of land previously held by white-settlers were purchased and distributed to medium- and small-scale African producers as part of the transition to independence. This case has direct salience for the debate over the economic viability of smallholder peasant cultivation that is taking place in South Africa and Zimbabwe.

The Kenyan evidence is significant, first, because it demonstrates that a relatively limited land reform in itself does little to counter widespread poverty and inequality. Despite the million-acre scheme, and some later improvements to include more poor Africans as beneficiaries,[109] the extent of rural poverty in Kenya remains a major reality. Second, however, the evidence from the rather limited Kenyan land reform does suggest the same point made by the five more fundamental land redistributions in Mexico, Bolivia, South Korea, Taiwan, and China: Smallholders can be efficient economic producers. The social gains of spreading access to rural resources more broadly can be matched by economic gains as well.

Thus in the settlement schemes in Kenya, the evidence is clear. As the pathbreaking ILO *Report on Employment, Incomes and Equality in Kenya* stated, "The second main thrust of agricultural strategy should be land distribution towards the smaller and more labour-intensive farm units. Far from leading to a sacrifice of output for the sake of more employment and better income distribution, evidence suggests that this is likely to lead to higher total output and incomes." Net profit per acre was 424 Kenya Shs. on smallholdings (under 10 acres), 139 Shs. per acre on somewhat larger plots (10-20 acres), and 81 Shs. per acre on large holdings (of 70 acres or more).[110]

Land reform, then, can be a key element in countering rural poverty, but by itself land redistribution can also, as in Mexico and Bolivia, produce only short-run gains against rural poverty. Such social changes can be important in changing rural political settings and opening up the possibilities of ongoing rural transformation that make a long-term economic *and* social difference. But no certainty exists that land reform will bring this about just in itself. In economic and technological terms, institutions to improve rural productivity for smallholders through Green Revolution innovations, upgraded infrastructure, and access to credit and marketing networks seem crucial to translating land reform into rural socioeconomic transformation.

With such elements, land reform, as in Korea and China, can bring about fundamental economic improvements in the rural world. But land reform, though it can play a powerful role, emerges as just one part of the package. Without Green Revolution dynamism, Bolivian peasants have seen yields decline for their basic food, and poverty has persisted for many. Left out of national agricultural planning, southern Mexican Indians have experienced a deepening poverty that has led to revolt, despite earlier land reforms. Even in China, a minority of peasants remain caught by environmental factors and difficult terrain that keep their villages poor, despite marked gains brought in to most people through land reform, Green Revolution innovation, and extensive irrigation.

For many peasants, land reform can work, when supported by the Green Revolution, infrastructure development, credit mechanisms, and efficient marketing. But winning the fight for land reform is not always an attainable political goal.

5: Conclusion

Of the more than 1.3 billion very poor people in the world — people with living standards of less than a dollar a day — most live in rural areas. Whether isolated Tanzanian peasants in rice-growing Ulanga, Bolivian potato-producers on tiny highland plots, Ghanaian women farmers pushed into growing low-nutrition cassava in the poor Volta region, peasants in remote mountainous areas of China that the Green Revolution has not been able to reach, or undernourished children in landless households hurt by shrimp-farming in southern Honduras, these hundreds of millions of poor people represent the global reality that Canadians must confront.

The first step in confronting this reality is to understand the dynamics of global poverty. The first and crucial point is that these hundreds of millions of people are not helpless victims. Most of them are agricultural producers and have shown a capacity to respond quickly and energetically to opportunities. But most peasant households also face heavy risks in producing crops and other output in the much more variable and uncertain climate and soil conditions of Southern environments. With few assets to fall back on, poor peasant households have had to stress *survival strategies*, which have often meant they stayed trapped in small-plot, limited-input, hardworking situations in which producing enough to eat year by year marks success.

Some peasant households, with more assets or especially fertile soils or other income sources, have been able to move ahead with cash-crop gains. But here, too, the price patterns in the international economy have often worked strongly against them. When they have made good incomes, large shares of the gains have often been taxed away by colonial and postcolonial governments for urban-based developments.

Peasant agriculture has remained at the heart of the rural poverty equation in most Southern countries. Gender inequality has emerged as a fundamental explanatory factor, with women-headed families now the focus of much analysis of rural poverty groups and male-female educational differences as basic ongoing elements preserving the rural poor. Environmental considerations in themselves, from increased drought, to deforestation, to loss of "commons" lands, to water pollution, have become increasingly major pressures blocking movement out of rural poverty. When combined, environmental and gender concerns become important interacting complications. Too often, as the Zimbabwe cattle case and the Sarawak lumbering example demonstrate, environmental threats are either worsened by gender inequalities or have the effect of worsening those inequalities. Gender inequalities and environmental pressures can clearly work together to deepen rural poverty in the South.

The Green Revolution of new high-yielding seed varieties and high fertilizer inputs has countered this poverty to some degree (although effects have depended on the crop involved, with rice in Asia appearing to have the most balanced distributional impact). But the revolution has been partial, limited to certain types of areas, and usually not enough in itself to overcome other sources of poverty persistence.

Land reform has been an essential additional requirement for making major progress against rural poverty. The case of South Korea has clearly demonstrated this need, as has China; and the earlier years of Bolivian and Mexican land reform brought important improvements for the rural poor. But Bolivia also demonstrated that a failure to stress continuing agricultural research, smallholder credit and marketing channels, and continuing efforts against poverty could result in the rebirth of entrenched rural inequity within decades. Those continuing efforts needed against rural poverty reflect the strength of other sources of rural deprivation.

But still, let me stress yet again, the hundreds of millions of rural poor are not helpless victims. The dynamics of peasant agricultural change in Southern countries do show signs of creative community-based initiatives to improve situations, as in the water provision developments that Canadians have been co-operating with in communities in Northern Ghana. What is striking is that this effort seems to be succeeding well, precisely because it is changing the gender inequalities of the past in many Southern countries. This initiative is drawing heavily on the dynamism and energy of women-based groups — and they are responding strongly and creatively to the empowerment they are now experiencing within their rural communities. Although rural poverty is indeed deeply rooted in many Southern countries, new currents do exist that can bring change.

Notes

1   Personal field notes, IRDC Files, "Economics of Rice Production in Ulanga," September 30, 1983.

2   See *Sebungwe Regional Study*, proceedings of a workshop, February 1982, Wankie, Zimbabwe — especially Malcolm Blackie, "A Time to Listen: A Perspective on Agriculture Policy in Zimbabwe," Appendix 2. This also reflects personal field visits in 1983 to the Sebungwe region.

3   See Stonich, "Struggling with Honduran Poverty: The Environmental Consequences of Natural Resource-Based Development and Rural Transformations," pp.389-94.

4   See C. Vlassof, "From Rags to Riches: The Impact of Rural Development on Women's Status in an Indian Village," *World Development*, vol.22, no.5 (1994), pp.707-19.

5   Personal field notes, IRDC Files, "Trip Report, Southern Africa, July 1982," pp.21-22. The research study being monitored was directed by Peter Hayward, University of Zambia.

6 See Amanor, "Ecological Knowledge and the Regional Economy: Environmental Management in the Asesewa District of Ghana," in *Development and Environment*, ed. Ghai, pp.55-64.

7 Quoted from East Africa Economic Commission, "Final Report: Part 1, 1919," p.19, in Wolff, *The Economics of Colonialism*, p.140.

8 For details see G.K. Helleiner, *Peasant Agriculture, Government and Economic Growth in Nigeria* (Homewood: Richard Irwin, 1966), pp.64-67.

9 See T.W. Schultz, "Effects of the International Donor Community on Farm People," *American Journal of Agricultural Economics*, vol.62, no.5, (1980), pp. 873-78.

10 See the detailed discussion of much greater climate variability in Gunnar Myrdal, *Asian Drama*, vol.III (New York: Pantheon), Appendix 10, (1968), pp.2133-34.

11 See the excellent discussion in Michael Lipton, "The Theory of the Optimising Peasant," *Journal of Development Studies*, vol.4 (1968), pp.327-51.

12 See Breslin, "U.S. Aid, the State, and Food Insecurity in Rural Zimbabwe: The Case of Gowke," pp.95-96.

13 See Carlsen, *Economic and Social Transformation in Rural Kenya*, pp.190-92.

14 Jette Bukh, *The Village Woman in Ghana* (Uppsala: Scandinavian Institute of African Studies, 1979), pp.38-40.

15 See Frances Moore Lappe and Adele Beccar-Varela, *Mozambique and Tanzania: Asking the Big Questions* (San Francisco: Institute for Food and Development Policy, 1980), p.86.

16 See Carlsen, *op. cit.*, chapter 2.

17 Carl Eicher, "Zimbabwe's Maize-Based Green Revolution: Preconditions for Replication," *World Development*, vol.23, no.5 (1995), p.809.

18 See Eric Wolf, "Peasantry and Its Problems," in *Peasants* (New York: Prentice-Hall, 1966), pp. 7-8.

19 Carlsen, *op. cit.*, p.52-73.

20 Malcolm Blaikie, "A Time to Listen," *Sebungwe Regional Study*, Appendix 2, p.8.

21 Charles Jebuni et al., *The State of the Ghanaian Economy in 1994* (Legon: Institute of Statistical, Social and Economic Research, July 1995), p.47.

22 Lionel Demery, "Côte d'Ivoire: Fettered Adjustment," in *Adjustment in Africa: Lessons from Country Case Studies*, ed. I. Hussain and R. Faruqee (Washington: World Bank, 1994), pp.120-23.

23 Alfred Maizels, "The Continuing Commodity Crisis of Developing Countries," *World Development*, vol.22, no.11 (1994), p.1686.

24 *Ibid.*, pp.1686-7.

25 Madhav Gadgil and Ramachandra Guha, "Ideological Conflicts and the Environmental Movement in India," in Ghai, *op. cit.*, pp.124-25.

26 See especially Wardrop Engineering Inc., *Case Study of the GWSC Assistance Project from 1990 to 1994*, report to GWSC Assistance Project: Community Management of Urban Water Supplies in Northern Ghana, CIDA, December 1994, chapter 8.

27 See Bukh, *The Village Woman in Ghana*, pp.88, 94.

28 See L. Haddad et al., "The Gender Dimensions of Economic Adjustment Policies," *World Development*, vol.23, no.6 (1995), pp.886-87.
29 See T. Turner and M. Oshare, "Women's Uprising against the Nigerian Oil Industry in the 1980s," *Canadian Journal of Development Studies*, vol.XIV, no.3, (1993), pp.340-42.
30 Janet Townsend, "Gender Studies: Whose Agenda?" in *Beyond the Impasse*, ed. Schuurman, p.171.
31 See World Bank, "Summaries of Poverty Assessments Completed in Fiscal 1995," Internet, 1996.
32 See Kojo Amanor, *The New Frontier: Farmers' Response to Land Degradation* (London: Zed Books, 1994), p.98.
33 Vivian, "NGOs and Sustainable Development in Zimbabwe," pp.179-80.
34 Joekes et al., "Gender, Environment and Population," pp.144-47, 151-53, 157-58.
35 Ibid., pp.147-50, 153-55, 158-60.
36 See E. Hviding and G.B.K. Baines, "Community-Based Fisheries Management, Tradition and the Challenges of Development in Marovo, Solomon Islands," in *Development and Environment*, ed. Ghai, pp.13-40.
37 See Peter Bartelmus, *Environment, Growth and Development* (London: Routledge, 1994), chapter 1.
38 Anil Agarwal and Sunita Narain, "Towards Green Villages," in *Global Ecology: A New Arena of Political Conflict*, ed. Wolfgang Sachs (London: Zed Books, 1993), pp.248-52.
39 Krishna Ghimire, "Parks and People: Livelihood Issues in National Parks Management in Thailand and Madagascar," pp.195-230, and Peter Utting, "Social and Political Dimensions of Environmental Protection in Central America," pp.236-39, in *Development and Environment*, ed. Ghai.
40 See Christian Aid, "After the Prawn Rush," 1996, One-World On-Line, Internet.
41 See Amanor, *The New Frontier*, pp.48-49, 206-16.
42 See Vivian, "NGOs and Sustainable Development in Zimbabwe," p.179.
43 See Ellen Bortei-Doku Aryeetey et al., "Review of District Assembly Capacity for Decentralization and Development Initiatives," report to CIDA, Accra, Ghana, 1994, p.19.
44 See Wardrop Engineering Inc., *Case Study of the GWSC Assistance Project from 1990 to 1994*, pp.45ff.
45 See World Bank, *World Bank Brief: Poverty Reduction*, August 14, 1996, Internet.
46 See John Wong, *ASEAN Economies in Perspective* (London: Macmillan, 1979), p.95.
47 See IFPRI, *2020 Vision*, Washington, from "People and the Planet," Internet source, 1995.
48 See ICARDA (International Center for Agricultural Research in the Dry Areas), *Wheat Research Pays Off for Egypt's Farmers*, Aleppo, Syria, September 1995.
49 See W. Ladejinsky, "Ironies of India's Green Revolution," in *Development Economics and Policy: Readings*, ed. Ian Livingstone (London: George Allen and

Unwin, 1981), pp.293-94.

50 See R. Barker, R.W. Herdt, B. Rose, *The Rice Economy of Asia* (Washington: Resources for the Future, 1985), pp.60-61.

51 Ibid., pp.63, 244, 251. China's rice output also expanded greatly by over 50 million metric tonnes of paddy, almost four times the increase in Indonesian output, and 15 million tonnes more than India's over the 1965-80 period.

52 See Eicher, "Zimbabwe's Maize-Based Green Revolution," pp.806-10.

53 See Ghana, *The Crops Research Institute*, Kumasi, 1995, p.7.

54 See *Research Briefs* (Bulletin of the Crops Research Institute, Ghana), May 1995, p.1.

55 ICARDA, *New Barley Boosts Chinese Agriculture*, Internet, July 1995.

56 See F.R. Frankel, "India's New Strategy of Agriculture Development: Political Costs of Agrarian Modernization," in *Development Economics and Policy*, ed. Livingstone, pp.290-91.

57 See Barker at al., *The Rice Economy of Asia*, pp.146-47.

58 Eicher, "Zimbabwe's Maize-Based Revolution," pp.808-9.

59 See Furtado, *Economic Development of Latin America*, pp.116-17.

60 Ibid., p.77.

61 See Barker et al., *The Rice Economy of Asia*, p.150.

62 Ibid., p. 153.

63 See Ladejinsky, "Ironies of India's Green Revolution," in *Development Economics and Policy*, ed. Livingstone, p.295.

64 Barker et al., *The Rice Economy of Asia*, pp.155-56.

65 See Pat Roy Mooney, *Seeds of the Earth* (Ottawa: Inter Pares, 1980), pp.40-44.

66 Eicher, "Zimbabwe's Maize-Based Green Revolution," p.807.

67 Interview with Emmanuel Addison, Director, Ghana Crops Research Institute, Kumasi, May 23, 1996.

68 See Barker et al., *The Rice Economy of Asia*, p.64.

69 See IFPRI, *2020 Vision*.

70 Interview with Tareke Berhe, Senior Agronomist, Saskakawa-Global 2000, Accra, May 22, 1996.

71 The estimate is by Dalrymple. See Barker et al., *The Rice Economy of Asia*, p.143.

72 Ibid., p.156.

73 Ibid., p.155.

74 Ibid., pp.144-45.

75 Ibid., P.157.

76 See Amanor, "Ecological Knowledge and the Regional Economy: Environmental Management in the Asesewa District of Ghana," in *Development and Environment*, ed. Ghai, pp.41-43.

77 Kothari, *Poverty*, p.129.

78 Eddie Koch, "'Power to the People' Land-Reformers Defy Critics," Panos, Internet, December 20, 1995.

79 World Bank, *South Africa: Stimulating Economic Growth*, Southern Africa Department, Washington, Internet, 1994.

80 See C. Bell and J. Duloy, "Formulating a Strategy" and "Rural Target Goups," in *Redistribution with Growth*, ed. H. Chenery et al. (London: Oxford

University Press, 1974).
81 *Ibid.*, p.97.
82 *Ibid.*, pp. 97-98.
83 See "Distribution and Growth: Complements, not Compromises," *World Bank Policy Research Bulletin*, vol. 6, no.3 (May-July 1995).
84 See Martin Adams, "Land Reform: New Seeds on Old Ground?" Overseas Development Institute, no. 6 (October 1995), p.4.
85 See Eric Wolf, *Peasant Wars of the Twentieth Century* (New York: Harper and Row, 1969), pp.16-18, 45.
86 See Peter Dorner, *Land Reform and Economic Development* (London: Penguin, 1972), pp.121-22.
87 Furtado, *Economic Development in Latin America*, pp.220-21.
88 See World Bank, "Mexico - Agricultural Development and Rural Poverty Project," Project ID MXPA7711," July 28, 1995.
89 See *Bolivia: A Country Study*, Washington: Federal Research Division of the U.S. Library of Congress, 1990, Internet.
90 Ibid.; see also Furtado, *Economic Development of Latin America*, pp.222-26.
91 Dorner, *Land Reform and Economic Development*, pp.89-90.
92 See *Bolivia: A Country Study*, "Land Use" and "Food Crops."
93 See *Bolivia: A Country Study*, "Land Use."
94 Irma Adelman, "Korea," in *Redistribution and Growth*, ed. Chenery et al., p.280.
95 See Ponna Wignaraja, "Rethinking Development and Democracy," in *New Social Movements in the South*, ed. Wignaraja, pp.14-15.
96 See Barker et al., *The Rice Economy of Asia*, pp.63, 68.
97 See Ibid., p.132.
98 See Deborah Brautigam, "What Can Africa Learn from Taiwan? Political Economy, Industrial Policy, and Adjustment," *Journal of Modern African Studies*, vol.32, no.1 (1994), p.117.
99 See "Land Reform: New Seeds on Old Ground?" Overseas Development institute, no. 6, 1995.
100 See Dorner, *Land Reform and Economic Development*, pp.88-89.
101 Brautigam, "What Can Africa Learn from Taiwan?" p.117.
102 See Barker et al., *The Rice Economy of Asia*, p.248.
103 Ibid., p.132.
104 See E.L. Wheelwright and B. McFarlane, *The Chinese Road to Socialism* (New York: Monthly Review Press, 1970), pp.32-33.
105 Brian Hook, ed., *The Cambridge Encyclopedia of China* (Cambridge: Cambridge University Press, 1991), pp.55-56.
106 See Barker et al., *The Rice Economy of Asia*, pp.84, 247-49.
107 World Bank, "Poverty Project Summary," Internet, 1996.
108 See Ibid.; also State Science and Technology Commission of the People's Republic of China, *Proposal: System for Co-ordinating Development of Technology and Environment in China's Poor Areas*, Beijing, 1993, pp. 2-3.
109 See *Ethiopia: A Country Review*, "Land Reform," U.S. Library of Congress, Internet. Also personal field notes, 1982-83.

110 E.S. Clayton, "Kenya's Agriculture and the ILO Report - Six Years After," in *Papers on the Kenyan Economy*, ed. Tony Killick (Nairobi: Heinemann Educational Books, 1981), pp.147-48.

111 International Labour Office, *Employment, Incomes and Equality: A Strategy for Increasing Productive Employment in Kenya* (Geneva: ILO, 1972), pp.165-67.

CHAPTER 5

Industry and Labour

In 1960 South Korea produced virtually no steel; by 1980 it was one of three Southern countries (along with Brazil and India) that were factors in world steel production. By 1990 it had exceeded the output of its two much more populous Southern counterparts and was manufacturing 23 million metric tons of steel per year (50 times its 1970 level).[1]

In 1960 Kenya produced no cotton cloth, despite widespread cotton-growing near Lake Kisumu and elsewhere. By 1977 an influx of five foreign-controlled textile subsidiaries had resulted in the production of 67 million metres of cloth per year (71.1 per cent from the foreign firms). Yet by 1983, the four largest of those foreign enterprises had collapsed in major bankruptcies, costing the Kenyan government millions of dollars, throwing thousands out of work, and pushing textile production towards synthetic materials despite the cotton available in Kenya.[2]

Brazil has stressed the development of indigenous technological capacity and invested in internationally expanding sectors such as small aircraft and steel. In the 1970s these efforts seemed to expand regular wage (or "formal-sector") jobs significantly, but incomes declined over the 1980s for all income groups, with decreases hitting those at the bottom especially hard. Urban poverty increased faster than in most Southern countries, and the most recent analysis suggests this is because "fewer adults, particularly women, in poor urban households work than in better off households." This leaves many of the Brazilian poor caught in irregular, shifting, and vulnerable "informal-sector" self-employment situations.[3]

In Canada, early in 1993, in Windsor, Ontario, the 300 long-time employees of the Wyeth Canada pharmaceutical subsidiary learned they were to have their very profitable factory closed by their American Home Products parent company — just a few months after the federal government had passed laws improving protection for the established drug subsidiaries in Canada (in return for promises from those companies to expand jobs in Canada). Various factors stood behind this decision, but one

101

was special tax benefits that U.S. firms could receive for increasing their investment and production in certain lower-wage Southern countries.

What do these patterns mean? What do they suggest about global industrial change, world poverty, and responses to it?

1: Global Industrial Production Patterns

There was a period in the 19th century when Great Britain was by far the dominant industrial producer in the world, and then a later period in which countries like the United States, Germany, France, the Netherlands, and Canada came to share with the British that primary industrial role. Even as late as the 1950s, major Southern analysts such as Latin America's Raul Prebisch stressed the overwhelming predominance of the richer countries in industrial production and exports as the heart of their economic advantage over the poorer countries in Asia, Africa, and Latin America.[4] This focus on the goal of industrialization as the core of economic development was evident in the theories of development from 1945-70.

What is striking is that powerful forces were already at work in the global economy encouraging industrial expansion in the South. By 1970, some 15 per cent of world manufacturing value-added was to be found in poorer Southern countries, and some 7 per cent of world manufacturing exports was coming from the same sources. This was a growing trend, with the Southern share of value-added up to 17.5 per cent by 1976, and the manufacturing export share up to 8.4 per cent.[5] This industrial export growth continued during the 1980s (to over 13 per cent of the world total), even though the overall Southern share of manufacturing value-added stayed fairly stable; but increasingly the export increase was concentrated in a small number of so-called "NICs" — the newly industrializing countries of East Asia (the "Four Tigers" — South Korea, Singapore, Hong Kong, and Taiwan), Brazil, and Mexico. This small number of NICs increased its share of world industry to 8.5 per cent by 1984 and accounted for the entire increase in the Southern share of world manufacturing exports between the mid-1960s and the mid-1980s.[6]

By 1994 this pattern was beginning to widen somewhat, although concentration by country was still evident. In international equity investment in Southern countries in the 1991-94 period, Asia and Latin America were still dominant, with 93 per cent of such equity capital going there in 1994; some 25 per cent of this private investment was in industry. But China, India, Indonesia, Thailand, and the Philippines had joined the "Four Tigers" to become continuing important Asian targets of international equity investment over 1991-94; and Chile and Argentina had joined Brazil and Mexico as major expanding investment areas in Latin America.[7]

This extensive yet uneven pattern of international change was influenced by five interconnected factors: a) the strong drive for new sources of raw materials to supply expanding consumption and investment in the Northern countries; b) the increasing competition among large Northern corporations to capture Southern country market advantages in a postcolonial context; c) the rising importance to firms in some industries of breaking out of union-led higher-wage frameworks in postwar consensus societies in the North, by relying on some production in non-union lower-wage environments in the south, thereby being able to outcompete counterpart firms in certain sectors; d) the opportunities open to commercialize technological and managerial advantages fully by internationalizing completely in the case of some multinational enterprises; and e) the leverage that some Southern states used to accelerate their entry into the emerging more fluid international economic system.

The traditional production investment from abroad in Southern countries has been in the resource-extraction sector, and this focus has continued to be important as the base of raw materials has declined in the United States and Western Europe. This pressure pushed the leading U.S. resource firms to increase their non-petroleum extractive industry operations abroad from 31 in 1945 to 67 in 1967, and to extend foreign petroleum extraction operations from 20 in 1929 to 60 in 1967.[8] Many European resource firms did likewise, and Japanese enterprises were especially active in resource industry investments to cover raw material scarcities at home.

This process created resource-extraction enclaves that are the classic historic case of direct foreign investment in Southern countries — with concentrated effects, often considerable profit-making, and powerful multinational corporations (MNCs) involved — such as the petro giants in the Middle East and Venezuela, Royal Dutch Shell in Nigeria, U.S. and Canadian multinationals in copper in Chile, Anglo-American in Zambia, Rio-Tinto-Zinc in Papua-New Guinea, Inco in nickel in Indonesia, and U.S. aluminium giants in bauxite in Jamaica. The very large capital requirements for these operations, the highly oligopolistic world industry structure for most mineral trade and production, and often the complexity involved in finding and developing any mineral source gave these multinationals considerable bargaining power at the start of projects, but this power usually shifted over time once the capital was committed and learning effects in the Southern country began to take place. Hence a dynamic bargaining framework often emerged, within the context of a varying world and domestic political economy.[9] This resource-based role has been especially prominent for Canadian MNCs, such as Alcan, Inco, Noranda, and Sherritt-Gordon.

The second process of changing industrial location was somewhat more complex. In the 1960s and 1970s, two combined trends significantly increased the manufacturing of previously imported industrial goods in most Southern economies. On the one hand, the manufacturers of many products were confronting increasing competition in their international exports, and they found that they could outcompete rivals or better dominate local Southern country markets by establishing producing subsidiaries behind protective barriers within such markets. On the other hand, Southern governments found they could spur new investments and manufacturing jobs by working out agreements to set up such protective barriers and other forms of incentives. The combination led to marked increases in protected import-substituting industrialization ("ISI") in many Southern countries.

There were often important problems associated with this ISI process. The products being manufactured were often of questionable benefit (such as the infant bottle-feeding formula that advertising persuaded mothers to use, rather than much safer and more nutritious breastfeeding).[10] The level of barriers established to protect new industries was often extremely high; and this protection tended to be highest for simpler consumer goods and lower for the intermediate goods production that should be encouraged to follow next — meaning that Southern ISI often stalled at producing just the simpler items. Thus Canadian economist Gerry Helleiner notes that the effective protection for consumer goods in Brazil in 1966, for example, was 230 per cent, while intermediate goods production was protected at a rate of just 68 per cent.[11] These high protection levels also meant that the prices of manufactured consumer goods in Southern countries rose very much higher than prices of rural agricultural goods, worsening badly the poverty of peasants and landless labourers in the rural areas. The reality, said Michael Lipton in *Why Poor People Stay Poor*, was that "most modern industry in most poor countries is an exotic, artificial, fragile plant ... because it survives largely by compelling governments to grant it permanent and prohibitive protection against imports, at the expense of farmers, consumers, and national efficiency and development."[12]

Yet the growth of ISI manufacturing did generate learning effects among Southern workers and managers, and it could become the basis for industrial expansion with considerably greater and more dynamic spread effects.

A factor that could and sometimes did intervene in this context was the process of cost-driven competition in OECD markets themselves, in societies in which post-World War II full employment and more egalitarian social policies had come to prevail, raising wages to OECD workers. Especially in sectors of highly labour-intensive, relatively standardized manufacturing, new imports from lower-wage Southern countries grew in importance. The classic cases here of direct industrial relocation include the shift of German and Dutch clothing manufacturing to Tunisia, Egypt, and other south Mediterranean countries, the U.S. investment in the *maquiladora* sector along the Mexican border, and the transfer of electronics components assembly to Southeast Asia. But there are also important examples of arms-length import increases, in textiles and in standard plywood, for instance, that were sometimes regulated by quotas (as with the Multifibre Agreement) and sometimes not. These cost-based export gains from Southern countries could then set off major patterns of industry-by-industry restructuring in OECD countries, with consequent product and technology upgrading in OECD production facilities (along with jobs shifts or job losses, depending on national policies). At the same time, this OECD restructuring could spur further manufacturing expansion in Southern countries.

This set of forces could be seen at work in Northern Europe in the 1978-84 period. Increased lower-cost textiles and standardized plywood exports were coming from Indonesia, Malaysia, and China. In the Netherlands, workers, employers, and the government organized major restructuring of both the plywood and textile industries, closing down much standard production, helping firms shift into higher-technology product areas (such as special sailboats in one large textile company), and providing up to two years of paid retraining for textile workers in less-advantaged parts of the country. The transition in the Dutch industry, as a result of this proactive industrial policy, was much faster than in France, where workers held on longer in failing firms at low wages (spurring an OECD poverty problem in the process). At the same time, Dutch investment went into Asian textile production, Tunisian clothing manufacturing, and certain parts of Sub-Saharan Africa, not only expanding export-oriented plywood mills so that African countries could share in the new OECD market gains, but also upgrading a veneer factory in the Congo to provide specialized wood veneer imports to assist the restructuring of Bruynzeel, the main Dutch plywood manufacturer near Amsterdam.[13]

Further spin-offs came from the expansion of both the ISI subsidiaries and the cost-related relocation subsidiaries. Once an enterprise network exists internationally, then the question of internalizing costs to maximize profits emerges powerfully. Information flows become well-established within the network, and these flows can be more fully utilized to benefit as much as possible from the managerial and technology-transfer advantages of not having to measure and cost these flows.[14] In practice, worldwide information can be used to place new investments in sites that can make the differing parts of the investment conform best to the attributes most essential to particular aspects of the production process. Indeed, it is even possible to use information flows within the enterprise network to train workers for higher-skilled labour requirements in a location where lower-wage levels prevail.

Such pressures to make full use of information networks led to further MNC industrial growth that is much less connected to either local Southern market orientation or to an established basis of existing export competitiveness. As Joekes puts it, "The process of international specialization and integration of production units by TNCs in this way is one of the key features of economic globalization. As an example of how developed the process has become: the production schedules of a machine tool plant in the Philippines, part of and serving other units in a global TNC, are subject to more or less continuous updating by telecommunications according to the evolving production requirements of the other units round the world."[15]

After a period of relative stagnation in direct foreign investment in Southern countries, over 1980-87, there was thus a rapid increase in recent years, from a total of some $11 billion in 1987 to some $36 billion in 1992.[16] This period is when the parent-company shift of production to the South by the MNC American Home Products led to its subsidiary's Canadian Wyeth closure.

Still, Southern countries have not simply been required to accept whatever is generated by international investment trends. Another factor in analysing industrialization is the activism that certain Southern countries have shown in shaping their own industrial development. Policy actions by Southern governments were certainly a widespread consideration in ISI expansion, with extensive forms and levels of internal market protection commonly being established. But what is especially significant is the much more aggressive trade and industrial policy initiatives by a number of countries to drive the industrial growth process beyond the ISI pattern and its limitations — and how these countries had internal social equity and educational depth to sustain these initiatives and this growth.

Korea, Singapore, and Taiwan were particularly energetic in setting in place extensive incentives for industries to move into export manufacturing as well, once an ISI base had been established. Rather than stressing a minimal state role, as some more market-oriented analysts have recommended to expand exports, these three states established clear industrial strategy goals and intervened deeply in the economy to achieve dynamic export gains.[17]

In Korea, there was a rapid shift to requiring export earnings to get access to import licences; an Economic Planning Board using state control of banking and other finance to focus new Korean investment in strategic areas in which exports could be achieved; a heavy emphasis on training and on developing technological capability in industry through various technology agreements; and a strong interaction with the large Korean-owned *chaebol* conglomerates, and strict control of any foreign direct investment.[18] In Taiwan the government added to its import controls a heavy stress on duty drawbacks for exports and establishment of the world's first export-processing zones after 1965; also, highly interventionist policies on differential exchange rates and interest rates, with over 75 per cent of the loans to industries targeted by the government through state-owned banks; and,

again, a heavy emphasis on education, and only selective and limited use of
direct foreign investment.[19] In Singapore, the move to export-manufacturing expansion after 1965 relied more on multinational enterprises, and gen-
erous tax benefits and constraints on the labour movement were a major
part of the strategy; but as this approach began to lead to lower growth rates
in the mid-1970s, the Singapore government deliberately shifted strategy
towards a higher-wage, higher-value-added manufacturing structure that
pushed many low-wage assembly subsidiaries out, emphasized education
and training, and transformed the role of women in the workforce, for
instance, from low-wage, short-term patterns to higher-wage permanent
patterns based on state assistance for child care and non-discrimination in
employment.[20]

These Asian interventionist strategies led to particularly rapid and diversified export-manufacturing gains. As the World Bank notes, the 23 East
Asian economies were the fastest-growing in the world between 1965 and
1990, and in these countries, "Government interventions sometimes
resulted in higher and more evenly distributed growth than otherwise
would have occurred."[21] This is difficult for the Bank to concede, given its
usual strong emphasis in favour of reliance on the market and against state
intervention. But the evidence is simply too strong to deny in the case of
Korea (and Singapore and Taiwan).

Other countries also promoted dynamic export-manufacturing growth,
but with less success. Brazil, for example, put considerable support behind
the development of capital-goods production, working out a technology
strategy to build up the knowledge and expert inputs required to allow it to
compete in relatively complex sectors such as commuter aircraft. But in
general the country did not have much export success in these sectors on
which it concentrated. Argentina, too, put considerable effort into some
capital goods production (for example, CNC lathes), with very little export
success.[22]

Overall, then, the international division of industrial production does
seem to be changing. Virtually all Southern countries have experienced
some industrial development, although much of this has either involved
enclave-like resource extraction, with few widespread effects transforming
the broader economy, or import-substituting industrialization, which has
often been costly for consumers and rural areas and questionable for some
of the products being transferred for local production. Some Southern
countries, however, have been the focus of multinational corporation cost-
based relocation, with restructuring consequences for OECD country
workers. And, finally, a number of Southern nations (the NICs) have been
able to capture the majority of the South's world export-manufacturing
increases, especially in the context of aggressive and successful government
policy interventions to achieve dynamic export performance.

Expanding industrial growth, it has turned out, though, has not always meant improved employment conditions for labour. There was improvement in Korea, where export-manufacturing expansion increased employment in urban areas from 3.25 million in 1963 to 10.23 million in 1982, cutting the urban unemployment rate over the same period from 16 per cent to 6 per cent, and raising average real wages in manufacturing by 7.9 per cent per year.[23] But Brazil and Mexico have both experienced increases in urban unemployment and decreasing urban real wages despite industrial expansion, and Argentina has seen large unemployment increases over 1991-94, and a one-third fall in manufacturing real wages over 1985-94, despite the recent investment expansion — only Chile has seen urban employment and wages improve over the 1990-95 period.[24] The Asian downturn of 1997 has also revealed some serious instabilities in the expansion model, even in the cases of Korea and Brazil. Moreover, there is no doubt that many Southern countries, especially in Africa, have gained little from the changing international division of industrial production, and that they appear to have been increasingly marginalized in the emerging global economy.

2: Gender and Industrialization

Questions about the employment and income impact of industry become even more sceptical in the context of gender-equity concerns. The earlier Southern industrialization around resource extraction and protected formal-sector ISI was strongly oriented almost everywhere to male employment.

Thus the migrant-labour movement of males to the Copperbelt in Zambia, and the new jobs opened up in the ISI tire, detergent, or footwear factories of Kenya and the Ivory Coast raise gender-related employment discrimination issues. This discrimination could mean that women were consigned to lower-income, less-secure informal-sector service and trade roles; it could mean that far fewer emerging economic opportunities appeared for women; and it could mean that many women were left to care for the children and small pieces of land in the rural areas — land that provided meagre living standards in the absence of the males who had been essential for heavier land-clearing roles.

During this "first" pattern of industrialization in many Southern countries, men often had many more educational advantages to draw on, and they showed much higher migration rates in search of the newly emerging industrial jobs. In Bukh's detailed study of eastern Ghana, for instance, 82 per cent of Tsito boys aged 13-15 were in school in 1976-77, compared to 56 per cent of girls — with the percentages even wider for the 16-18 age range, where boys were at 78 per cent and girls at 38 per cent. This coincided with migration levels of 66 per cent for males aged 15-29, compared to only 36 per cent for women in that age range.[25] Saffioti documented the same marginalization of women in the expansion of ISI manufacturing in Brazil, with women making up only 12.2 per cent of industrial workers there in 1970, despite having had a much larger share of the traditional textile industry in the 1870s.[26] As Joekes's provocative analysis suggests, the growth of ISI "provides 'jobs for the boys', i.e., for a male 'labour aristocracy.'"[27]

As the trends took Southern countries more in the direction of MNC-relocation and export-strategy directions, however, the more labour-intensive assembly and processing enterprises that were becoming more important brought about quite different gender effects. As Joekes put it, "In the contemporary era, no strong export performance in manufactures by any developing country has ever been secured without reliance on female labour."[28] This tendency could be seen in a broad variety of statistical indicators, showing women's employment in manufacturing growing especially in such export-oriented countries as South Korea (the female manufacturing labour share went up from 26.4 per cent in 1960 to 40.5 per cent in 1987), Singapore (34.3 per cent in 1970 to 47.5 per cent in 1987), Hong Kong (34.8 per cent in 1961 to 49.6 per cent in 1987), Mauritius (6.6 per cent in 1972 to 59.1 per cent in 1983), Sri Lanka (17.9 per cent in 1963 to 45.3 per cent in 1986), and Thailand (27.1 per cent in 1960 to 45.2 per cent in 1986).[29]

The increased manufacturing export emphasis created significantly more economic opportunities for women, but to a considerable extent these fast-growing opportunities seemed to be building on and confirming the markedly lower wages paid to women workers than to men. Women were playing particularly prominent roles in three broad areas of export expansion and low-wage advantages were important in each. First, in a set of mainly locally run, standardized technology sectors, the high labour-intensity of production made labour costs crucial if exports were to successfully penetrate Northern country markets. Clothing, the classic industry in this category, characterized the expansion of women's employment in countries such as Bangladesh, Sri Lanka, and Mauritius (in 1993, clothing represented 56 per cent, 49 per cent, and 53 per cent of the merchandise exports of these three countries). Second, another grouping of much higher-technology enterprises relocated the labour-intensive parts of their electronics and communication operations in lower-wage countries. MNCs were especially active in this area, drawing in new women employees especially in Korea, Hong Kong, and Malaysia, where the higher educational level of women relative to Bangladesh or Indonesia was also an important factor. (Korean women in 1992, for instance, had an average of 6.7 years of schooling; the Hong Kong average was 5.4 years; and Malaysia was 5 years; while the average for Indonesian women was 2.9 years, with the Bangladesh average at 0.9 years.) Third, export-processing zones (EPZs) developed with a more diverse range of firms in many countries, often drawing on women as workers in the earlier days because low wages were especially crucial concerns and younger women might be expected to be more easily disciplined and controlled than older male workers from other manufacturing backgrounds, men who might bring trade union experience with them. EPZs were especially important in Singapore, Mauritius, and Mexico.[30]

Almost all these situations had a high level of wage discrimination against women, even accounting for different educational levels. An analysis of 11 Southern countries that examined export-manufacturing wage patterns concluded that the average wage gap was 10-25 per cent in favour of men, and in some countries (such as Korea) the difference was much greater.[31] Only in a few countries (such as Bangladesh and the Dominican Republic) does the evidence suggest similar wage levels for men and women. Moreover, there appears to be no overpowering trend towards the narrowing of these Southern gender wage gaps. A study of 15 countries in the 1990s shows some decrease in the gap in ten countries, but an increase in four other cases; and data from some of the larger export-processing zones show both increases in male-female wage differentials, and decreases in the share of women employees, as more diversification of activities in these zones takes place. (Joekes notes that this is the case in both Mexico and Singapore.)[32]

Beyond these typical areas of export-manufacturing, Joekes perceives some new, emerging patterns of economic activity that have important gender implications in some Southern countries. Noting that much MNC investment is now moving into service and ancillary-operation areas that are being relocated to Southern countries, Joekes sees that new employment is expanding for Southern women in information-intensive sectors such as data-processing, accountancy, and computerized communication technology. Pointing to Jamaica, where women have higher educational levels than males in the labour force, and where there has been a strategic effort to build a presence in this area via an EPZ-like "Digi-port" for telecommunications processing, Joekes suggests optimistically, "There is a real prospect of a high level of women's involvement without compromise of employment quality. The newness of these sectors may have allowed them to escape the fixed patterns of gender stereotyping which have confined women to inferior occupational positions in industry."[33]

As Pearson notes, this emphasis on the female role in export-manufacturing and these hopeful perspectives about MNC relocation of new functions seem to miss several crucial points.[34] First, the MNC role does appear to exhibit major limitations so far as having broadspread effects that can transform poverty conditions in many Southern countries. In small, compact island economies such as Singapore, the MNC impact may be wide enough to bring dynamic results, but more appropriate technology with greater local employment and linkage effects seems essential in most larger economies. Second, the reality is that the great majority of women seeking economic opportunities are coping with the realities of the informal sector, with its myriad of small-scale, unregulated activities, rather than the formal employment structures of EPZs or MNCs. In Ghana, for example, while total female formal-sector employment in 1990 declined to 229,000, female informal-sector jobs rose to 346,000 (compared to 303,000 in 1985).[35] Analysis of female poverty reduction in Ghana suggests the expansion of such non-formal off-farm economic options can make a critical difference for women.

Detailed study of formal-sector employment of women, centred on export-oriented factories, then, may in its own way represent as much of a focus on a "labour aristocracy" as Joekes claims is implied by the ISI strategy for male industrial workers. In most Southern countries, the great majority of women workers are in the informal sector, where Joekes concedes that incomes and working conditions are significantly worse,[36] yet her lengthy review of employment and gender ignores the dynamics and policy concerns of that sector.

3: Industry and the Informal Sector

Kenyans commonly refer to the small-scale, less-regulated business activities of the informal sector in Nairobi as "*jua kali*" (Swahili for "hot sun"), because they are mostly carried on in open fields without adequate shelter or shade. Yet, as Kinuthia Macharia's research shows, people in this sector are "legitimately engaged in a wide variety of very useful occupations, especially the metal artisans, garment/footwear makers, and food preparers/sellers, as well as the vendors of a wide range of household goods and personal requirements.... Informal sector activities conserve scarce foreign exchange, require very little capital to create jobs, rely primarily on family savings, provide their own training in useful skills at no public cost, and offer an arena for the first-hand acquisition of entrepreneurial attitudes and expertise."[37]

Macharia's view is the first-hand perspective of a Kenyan African sociologist who was personally present when Kenyan authorities destroyed the homes of thousands of informal-sector participants in Nairobi. Yet others have seen the small-scale, diffuse efforts of thousands of poorer Africans not as legitimate and valuable economic enterprise, but as the residual underemployment (or even unemployment) of thousands of unnecessary urban migrants who should go back to the rural areas to find productive work to do. In some cases, such as Maputo in Mozambique, and Dar es Salaam in Tanzania, Southern governments went further than just demolishing informal sector housing (as Kenya did); they repatriated large numbers of people from national capitals long distances out into the countryside. Hostility and harassment, then, were at one point the common experience of informal-sector entrepreneurs and workers, and evidence of this perspective can still be found (as in the Nairobi case in 1990).

It was the work of Keith Hart in Ghana and the impact of follow-up studies by the International Labour Office that led to some shift in this negative view of the "problem" of overcrowded and redundant urban migrants. Hart's urban research stressed how important it was to the urban poor that "the range of opportunities available outside the organized labour markets is so wide that no one need be totally without income of some kind, however irregular."[38] Analysts such as Kenneth King then followed up this insight by investigating the training mechanisms by which African artisans developed their skills for informal-sector activity, and the often complementary relationship between informal- and formal-sector activities in some Southern economies.[39] Gradually, out of parallel work on urban small-scale economic activities in Asian, Latin American, and other African cities, a more positive perspective emerged of the potential contribution of the informal sector to economic expansion and income provision.

Thus, in the 1990s, the analytical focus is more on the constraints to informal-sector enterprise that need to be overcome, and the means by which the informal sector might best be encouraged. One key constraint is the powerful competition from formal-sector firms. Another is interest-rate advantages enjoyed by the formal sector over the informal with respect to credit.

The bread industry in Kenya provides an important example of the first constraint to the informal sector. Two broad options in the industry can be analysed.[40] The formal sector is dominated by Elliots Bakery, a spin-off from the mainly white-settler-run Kenya Farmers' Association (KFA) of wheat producers. This single firm accounts for some 63 per cent of bread production in Kenya, using automatic tunnel technology centralized in two huge bakeries — highly capital-intensive and using much less labour (per unit of output) than the informal-sector alternative. The small-scale, low-capital informal-sector option is represented by many more simple brick-oven bakeries scattered throughout the country in a much more decentralized way. What is striking is that comparison of the two technologies showed that "The rate of profit of the small-scale, predominantly rural brick-oven bakeries was substantially higher than their predominantly urban-based and larger-scale mechanized counterparts."[41] Wider consideration of "social profitability" measures simply accentuated the advantages of the brick-oven option. Yet the formal-sector bakery giant is far and away the dominant factor in the Kenyan bread market, acting as a major blockage to rapid expansion of the informal-sector alternative.

Why is this the case? For one thing, Kaplinsky suggests, the white-settler wheat farmers were able to perpetuate their market power in grain-milling, even after colonial independence, through a complex series of interlocking corporate share connections, as a result of which Elliots continued to serve as one source of realizing grain-milling profits and thereby received various benefits from the KFA-descended Unga-Maida grain-milling conglomerate (including loans and automated transfer of wheat directly from the Nakuru grain mill into one of the large tunnel bakeries). These intracorporate advantages were important. A second advantage was how the Kenyan state tended to skew its interventions in favour of the large-scale, powerful Unga-Maida empire and its Elliots Bakery affiliate. Thus credit did not go to the small-scale brick-oven bakeries, and price controls on bread were maintained as Elliots wanted, rather than lowered (which would have helped the more competitive brick-oven producers). Yet another advantage came from Elliots' long-term, high-pressure marketing efforts, which led to strong consumer preferences among many Kenyans for the firm's wrapped loaves of brand-name bread.

A second constraint that favoured formal-sector enterprises over the informal sector was differential interest rates on credit needed for working capital and for expansions. To some degree this could simply be seen as more evidence of state discrimination against the informal sector. But there are also structural factors at work, because financial institutions usually base their granting of credit on records of reliability in repayment and on the extent of assets that can be used as collateral. Given that informal-sector records and activities are often irregular and shifting, and that low investment means that fixed assets are also usually meagre, lenders have some justification for considering the risks of credit provision to the informal sector to be higher. Nevertheless, the result is usually wide differentials in interest rates that seem to overemphasize these structural points (see Table 5.1).

These differentials show the disadvantages that the informal sector faces in making use of credit; but even more important, they suggest the difficulty that informal-sector entrepreneurs have in even obtaining credit (given the huge risk premium that they clearly confront). Even more so, the low and commonly negative interest rates experienced by the formal-sector show again another way in which state policy, in this case in the financial sector, is biased in favour of formal-sector activities. It is true that there have been increasing attempts on the part of some Southern governments to overcome informal-sector constraints and build new economic opportu-

Table 5.1: Real Interest Rates for Formal & Informal Sectors (% per year)

Country	Informal Sector	Formal Sector
Ethiopia	66%	8%
Ivory Coast	145	6
Nigeria	192	-2
Sudan	120	7
Sierra Leone	60	-3
India	15	-1
Indonesia	29	3
Malaysia	58	16
Pakistan	27	4
Korea	49	5
Sri Lanka	20	-1
Bolivia	96	5
Brazil	38	-7
Chile	52	-16
Colombia	40	16
Costa Rica	20	4
Mexico	57	7

Source: R. Kaplinsky, *The Economics of Small*, 1990, p. 208.

nities around the dynamism of small-scale, less-regulated enterprises. A 1994 study in Ghana of 133 small enterprises showed strong demand for credit and indicated that half of the micro-enterprises sampled had received loans from the government-organized Program of Action to Mitigate the Social Costs of Adjustment (PAMSCAD). This credit availability clearly had an impact, because capital growth in the micro-enterprises was highest of all the small firms (at 13 per cent per year) and brought employment increases of 7 to 9 per cent annually.[42]

In many Southern countries, other forms of help also appear for small-scale entrepreneurs. It is common to see small enterprise estates, as in Arusha, Tanzania, or Kumasi, Ghana. Appropriate technology centres are found in Addis Ababa, Ethiopia, in Nairobi, Kenya, and elsewhere. Canadian business and aid agencies support prominent programs to send second-hand industrial equipment to small firms in Peru.

But such initiatives almost inevitably have a "formal-sector flavour" to them and fail to achieve broad-based informal-sector expansion. The real issue is the advantages and privileges of the formal sector that discriminate against the urban informal sector and the rural majorities of most Southern countries.

Over the 1985-90 period, Ghana dismantled many of these formal-sector privileges, severely cutting urban industrial protection, ending many special credit and tax privileges, and devaluing the exchange rate dramatically so that special foreign exchange arrangements could no longer favour the formal sector. Formal-sector employment fell from 464,000 in 1985 to 186,000 in 1991, while informal-sector jobs grew from 946,000 in 1985 to 1,266,000 in 1990.[43] Agricultural output grew in response to the much stronger incentives this created for rural economic activity. And, most significant in the context of this present discussion, there were also important shifts in living standards. As recent research has discovered, "Between 1987-88 and 1991-92, Ghana's poor fell from 37 percent to 31 percent of the population. This reduction was widespread and broad-based, benefiting mainly rural areas and the most vulnerable group — female headed households. Almost all of the reduction can be traced to economic growth in general and growth in non-farm self-employment in particular. Growth in private-sector services, especially wholesale and retail trade, has been the driving force behind non-farm self-employment."[44] Such non-farm self-employment represents the heart of informal-sector activity in Ghana and can be seen dynamically responding to dismantled formal-sector privileges from Tamale, to Techiman, to Sunyani, to Kumasi, to Cape Coast, to Tema, to Accra — in the "*jua kali*" right across the country.

It is especially important that research in Ghana is indicating that such informal-sector buoyancy is of particular benefit to female-headed households, because other research, in Mexico, has clearly set out the extreme difficulty faced there by one set of informal-sector women workers — the flower sellers of Xochimilco, a suburb some 13 kilometres south of Mexico City. In their case, the double responsibility they have for household tasks and for a key part of income-generating activities has led to increases in poverty and (in the face of increasing water pollution in the area) to worsening health problems for their families. In addition to low returns for their services related to gender, they also experience male domestic violence that adds to their gender subjugation.[45]

Constraints confronting the informal-sector clearly exist — including difficulty obtaining credit, marketing obstacles from some formal-sector firms, and harassment from state policy. To these must be added special constraints that women face because of their gender. In many Southern countries they have found it even more difficult to gain access to credit; and in other cases, informal methods of training through what are in effect forms of apprenticeship have often been far less open to them.

This is why increasingly the focus of gender-equity efforts in Southern countries is turning away from exclusive concern with wage comparisons and other policy issues in the formal sector (whether export-oriented or ISI) and placing more emphasis on the much larger number of women in the informal sector. As a recent United Nations analysis has put it, "The unfavourable work environment as well as the limited number of employment opportunities available have led many women to seek alternatives. Women have increasingly become self-employed and owners and managers of micro, small and medium-scale enterprises. The expansion of the informal sector, in many countries, and of self-organized and independent enterprises is in large part due to women, whose collaborative, self-help and traditional practices and initiatives in production and trade represent a vital economic resource."[46]

This reality has led to women's access to informal-sector credit, training opportunities, and improved legal status becoming key parts of gender-related industrial policy efforts in the later 1990s. Thus in Cambodia, for instance, Khemara house, with World Bank support, is training over 300 women in technical and business courses of three to nine months, so the women can make use of credit to set up small weaving, food-processing, printing, and services businesses in villages around Phnom Penh.[47] In Kenya, too, a Micro and Small Enterprise Training and Technology project is being established with an explicit goal of "increasing women's representation in manufacturing through skills training and technology development suitable for upgrading their enterprises or bringing them into the sector."[48] In Benin, another project also aims directly at women in the informal sector, planning to "provide resources and training to make their micro enterprises viable and sustainable, and should improve self-employment opportunities for poor women."[49]

Gender concerns in industrial development, then, ultimately come to focus, too, on the privileges and favoured benefits enjoyed by formal-sector industry. ISI, as an industrialization process, rested quite starkly on such privileges of import protection and state financial support. Export-oriented industry in practice, through low-interest credit and special import bonus arrangements, often did likewise. Women came to share more in these special benefits as export gains grew, although the evidence indicates that their wages still lagged behind those of men. But the truly stark inequality is the much greater gap between the unregulated, vulnerable informal sector and the privileged formal sector of employment. That gap, which most seriously undercuts the incomes of the great majority of non-farm women, is the one that is just beginning to be addressed.

4: Multinational Corporations and Industrial Production

At the same time as large, Northern-based corporations with operating subsidiaries throughout the world have dominated much Southern resource-extraction investment, been key factors in import-substituting industrialization, and extended or built their international networks around cost-related industrial relocations and exports from Southern countries, it is striking that the most successful Southern industrial expansion cases, such as Korea, Taiwan, and Thailand, have relied very little on such MNCs and had rigorous regulatory mechanisms to control them. This points to the analytical dilemmas raised by the MNC role in Southern countries, and to a fundamental question. There is no doubt, given the extensive growth in direct foreign investment in Southern economies, that MNCs will continue to play a role in Southern industrial expansion. The key question is whether Southern industrialization should rely on that MNC role, or if the evidence suggests that it is possible and desirable to rely on locally controlled alternative enterprises of a different kind.

The heart of MNC strength in the world economy is their technological capacity and control over specialized information and knowledge. This capacity and control increasingly lead MNCs into technology-related joint ventures and agreements: over 95 per cent of these sophisticated knowledge-based arrangements occur within the OECD countries, with 2 to 3 per cent involving the NICs, and well under 2 per cent involving other Southern countries.[50] With capital now more widely available from international money markets, the MNCs draw on these technology and knowledge factors as the crucial elements for their bargaining advantages in Southern countries; and in turn Southern countries too have come to feel an urgent need in many cases.

This is true even in the traditional resource-extraction cases. In the ongoing bargaining dynamics of such large, complex projects, once they have been built and learning effects have spread among Southern personnel, Southern governments have a basis for increased bargaining strength in dealing with the MNC involved. But the MNC will often have learned a great deal from previous projects and similar bargaining situations and be able to rely on continuing technological developments and to adjust financial arrangements to maintain advantages. As the managing director of Rio Tinto Zinc once told a seminar at the University of Sussex in the United Kingdom, with respect to maintaining financial gains for his MNC in a Southern copper project, "We've been around a long time, and we know there are all kinds of ways of killing a cat."

In a review of the large oil subsidiary in Trinidad and Tobago,[51] Farrell illustrates this MNC bargaining strength. Everything depends, Farrell concludes, on technology transfer, the "essence" of which is "knowledge." Analysing that technology requires a detailed and careful breakdown of tasks and skill requirements associated with those tasks; one must distinguish between *static technology* and *dynamic technology*, with the latter as crucial. "This then implies in turn that a key question is whether the corporation transfers the dynamic technologies that are key to this ability to run an industry successfully over time." Despite over two generations of

MNC activity in Trinidad and Tobago, "What emerged from the detailed examination of the data," Farrell shows, "was that the country suffered from certain serious weaknesses in the area of dynamic technology." Thus the Trinidad and Tobago government had very little ability to improve its position in dealing with the subsidiary. Developing local technological capability, then, becomes crucial to any efforts at greater long-run national leverage in complex resource sectors.

China has been carefully trying to build such technological capability in its offshore oil industry, via the Chinese National Offshore Oil Corporation (CNOOC).[52] Warhurst, reviewing the strategy, shows how it developed effectiveness over time, evolving into realistic negotiation and interplay on a company-by-company basis — built on targeting of strengths of various partners, on less emphasis on proprietary knowledge and more stress on state-of-the-art acquisition efforts, and on long-term human-resource upgrading strategies, often for periods abroad of two to three years. This was very much a "joint-venture" strategy, based on training abroad and on decentralized decision-making — with good results at the company-by-company level, especially where groups were involved together over time. The project also had a strong emphasis on problem-solving approaches; a stress, in choosing partners, on separating equipment supply from technology transfer, to get the knowledge transfer done right; and a recognition that the technology transfer agreement had to be of an ongoing character to be able to modify and improve technology. Still, complications often marked technology transfer, such as language problems, differing educational backgrounds, and other technology gaps outside the oil sector. In general, though, the CNOOC case shows it is possible to develop a successful local technology capacity strategy, even in the complex area of offshore oil.

The potential revenue gains to the Southern country could justify such major efforts and strategic work in given resource-extraction sectors. In the case of manufacturing operations, however, the wide number of firms involved and the diversity and smaller scale of enterprises mean that a company-by-company bargaining focus works less effectively for Southern countries. When firm-specific bargaining has taken place with MNCs, as examples from Nigeria, Kenya, Tanzania, and the Andean countries in Latin America show, the negotiation process was often a means by which MNCs won import protection, taxation benefits, and state financial help — rather than a process by which Southern governments improved local access to or control over technological knowledge.[53]

For Southern governments, then, technological capacity remained the core advantage of the MNCs in the manufacturing context, too.

To protect this advantage, MNC subsidiaries in Southern countries often did not transfer crucial technology elements to local workers. A common reality in many subsidiaries was for the production manager and key technical personnel to remain expatriates, often direct employees of the parent company. The result could mean no real local absorption of key technological knowledge. The MNC might carefully preserve key elements of technological knowledge (the formula for producing Coca-Cola). It might control continuing innovation in process or product technology (as with some microchip electronic producers, who have been able to simply shift production facilities from country to country, because the key element in the MNC branch-plant operation is the technical know-how). Or it might simply freeze out local personnel from crucial higher-technology areas (as in some synthetic textile production cases in Kenya).

Then there is the question of the cost of technology transfer. As Vaitsos shows, there are two sorts of costs that must be analysed: the impact of restrictions associated with MNC technology commercialization (such as export limitations, or requirements to buy expensive inputs only from the parent company); and the actual financial costs of technology (measuring *all* elements of the financial outflow involved). The nature of the market for technology is such (the demand side often involves high uncertainty and high costs of reproducing such specialized knowledge, while the supply side involves low marginal costs for further usage of specialized knowledge that has already been paid for) that a wide range of acceptable price outcomes could be possible — meaning that the final price established is very much a result of bargaining in what is really a non-market context.[54] The result can be very high costs, indeed.

Thus in three Andean pact countries analysed, for instance, Vaitsos found 92 of 136 MNC contracts had tie-in clauses enforcing imports from the parent; in four Andean countries, export bans were in place in 81 per cent of the 247 MNC contracts reviewed. Beyond these economically costly restrictions, the Vaitsos evidence also shows huge outflows from Colombia to MNC parent companies in the form of imports from the parent at "transfer prices" paid that were 51 per cent to 77 per cent above the usual world prices for those items (depending on the industry). These transfer-pricing outflows far exceeded declared profits and royalty payments from the subsidiaries to their parent companies (in pharmaceuticals, for example, reported profits made up 3.4 per cent of the effective returns to the MNC parent, royalties contributed another 14 per cent, and overpricing of imported inputs accounted for 82.6 per cent of the total).[55] Research in Kenya also discovered widespread MNC use of transfer-pricing to understate profits.[56]

Then there is the question of the appropriateness of the technology being transferred. Various studies have sparked analytical scepticism on this point, including a detailed review by Cooper of metal-can manufacturing in Thailand. This research found that two broad choices were economically feasible for manufacturing firms: one used over 11 workers on lower-cost semi-automatic machinery to produce 100,000 cans per hour; the second (chosen by MNCs) used 3 workers to produce the same level of output on much more expensive, continuous, automated machinery also used in the British parent. The MNC option led to output costs per unit (even standardizing at the wage rates paid by the MNC) some 42 per cent higher than the more labour-intensive local alternative.[57] Yet the MNC used the advanced technology employed throughout the international enterprise because this was most efficient to the MNC's notion of "internalizing" technology strategy, reducing enterprise costs of transferring personnel to different global production locations, maintaining uniform specifications for production internationally, and minimizing overall corporate technology-option search costs. But this approach meant rejection of a more "appropriate" technology for Thailand — an approach that would have had wider employment effects and more potential linkage benefits to production of the simpler machinery that could have been much more readily manufactured locally.

Increasingly the notion of "appropriate" has come to incorporate dimensions of: i) greater employment provision than alternatives; ii) high levels of interaction with the rest of the local economy (usually thought of as linkage effects); iii) contributing to indigenous technological capacity, to keep the innovation process under local control and subject to local factor endowments; iv) relatively small-scale, to maintain ties with the community that are not dominant; v) resource and energy-conserving, to preserve opportunities over the long run; and vi) respectful of the environment, to not impose negative external costs on other members of the community.

The question then becomes one of how appropriate technology can be transferred by MNCs, or of whether this requires the development of indigenous technological capacity as a conscious strategy. Jenkins, providing an answer to the first part of this question, shows that MNC subsidiaries abroad not only tend to stress the products and production technology that they use in industrial countries (as in the Thai can-making case), but also have the effect where they are predominant of pushing larger Southern firms in the same technology-choice and related linkage directions.[58] Reliance on MNCs, then, would be unlikely to lead to industrial growth with the widespread effects and broad job spinoffs suggested by the perspectives of appropriate technology.

But is it possible to rely on an alternative strategy? Do other options beyond MNC technology reliance exist? This may not be a blanket question, but a specific sector-by-sector, product-by-product issue. For instance, if the goal is reproduction of an international tourist-oriented soft drink, the alternative to Coke may simply be Pepsi. But if the goal is production of a thirst-quenching carbonated beverage, relying on local fruit concentrates, the alternatives to Coke might be much wider. The development of technology centres, often on a regional basis (such as the Caricom Technology Centre in the West Indies), helps document and organize such alternative options. Another approach could be to use foreign technology suppliers, but only those independently based and providing their expertise (for a fee) directly to a local company. This was successfully done, for example, by a local Jamaican entrepreneur in building up a locally controlled welding electrode-manufacturing enterprise over the 1972-85 period, in the process expanding employment, improving local training, and building the firm's ability to make appropriate technology choices itself in the future.[59]

Analysis of the textiles and wood-products sectors in Kenya shows the contrast in practice between relying on MNCs and relying on more appropriate local enterprise and technology capacity.[60] In both industries, the more profitable, export-oriented and viable firms in Kenya (over the long term) were those locally controlled alternatives that developed indigenous technological capability — either in a slow process of learning-by-doing, or as part of a deliberate strategy of building their own technology capacity (through research and development efforts, training, and independent technology-supply advisors). This direction contrasted dramatically with companies that relied on MNC technology transfer — like CFG in Gabon in plywood manufacturing, and the large foreign textile subsidiaries in Kenya. In the case of CFG, reliance for technology inputs on Bruynzeel of the Netherlands in the post-World War II period led only to deeper reliance on that same foreign MNC when the company had to restructure into new production areas in the face of competition with Asian plywood suppliers in the later 1970s. In the case of textiles in Kenya, the German-Dutch technology inputs to Rivatex, the British inputs to the Lonrho subsidiary, the India technology basis of Kisumu textiles, and the German inputs into Kenya Fine Spinners all led to bankruptcy and massive losses for the Kenyan state. Of the large Kenyan textile projects based on foreign MNCs, only KTM, based on Japanese technology that the Kenyan state industrial holding company transformed to much greater local technological control through heavy emphasis on local training and R & D, managed to maintain itself as a viable firm (despite the early period in which it generated heavy outflows to Japan through purchase of synthetic textile inputs at higher than world prices). In general, the local alternatives, relying on indigenous technological capacity, had significantly higher employment and linkage effects than the MNC subsidiaries.

There are, then, serious economic and social costs of MNC technology reliance, but alternative approaches can be developed. The counterdirection would aim to build indigenous technological capability, promote broad product technology alternatives, develop greater technological independence in small local firms, and encourage the production directly of more appropriate technology in domestic capital goods production.

The "informal sector" of small-scale, indigenous, less-regulated enterprises in Southern countries can provide one important source from which such Southern entrepreneurial and technological capability can often emerge.

5: Conclusion

The international division of industrial labour underwent a remarkable change after 1945. New factories, mines, oil fields, and infrastructure expanded dramatically in the South, alongside extensive industrial restructuring in Northern countries. Basic forces have been at work, including Northern drives for new raw material, the rise of MNCs that first sought Southern market penetration and then used the South as new bases of operation worldwide, and changes in political forces that gave some Southern countries the institutions and determination to reshape their trade and industrial policies to compete against the North.

Yet as these powerful new factors played themselves out, four essential realities emerged that explain why changing industrial patterns have not swept away Southern poverty.

First, only a restricted number of Southern countries have achieved powerful industrial transformation in a way that has brought about dynamic social change. Korea, Singapore, Mauritius, Thailand, perhaps Chile in the last ten years, and perhaps China in the same period have grown at rapid rates and seen that growth spreading itself broadly throughout the society, enough to improve markedly the conditions of many of the poor within their boundaries. But few other countries have matched this record, and many Southern countries have been marginalized almost entirely in this process of change. This is especially true for much of Africa, where the collapse of ISI largely meant the retrenchment of industrialization rather than a change in its orientation. Increased reliance on traditional raw materials and high international oil prices have simply meant crippling debts left from better times and large devaluations that have maintained poverty intact.

Second, increased Southern industrial competition from low-wage countries has undercut some of the earlier Southern leaders, including Mexico and Argentina. Recent wage decreases in those two countries and in Brazil are signs that industrial growth in itself cannot generate social transformation in larger Southern countries. This seems to be particularly true when countries rely on MNCs, as Mexico and Argentina have done. MNCs will undoubtedly be continuing factors in the industrial change process in most Southern countries, but their record does not show the broad employment effects, extensive linkages, and positive encouragement for local small-scale industry that would lead to a marked poverty reduction in the South.

Third, gender-based inequalities remain strong in the industrial sector, limiting the impact of industrialization on poverty. While export-oriented manufacturing drew more women into employment than ISI, the wage discrimination practised against women remained strong. And where women are being paid the same as men in export processing zones (as in the Dominican Republic), it is because men are being forced to accept the lower wages that women have had to take.

Fourth, and finally, for most Southern countries there seems to be a strong case to be made for more appropriate technology choices, based on improved technological capability, and promoting more local employment and linkage effects. The informal sector can be a source for this direction, and for broader income opportunities for many poor people (women and men), but the privileged competitive advantages, training, and credit access of the formal sector must be broken down to encourage informal-sector expansion. Not surprisingly, formal-sector industrial firms, both MNC and domestic, are not encouraging changes of this kind.

The reduction in poverty levels in Ghana, based on removal of formal-sector benefits, and resulting in informal-sector growth (especially among women), is a sign of the consequences that a new industrial policy direction could assist. The political question in many Southern countries is whether the social forces that represent the poorer majority, in the rural areas, and in the informal sector, will be able to enforce such a policy change.

The political economies of many Southern countries are now very much under pressure. The international conditions facing most countries have brought forth hard choices for Southern governments, as they have tried to maintain viable macroeconomic policies despite debts, falling terms of trade, and tough restructuring efforts by the International Monetary Fund and the World Bank. These realities and the conflicts they set off have often led to movements towards democracy in Southern societies, and this move to democracy may finally reshape industrial expansion so that it does indeed contribute more to poverty reduction in the South.

Notes

1 See A.P. D'Costa, "State, Steel and Strength: Structural Competitiveness and Development in South Korea," *Journal of Development Studies*, vol. 33, no.1 (1994), p.52.
2 See Steven Langdon, "Industrial Dependence and Export Manufacturing in Kenya," in *Africa in Economic Crisis*, ed. John Ravenhill (London: Macmillan, 1986), pp.184-99.

3 See World Bank, *Summaries of Poverty Assessments Completed in Fiscal 1995*, Internet, 1996.
4 See the classic R. Prebisch, "The Economic Development of Latin America and Its Principal Problems," *Economic Bulletin for Latin America*, March 1961.
5 See UNIDO data presented in *Industry and Accumulation in Africa*, ed. M. Fransman (London: Heinemann, 1982), pp.395, 400.
6 Rhys Jenkins, "Industrialization and the Global Economy," in *Industrialization and Development*, ed. T. Hewitt et al. (Oxford: Oxford University Press, 1991), pp.18-20.
7 See International Monetary Fund, *Private Market Financing for Developing Countries* (Washington: Policy Development and Review Department, IMF, 1995), pp.25, 78.
8 See Raymond Vernon, *Sovereignty at Bay* (London: Basic Books, 1971), pp.32, 39.
9 See Carlos Fortin, "The State, Multinational Corporations and Natural Resources in Latin America," in *Transnational Capitalism and National Development*, ed. Villamil, pp.205-22.
10 A detailed discussion of the continuing damage caused by baby formula multinationals is found in UNICEF, *The Progress of Nations*, 1997.
11 See G. Helleiner, *International Trade and Economic Development* (London: Penguin, 1972), p.131.
12 See M. Lipton, *Why Poor People Stay Poor* (London: Temple Smith, 1977), p.41.
13 See S. Langdon, "North-South, West and East: European-African Industrial Restructuring in the World Economy," *International Journal*, Fall, 1981; FMO (Netherlands Finance Company for Developing Countries), *Annual Report 1979*, The Hague, 1980.
14 See the discussion of this "internalization" perspective in Peter Buckley and Mark Casson, *The Future of the Multinational Enterprise*, Second Edition (London: Macmillan, 1991), chapter 2.
15 See Susan Joekes, *Trade-Related Employment for Women in Industry and Services in Developing Countries*, United Nations Research Institute for Social Development, Geneva, August 1995, section 2.4.
16 See R. Miller and M. Sumlinski, "Trends in Private Investment in Developing Countries 1994," *International Finance Corporation*, discussion paper 20, Washington, 1994, p.6.
17 See David Evans, "Visible and Invisible Hands in Trade Policy Reform," in *States or Markets?* ed. C. Colclough and J. Manor (Oxford: Clarendon Press, 1991), pp.48-77.
18 See Chung H. Lee, "The Government, Financial System, and Large Private Enterprise in the Economic Development of South Korea," *World Development*, vol.20, no.2 (1992), pp.187-97; Anthony D'Costa, "State, Steel and Strength: Structural Competitiveness and Development in South Korea," *Journal of Development Studies*, vol.31, no.1 (1994), pp.44-81; Larry Westphal, Yung Rhee and Gary Purcell, "Sources of Technological Capability in South Korea," in *Technological Capability in the Third World*, ed. M. Fransman and K. King (London: Macmillan, 1984), pp.279-300.
19 See Brautigam, "What Can Africa Learn from Taiwan?" pp.111-38.

20 See Cheah Hock Beng, "Export-Oriented Industrialization and Dependent Development: The Experience of Singapore," *IDS Bulletin*, vol.12, no.1 (1980), pp.35-41; Ruth Pearson, "Gender Issues in Industrialization," in *Industrialization and Development*, ed. T. Hewitt, H. Johnson and D. Wield (Oxford: Oxford University Press, 1991), pp.237-38.

21 See "The Making of the East Asia Miracle," *World Bank Policy Research Bulletin*, vol.4, no.4 (August-October 1993), Internet.

22 See Daniel Chudnovsky et al., *Capital Goods Production in the Third World* (London: Frances Pinter, 1983), chapter 3, pp.138-47.

23 See Chung H. Lee, "The Government, Financial System, and Large Private Enterprise in the Economic Development of South Korea," *World Development*, vol.20, no.2 (1992), pp.187-97.

24 See CEPAL, *Preliminary Overview of the Latin American and Caribbean Economy, 1995* (Santiago de Chile: United Nations, December 1995), pp.50-51.

25 See Bukh, *The Village Woman in Ghana*, pp.66, 115.

26 See Ruth Pearson, "Gender Issues in Industrialization," p.228.

27 See Joekes, *Trade-Related Employment for Women in Industry and Services in Developing Countries*, section 2.1.

28 *Ibid.*, section 2.1.

29 Pearson, "Gender Issues in Industrialization," Table 8.1.

30 See discussion in Joekes, *Trade-Related Employment for Women in Industry and Services in Developing Countries*, section 2.

31 *Ibid.*, section 2.3.

32 *Ibid.*, section 2.5.

33 *Ibid.*, section 3.3.

34 See Pearson, "Gender Issues in Industrialization," section 8.4.

35 See reports in Institute of Statistical, Social and Economic Research (ISSER), *The State of the Ghanaian Economy in 1994* (Legon: University of Ghana, July 1995), pp.139, 142.

36 See Joekes, *Trade-Related Employment for Women in Industry and Services in Developing Countries*, section 2.3.

37 See Macharia, "Slum Clearance and the Informal Sector in Nairobi," pp.221-36.

38 See K. Hart, "Informal Income Opportunities and Urban Employment in Ghana," in *Third World Employment*, ed. R. Jolly et al. (Harmondsworth: Penguin, 1973), p.89.

39 See K. King, *The African Artisan* (London: Heinemann, 1977), especially chapter 2.

40 See Kaplinsky, *The Economics of Small*, chapter 3.

41 Ibid., p.53.

42 See Ernest Aryeetey et al., "Supply and Demand for Finance of Small Enterprises in Ghana," discussion paper no. 251, World Bank, Washington, 1994, Internet.

43 See reports in ISSER, *The State of the Ghanaian Economy in 1994*, pp.139, 143.

44 See World Bank, "Ghana — Growth, Private Sector, and Poverty Reduction: A

Country Economic Memorandum," Report no. 14111, Washington, May 15, 1995, Internet.

45 Joekes et al., "Gender, Environment and Population," pp. 150-51, 155-56, 160-62.

46 See United Nations, "Women and the Economy, 1996" [Internet document - UN Home Page].

47 See World Bank, "Women in Business – Cambodia," *Project Description*, 1996.

48 See World Bank, "Kenya — Micro and Small Enterprise Training and Technology Project," *Project Description*, 1995.

49 See World Bank, "Benin — Women's Initiative Pilot Project," *Project Description*, 1994.

50 See C. Freeman and J. Hagedoorn, "Catching Up or Falling Behind: Patterns in International Interfirm Technology Partnering," *World Development*, vol.22, no.5 (1994), pp.771-80.

51 See Trevor Farrell, "A Tale of Two Issues: Nationalization, The Transfer of Technology and the Petroleum Multinationals in Trinidad-Tobago," *Social and Economic Studies*, 28, 1979, pp.234-81.

52 See A. Warhurst, "Technology Transfer and the Development of China's Offshore Oil Industry," *World Development*, vol.19, no.8 (1991), pp.1055-73.

53 See D. Gachuki and P. Coughlin, "Structure and Safeguards for Negotiations with Foreign Investors: Lessons from Kenya," in *Industrialization in Kenya*, ed. P. Coughlin and G.K. Ikiara (Nairobi: Heinemann Kenya, 1988), pp.91-111; S.M. Wangwe, "Industrialization Experiences from Tanzania 1965-1985," in *Industrialization in Kenya*, ed. Coughlin and Ikiara, pp.71-90; T.J. Biersteker, *Distortion or Development?* (Cambridge: MIT Press, 1981), pp.69-75; L.K. Mytelka, *Regional Development in a Global Economy* (New Haven: Yale University Press, 1979), pp.138-89.

54 See C.V. Vaitsos, *Intercountry Income Distribution and Transnational Enterprises* (Oxford: Clarendon Press, 1974).

55 Ibid., pp.45, 54, 90, 119-42.

56 See R. Kaplinsky, "Report on Foreign Exchange Leakages with Particular Reference to Transfer Pricing," Kenya Ministry of Commerce and Industry, Nairobi, 1978.

57 See C. Cooper et al., "Choice of Techniques for Can Making in Kenya, Tanzania and Thailand," in *Technology and Employment in Industry*, ed. A.S. Bhalla (Paris: OECD Development Centre, 1975), pp.85-121.

58 See Rhys Jenkins, "Comparing Foreign Subsidiaries and Local Firms in LDC's: Theoretical Issues and Empirical Evidence," *Journal of Development Studies*, vol.26, no.2 (1990), pp.205-28.

59 See Norman Girvan and Gillian Marcelle, "Overcoming Technological Dependency: The Case of Electric Arc (Jamaica) Ltd., A Small Firm in a Small Developing Country," *World Development*, vol.18, no.1 (1990), pp.91-107.

60 See S. Langdon, "Indigenous Technological Capability in Africa: The Case of Textiles and Wood Products in Kenya," in *Technological Capability in the Third World*, ed. Fransman and King, pp.355-74.

CHAPTER 6

Debt, Downturns, and Crisis

I n Mozambique, in the aftermath of a bloody civil war, analysts write that
the nation is now "the most heavily indebted country in the world" and
has been forced by its overall economic situation to accept dependent
"vassal status," with World Bank economists setting its policies.[1]

In Brazil the industrial growth of the 1970s collapsed in a 1983 decision
to default on the country's debt repayments, leading to a number of debt
and debt-service reschedulings that, in 1988 for instance, rolled over U.S.
$30 billion into new 30-year bonds, all in the context of IMF-led policy
changes responding to widespread Southern country debt burdens.[2]

And in the Central Asian republic of Kazakhstan, independent since the
break-up of the former Soviet Union in 1991, the 17 million citizens (who
have experienced a 50 per cent fall over three years in their per capita
average incomes) have been advised by the World Bank officials assisting
them that one key solution to their macroeconomic problems is to reduce
the numbers of schools and hospitals in the country.[3]

As in these three examples, in any given Southern society macroeconomic forces — an overall mix of exchange rate, fiscal, and monetary policies across the national level — work to shape the budgetary, inflation, and
international trade and finance conditions that influence people's lives. In
recent years in most Southern countries, two broad forces stand out as
having an impact on macroeconomic realities. The first is the many international economic shocks that hit the global economy in the 1973-98
period, reflected in massive energy price shifts and related capital flows that
resulted in Southern country debts. The second is the extensive and activist
role established in Southern countries by the international financial institutions (the World Bank and the International Monetary Fund) in direct
response to the serious macroeconomic problems created by these global
shocks. The interaction of these two forces had significant consequences,
spurring downturns for many sectors and social costs for many groups
within Southern countries.

1: Debts and Downturns

In 1970 Saudi Arabian light crude oil was selling at U.S. $1.30 per barrel. Over October-December 1973, thanks to united political action from OPEC (the Organization of Petroleum Exporting Countries), the price per barrel was raised to $11.65. An extra $65 billion flowed to the OPEC countries the next year alone, some $10 billion of it from non-oil-producing Southern countries.[4] Then in 1979 came a second oil shock as OPEC reacted to oil supply reductions caused by the Ayatollah's revolution in Iran. That year oil prices were raised to five times the increased 1973 levels.

These price increases had powerful effects on non-oil-producing Southern countries. Their import bill for oil over the 1973-83 decade was $250 billion higher than it would have been if prices had remained stable. While the recycling of mainly Arab petro-profits through the unregulated Eurocurrency market vastly increased the capital available for borrowing to offset this huge change — raising Eurocurrency loans over five times higher to some $1,600 billion between 1973 and 1982 — some of these higher loans were channelled to non-oil-producing Southern countries (mainly in the years after the first oil price shock), but this support began to falter after the second oil price hike. In 1980, for instance, short-term bank lending to Southern countries was $26 billion and private export credits were $11.1 billion — but in 1982, short-term lending fell to $15 billion and private export credits to $7.1 billion.[5] During the 1972-82 period, after the first OPEC-based oil price escalation, Southern countries were able to borrow on average U.S. $21 billion per year to counter the severe oil price pressures of the shifting international terms of trade produced by the OPEC cartel. But an outflow of finances of U.S. $21.5 billion per year took place from Southern countries over 1983-90, after the second large increase in oil prices, leading to Southern foreign debts by 1990 of 13 times the 1970 levels, or some U.S. $1,350 billion — a dramatic, damaging shift.[6]

During the 1973-80 period, most non-oil-producing Southern countries had benefited from increased world prices for their export products, which helped offset the increased foreign exchange costs of their oil imports and seemed to make international borrowing viable. (In 1977, for instance, international terms of trade for these Southern countries improved by 6.3 per cent, despite the higher oil prices they were paying.) But the second oil price shock hit OECD economies with a considerable negative impact, during a time when OECD monetary authorities were already trying to counter inflationary pressures with higher interest rates — thus pushing the OECD economies as a group into recession, with even larger interest rate increases, high levels of unemployment and consequent reductions in demand for Southern country products. International terms of trade for

Graph 6.1 Net Long-term Financial Transfers to Developing Countries, 1972-90

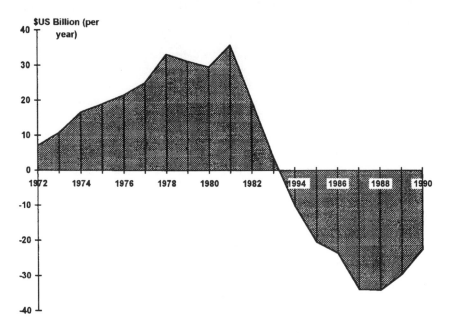

Source: based on UNDP, *Human Development Report, 1992*, New York, 1992, p. 50.

the non-oil Southern countries declined, as their non-oil-producing imports went up by over 20 per cent in price in 1980.[7]

Over the next decade the crisis created by these factors in most Southern countries played itself out in three major ways.

First, the high level of debt built up by many countries proved to be impossible to service in the circumstances of high interest rates, even higher oil prices, and less buoyant international trade demand imposed by OECD economic stagnation. This led to dramatic Southern country decisions to suspend repayment of even the most sacred of debt obligations, loans received from the IMF (recognizing that without such repayments, the country would be effectively frozen out of virtually any form of international borrowing). Until the 1980s, the IMF had never experienced a formal default — a situation that, as Killick notes, "changed dramatically during the 1980s."[8] By 1990, 11 countries were in arrears, owing 13.9 per cent of total outstanding IMF credits.

This grim reality pushed leading IMF members such as the United States to take the Southern country debt problem much more seriously and to propose two increasingly activist plans (the 1985 Baker proposals, and the 1989 Brady plan) to assist debt reduction and rescheduling. As a result, regular negotiations between individual Southern country governments and the creditor countries, under the semi-official auspices of the "Paris Club," have become a fundamental feature of the new global political economy.[9] Even more complex have been the various debt rescheduling and reduction agreements negotiated by the private banking institutions, with assistance from the IMF. Between the start of 1986 and the middle of 1995, a total of 34 countries negotiated such arrangements, with the largest amounts involving over $46 billion for Mexico, over $30 billion for Brazil, over $19 billion for Argentina, over $5 billion for Nigeria, and over $5 billion for the Philippines. The Philippines bought back half this debt at just over 50 cents on the dollar, and Nigeria bought much of its debt back at 40 cents on the dollar, but Brazil and Argentina have concentrated more on important interest rate reductions and rescheduling repayments for 30 years in the future.[10]

The second feature of the new landscape involved the decisive withdrawal of private bank lending from many poorer Southern countries, particularly in Africa. New medium-term and long-term loan commitments to Southern countries remained high in 1993-95 ($53 billion, for instance, in 1994,) but 62 per cent of these loans were to go to Asian countries and 8 per cent to Latin America, with only 1.5 per cent to Sub-Saharan Africa. Asian and Latin American countries were even more overwhelmingly dominant in the pattern of new international bond issues by Southern countries over the 1993-95 period.[11] Helleiner underlines the same point in reviewing private long-term loan transfers to Sub-Saharan Africa over the 1980s: From positive flows in the 1980-83 period, these statistics consistently began to measure *outflows* (or net repayments) from the region each year from 1984 to 1990, with levels as high as $2.6 billion in 1985 alone.[12] As a result, dealing with the accumulated debt burden has been a powerful continuing preoccupation for many poorer Southern countries, despite the reductions and reschedulings that have helped a minority of countries. As the World Bank put it in its 1994 report on Africa, "The external debt burden continues to be large for many countries, and a sustainable solution to the debt problem is still elusive." That same report noted that even with the "Trinidad terms" of debt reduction for the poorest countries (a 67 per cent reduction level), 15 of the 21 severely indebted African countries (including Kenya, Zaire, Zambia, Uganda, Tanzania, and Mozambique) would have debt-service burdens that were unsustainable given their annual level of exports.[13] Taking total external debt, and annual debt service, as a percentage of exports, such Latin American and Caribbean countries as Haiti, Peru, Bolivia, and Argentina still remain vulnerable, too, although 1995 debt renegotiations improved the situation somewhat for Peru and considerably for Nicaragua.[14]

The third reality for many Southern countries has been that the persistent slowdown in OECD economies since the 1980-81 response to the second oil price shock (a response that stressed higher interest rates and budget cutbacks to reduce inflation and slow down demand growth for OPEC oil) has in turn hurt their economic prospects. The prices and quantities demanded of many Southern raw material exports to the North have been cut back, contributing to the negative international terms of trade for Southern producers. In addition, the continuing budget cutbacks in most OECD countries have hit hard at international assistance flows to poorer Southern countries.

To some degree, increased direct foreign investment flows have counteracted these external financial blows. There has clearly been a recovery in international lending to Southern countries, too, as the 1993-95 data indicate. But the harsh reality is that these investments were responding overwhelmingly to the fast-growing NICs and their few rising partners, while the majority of poorer Southern countries were experiencing the brunt of economic downturn. The new loans went mainly to Korea, Thailand, China, Hong Kong, Malaysia, and Indonesia — and the international bond issues went mainly to the same countries, plus Argentina and Brazil. In Sub-Saharan Africa, only South Africa has been a notable recipient of large-scale capital flows.[15]

This state of affairs has led to considerable pressure on the IMF and the World Bank to fill the gap in responding to the triple combination of massive oil price increases, consequent heavy Southern debt loads, and economic slowdowns in OECD countries. Many Southern countries have faced difficult adjustment challenges in their economies, and the two international financial institutions (the IFIs) have been seen as key agencies to participate in responding to these problems.

The IMF was originally charged with responding to the short-term liquidity problems of its members in an international currency system in which fixed exchange rates were the norm. But the world movement to flexible exchange rates, no longer tied to a particular value for gold, reduced the importance of this role, at the same time as Southern countries were having to cope with the pressures forcing adjustment in their internal financial situations. The IMF accordingly began the establishment of what has become a series of longer-term financing facilities — beginning with an extended fund facility usually lasting three to four years (EFF) and culminating in the structural adjustment facility (SAF) and the enhanced structural adjustment facility (ESAF). These initiatives took the IMF fully into the structural adjustment area and saw it arranging detailed conditional agreements with developing countries in policy areas in which the World Bank had previously been the main actor. Between 1980 and 1986 IMF lending to Southern countries increased from U.S. $9.5 billion to $42.4

billion.[16] Meanwhile the World Bank had expanded beyond its original focus on project-by-project financing, also in response to the balance of payments and debt-servicing problems of developing countries in the post-OPEC oil shock era. It began a series of policy-based structural adjustment program loans (SAPs) and then sectoral adjustment program loans (SEPALs) — again provided on a conditional basis.

Both of the IFIs became active in the acute macroeconomic crisis in many Southern countries. As of March 1994, for example, the IMF had 49 agreements in place, 39 of these with Southern nations (20 of them involving the new ESAFs — mostly in Sub-Saharan Africa).[17] During the 1988-91 period, some 35 Sub-Saharan African countries had been involved in IMF agreements.[18] At roughly the same period, the World Bank had adjustment agreements in place with 29 Sub-Saharan African countries.[19] As a result, considerable overlap existed, despite IFI efforts at co-ordination. All of this activity increased the influence of the IFIs in many Southern countries. But it also made for heavy negotiation and discussion burdens in the South. As Tony Killick, of the UK Overseas Development Institute, notes, over 1980-92 African countries conducted some 8,000 separate negotiations with creditors, tending to "swamp" African policy advisors.[20]

This, then, was the context within which Southern governments faced macroeconomic crisis. The external environment was in turmoil, traditional aid relationships were being cut back, and outside agencies were exerting influential new pressures within domestic political economies. The challenge of major adjustment could not be ignored, or the negative effects of external change would simply become worse. Yet the choices to be made were complex, often politically difficult, and complicated by the new pressures of outside agencies.

2: The Macroeconomics of Crisis

For many Southern countries the external economic shocks of the 1973-82 period hit their societies during a time when limitations in agricultural strategy and industrial policy were already causing internal social division and economic stress. Where land reform and strong rural support policies combined with export-oriented industrial efforts and encouragement for small-scale business, as in Korea, Taiwan, and Thailand, countries found they could adjust to the changed global economy. Thus despite being hard hit by the effects of external price changes on their balance of payments over 1979-82, both Korea and Thailand were back in a position of producing profitable economic expansion by 1981-83.[21] But for most Southern countries the existing policy context was different. ISI manufacturing investments had left them with enterprises highly protected and therefore very uncompetitive in the world economy; and the strong biases in pricing and marketing policies against peasant agriculture, combined with ISI-based urban-rural terms of trade that hurt rural production, meant that dynamic expanding agricultural sectors, able to respond to changed circumstances quickly, were rare. Larger-scale, favoured rural households had enjoyed most government benefits (often in quite localized parts of the country), and ISI "insider" enterprises had received privileges of protection, tax breaks, and low interest rates — generating few effects that would spread out to the broader economy.

But now external shocks began to shake what were previously often closely controlled, elite-directed political economy systems. The results involved certain common features, but also variations based on separate domestic situations, as a number of case examples show.

a) Ghana: The dominant common feature in most Southern countries was a large deterioration in international terms of trade, as import prices rose and export prices fell in real terms (by a combined 41 per cent in Ghana over the 1971-82 period). It became much more difficult as a result to import key inputs for the ISI manufacturing sector, leading governments to try to control foreign exchange allocations tightly to direct to favoured firms in that sector — yet also making the profitability of the sector more vulnerable, because less output was being produced in capital-intensive facilities (in Ghana, only 20-25 per cent of manufacturing capacity was being used, as a result, by 1983). Price controls were imposed to try to keep imported energy items from skyrocketing. And government deficits grew (to 11 per cent of Gross Domestic Product in Ghana in 1980) to finance subsidies to permit such controls. These deficits, plus loans to money-losing enterprises, were financed by large annual increases in the money supply (of over 30 per cent in Ghana.) This, in turn, brought inflation rate increases (these rose in Ghana from 9 per cent per year in 1970, to 30 per cent in 1975, to 50 per cent in 1980.)[22]

These patterns were usual in non-oil-producing Southern countries, nor was it uncommon to see GDP stagnate as a result, as it did in Ghana over the 1970-81 period. Yet in Ghana three distinct features of the crisis especially hit the country.

First, Ghana was one of a number of Southern countries, especially in Sub-Saharan Africa, that attempted to maintain a fixed exchange rate (tied to the U.S. dollar) rather than permitting devaluation of the exchange rate to take on some of the burden of adjustment to external shocks. (A lower value for the Ghanaian cedi would have helped reduce demand for imported products, increased domestic demand for products made in Ghana, and given more competitive lower prices — when calculated in foreign currencies — to exports from Ghana sold abroad.) This high-fixed-exchange-rate policy increased expansion of illegal foreign exchange dealings, illegal markets for many imported items that could not be brought in legally, severe cuts in the real prices received for agricultural exports through official channels, and hence huge declines in the use of those official channels, consequent cutbacks in state expenditure, and over 30,000 job losses in the formal sector between 1979 and 1983.

The second distinct feature of the situation in Ghana flowed directly from the pervasiveness of these illegal market transactions within a collapsing official economy. As Loxley describes the governmental context of the late 1970s – early 1980s, "State enterprises, licensing and controls had been used to line the pockets of senior state officials and, especially, larger traders, with black marketeering, overinvoicing and underinvoicing, tax evasion and corruption being widespread."[23] Herbst makes the same point, showing how overvaluation of the exchange rate by more than 2,200 per cent set up a system of "administrative allocation of foreign exchange" that government insiders could use to reward clients and illegal market organizers. "Many of these racketeers," Herbst concludes, "were either in government or had become the primary supporters of successive governments."[24]

The third key element in the Ghana situation has to do with how the economic and political crisis, as it squeezed people, badly damaged the social welfare of most of the population. This was not just a matter of the drastic downturns in real salaries and wages, or of an overall pattern that cut GDP per capita by 36 per cent between 1970 and 1983. Women and children were especially hard hit. There was reduced enrolment, especially of girls, in schools. UNICEF estimated that infant mortality increased in Ghana from 80 per thousand in 1975 to 110-120 by 1983-84. Death rates doubled for children aged one to four, and diseases such as yellow fever (which had been eradicated in Ghana) reappeared in northern regions. There was also an increasing incidence of child malnourishment, and deteriorations in the availability of health personnel and supplies.[25]

The result was what has been called a "calamity." Other observers have stressed that "the economy had been largely devastated. Signs of collapse were everywhere."[26] Ghana had been hit particularly hard by the external shocks internationally, because of its heavy dependence on a single export commodity, cocoa, that had already been suffering decline. Its major investments in larger ISI manufacturing enterprises had made adjustment harder. Marketing structures set in place to tax cash-crop agriculture exports heavily had undercut the responsiveness of peasant producers, and reliance on defending its fixed exchange rate had delayed adjustment efforts far too long, given Ghana's difficulties right from the start of the oil shock pressure. All of this, combined with the 1983 drought and Nigeria's repatriation of a million Ghanaians, made the crisis in Ghana especially severe, hurting all sectors of the economy and worsening social conditions in a widespread way.

The ultimate political outcome was the late-1981 overthrow of the elected government by a movement of younger military leaders, more alienated university faculty, students, and some trade union leaders. As their leader, they brought back into power Flight Lieutenant Jerry Rawlings (who had led a brief military takeover in 1979 that had tackled symptoms of corruption, then resigned after three months to allow a democratically chosen government to take power). After exploring various options in this situation of economic crisis and collapse, the new government decided that the fixed exchange rate had to be tackled and that working with the IMF and World Bank was crucial to escape the impasse confronting the country.

b) Costa Rica: If Ghana represents the problems of trying to insulate an economy from external shocks by defending a fixed exchange rate, Costa Rica presents the consequences of considerable debt reliance in responding to the first oil price shock.

Costa Rica made some use of changes in exchange rate policy throughout the oil shocks period. A relatively minor devaluation took place after the first oil price jump, reducing the value of the Costa Rican colon from about 15 cents U.S. to just under 12 cents. But that level was then maintained from 1974 to 1981.[27] The early decrease did assist in the adjustment process, but two other factors permitted much easier maintenance of the new fixed rate than in Ghana. First, coffee was the major export commodity from Costa Rica, and it increased significantly in price into the 1977 period. Second, Costa Rica's continued international borrowing led to large foreign debt accumulations.

Yet when the second oil price shock hit, ironically, this new external shock turned out to be more powerful in spurring an economic crisis, precisely because higher coffee prices and large foreign borrowings had helped insulate Costa Rica's response to the earlier changes in the global economy.

Thus the second oil shock hit at the same time as the coffee boom was disappearing, leading to a fall in international terms of trade of one-third over the 1977-81 period.[28] As of 1979-81, after borrowing on variable interest rates from the commercial banks (with those interest rates now increasing quickly), Costa Rica found itself with total external debt and interest service due (as a percentage of exports) that were 36 per cent above Central American and Caribbean averages for total debt and 58 per cent higher for interest due.[29] Continuing expansionist fiscal policies, set off in the coffee boom period, and the maintenance of the fixed exchange rate ultimately collapsed into a massive devaluation of the colon from the 12 cent U.S. level to a 3 cent U.S. level in 1981 and to inflation levels at almost triple digits — as well as a jump in external interest payments due, from 19.7 per cent of exports to 34.6 per cent of exports by 1982-83.

In general the country experienced a 14 per cent decline in real GDP over the 1980-82 period, a 23 per cent decline in average income per person, and a 25 per cent cut in real wages.[30]

As in Ghana, the depth of the crisis drew the IFIs actively into Costa Rica, with an IMF stand-by agreement over 1980-82 for SDR60.5 million, and negotiation of a three-year EFF in 1981 for SDR277 million. But unlike Ghana, it did not take the crisis to bring IFI entry — previous arrangements had already been negotiated. Also unlike Ghana, Costa Rica had less evidence of massive social welfare decline given the crisis. As a share of GDP, Costa Rica's government actually raised health spending from around 1 per cent over the 1974-78 period to some 7 per cent in 1981 and 1982. But housing and social security spending fell from the 5-7 per cent level over 1974-78 to the 3-4 per cent level, while there was little change in other socioeconomic spending (around 4 per cent).[31]

The oil price shocks and variations in international capital markets did bring economic crisis to Costa Rica, but the immediate 1980-82 impact — though very damaging — was not nearly the "calamity" it was in Ghana. Somewhat greater use of devaluation (in responding to the first oil price shock), much better performance by the main export commodity (coffee), and the use of international commercial borrowing helped to mitigate the external turmoil; and faster devaluation in 1981, plus continuing IFI involvement, meant that the adjustment process in Costa Rica started working itself through the economy more quickly than in Ghana. As a result in the shorter run the economic crisis did not bring as much negative social devastation as it did in Ghana. But the longer-term consequence of this pattern was that at the beginning of the 1980s Costa Rica had extremely high foreign debt loads that would curtail its social and economic development for the next decade.

c) **Kenya:** The case of Kenya mirrors some aspects of the experiences of Costa Rica (since both are major coffee producers) and of Ghana (both share the African process of marginalization in the changing world economy). But the key aspect of the Kenyan example may best be caught by a World Bank analysis that concludes: "Few country lending experiences have given the Bank so much cause for frustration."[32] Again and again, Kenya reached agreements with the IFIs, then failed to follow through on commitments made.

As elsewhere, the first oil price shock had a major impact in Kenya, bringing a 12.4 per cent decline in terms of trade in 1974 alone (a loss in foreign exchange of about U.S. $200 million), followed by a further 8 per cent decline the next year. This downturn at once fed back into the domestic economy, generating an increase in inflation and a decline in internal GDP. Unlike Ghana, however, Kenya made some use of exchange rate devaluation to respond, reducing the value of the shilling from 14 cents U.S. to 12 cents after 1974. But the 1975 coffee frost in Brazil then raised coffee prices from 65 cents U.S. per pound to 142 in 1976 and 229 in 1977 — and in turn pushed up tea prices from 65 cents U.S. per pound to 121 in 1976. As a major exporter of both products, Kenya gained more than U.S. $700 million in extra export revenues over the two years, and a failure to insulate the economy at all from this boom led to a 50 per cent increase in the money supply in 1977, to a 21 per cent increase in the lower-income consumer price index, and to a massive investment boom in the coffee- and tea-growing areas that pushed up import volume demands by 25 per cent in real terms between 1977 and 1978. With prices for tea and coffee beginning to moderate downward by then, and with world prices for imports rising quickly, Kenya rapidly found itself back in a balance of payments squeeze.

With the death of long-time president Jomo Kenyatta in mid-1978, and some resulting political uncertainty, the government was not prepared to devalue the exchange rate again (despite the activity of illegal currency markets, which were trading Kenyan shillings at prices much lower in foreign currency terms than the official rate) or to impose higher taxes on coffee and tea income or use other methods to reduce demand somewhat to stabilize the investment boom. As a result, by the end of 1978, despite the huge earnings of the coffee and tea boom period, Kenya was down to holding only 2.6 months of foreign exchange for trade purposes. This in turn pushed the government into more and more international commercial borrowing, raising its indebtedness.[33] All this made the damage from the second oil price shock much worse than was the case in Costa Rica. The Kenyan economy was already in trouble at the end of 1978, and then it was hit by another very large oil price increase.

By 1980 external terms of trade had again dropped dramatically, by 28 per cent. By 1981 the national budget deficit had increased to some 10 per cent of GDP. The debt service ratio had jumped from 4 per cent in 1977 to 13.2 per cent of exports in 1980.[34] These factors all pointed to problems for the future, and at the time the sudden impact of the oil purchase outflows severely contracted the economy. Real wages in manufacturing in Nairobi, for instance, declined by 8 per cent between 1980 and 1981, with the official minimum wage falling by 9.5 per cent.[35] Between 1982 and 1984 real private wages per capita declined by 16 per cent more.[36] By and large, throughout this period, the official exchange rate appreciated slightly in value, despite the unofficial rate in illegal markets being much lower. The result for ISI manufacturing was a dramatic decrease in domestic demand, severe difficulties in obtaining key imports for production, and reduced capacity utilization. GDP per capita also declined significantly across the economy. Meanwhile, social welfare expenditure as a percentage of GDP stayed at about the same level, rather than falling as it had in Ghana.[37]

The severe downturn in the economy, combined with the political uncertainties after Kenyatta's death and the continued inflation and external shocks, finally brought on major political unrest in 1982. A chaotic effort at a military coup took place, severely undercutting the sense of long-term security of the Asian community in Kenya, and revealing widely held resentments about inequalities and African poverty in the country. By that time the IFIs were working energetically on adjustment strategies with Kenyan officials, but the failed coup recast the political dynamics of the country in the direction of a more authoritarian approach by President Daniel arap Moi, movement on his part towards the building of a new political coalition of different social forces than the constituencies that had kept Kenyatta in power, and patterns of state policy implementation that complicated the IFI relationship.

The Kenyan crisis demonstrated again the impact of the oil price shocks and how countercommodity booms could (as in Costa Rica) postpone but not ultimately escape these. The case of Kenya also showed how this interplay could produce long-term debt load problems, and it underlined the weaknesses of the ISI industrial strategy. But, above all, Kenya's experience suggested how explosive the politics of international economic turmoil could be, both in shaping the political struggles of countries facing adjustment and in influencing the frustrations that could emerge in IFI-state relationships as external changes worked themselves out.

3: Conditionality and Adjustment

Many Southern countries emerged from the 1973-82 period bearing the grim effects of structural adjustment crises. External economic changes had hit the global economy and transformed it in ways that were not going to disappear — much higher energy prices, huge new burdens of international financing, slower-growth OECD economies, and powerful low-cost NIC manufacturing competitors were all persistent new realities. To take account of these new realities, Southern countries would have to restructure their internal economies and societies. This imposed need, fundamentally, placed structural adjustment priorities at the heart of Southern country development policy.

Countries could refuse to respond to these challenges — as Ghana did, in most important respects, over the 1973-82 period. But the result was stark and devastating in Ghana's case. The pervasive economic crisis simply played itself out in other ways, shaping a "calamity" for Ghana and bringing social devastation that was brutal, widespread, and especially harsh for women, children, and the poor. Huge increases in key import prices for essentials took place, and export revenues plunged because peasant producers would not sell at official exchange rates that could buy them nothing. Illegal markets replaced almost all trading and exchange mechanisms in the country, corruption flourished, and domestic fiscal and monetary policy became meaningless. Most manufacturing shut down, and employment collapsed and domestic infrastructure deteriorated. Eventually state structures themselves were taken over, and new political forces tried to set things right.

Costa Rica did not try to avoid adjustment, but responded to the external shock with a currency devaluation — and then with strategies that tried to minimize the restructuring required (thanks to the 1976-77 coffee boom and to much increased international borrowing). But this minimalist approach to adjustment ironically made the second oil price shock even harder hitting, because it came as coffee prices were again declining and it dramatically accelerated the burden imposed by high international borrowing (as a result of large interest rate increases).

Kenya's response to the first oil price shock was probably the strongest of the three cases, combining devaluation with moves supported by the IMF and World Bank to encourage small-scale agriculture and provide export-manufacturing subsidies. But these steps were quickly overshadowed by the coffee and tea boom and the inflation and investment boom set off by that success. By the time of the second oil price shock, Kenya's economy was much more vulnerable to an adverse external impact, especially because of failures to deal with its ISI manufacturing weaknesses. And in this context Kenya (like Costa Rica, but somewhat later) began to increase foreign commercial borrowing at a rapid pace.

Both Costa Rica and Kenya, then, did not try to avoid responding to the global restructuring challenge, but both failed to adjust their domestic economic structures nearly enough to be able to avoid the impact of macroeconomic crisis. In Kenya's case, the re-emergence of crisis in a much more unsettled political context led to near-political breakdown and the eventual movement towards a more authoritarian state. In Costa Rica democratic traditions were maintained, and the restructuring strategy adopted reflected that continuity to some extent.

Helleiner has identified three of the crucial and (in his view) positive elements of IFI emphases in conditional agreements with poorer Southern governments in this crisis context. "The most grotesque distortions," he suggests, are the highly overvalued exchange rates in most countries, and the very large fiscal budget deficits that are often related to these rates. The third point is the high productivity of increased external resource availability in the short and medium terms, related mainly to the contribution of such resources to restoring higher levels of capacity utilization.[38] These concerns all loomed high in the IFI involvement with the three case countries.

a) Ghana: In Ghana the combination of the IMF and the World Bank provided additional foreign exchange inflows of about U.S.$1 billion between 1983 and 1986. This improved international liquidity permitted increases in import volumes of 27 per cent between 1983 and 1984, and recovery of export volumes by almost as much between 1984 and 1985. Manufacturing value-added rose by 22 per cent as well in 1985, in another positive response to increased foreign exchange availability.[39] At the same time, the massive process of exchange-rate rationalization was moving forward quickly, using first the device of multiple exchange rates to sidestep the political explosiveness of straight devaluation, but achieving a 1090 per cent devaluation within five months in 1983.[40] These changes had powerful effects on peasant incomes and general income levels. The increase in real producer prices to cocoa farmers between 1983 and 1986 was 135 per cent, and cocoa exports rose almost 40 per cent. At the same time, real per capita GDP rose by 6.8 per cent in 1984, and by another 9.2 per cent over the two years 1985-86. The result was that the fiscal situation could be balanced, not as in many Southern country IFI cases by expenditure reduction, but by revenue and grant increases (from 5.5 per cent of GDP in 1983 to 14.4 per cent in 1986, while spending rose from 8 per cent of GDP to 13.8 per cent) — providing a small budget surplus.[41]

In the aftermath of tackling these basic adjustment issues, the IFIs then began to interact with Ghana regarding more complex questions, with somewhat more ambiguous progress. The points involved included:

i)   the degree of import protection in the economy, especially for the manufacturing sector (extensive tariff reduction was achieved);
ii) the extent of public-sector employment reduction that would provide the greatest possible efficiency, especially in agriculture marketing and other public-sector parastatals (public-sector numbers did fall dramatically);
iii) the degree to which privatization of government-owned bodies should be a priority (Ghana moved more slowly on this, but eventually quite decisively);
iv) the importance to give to financial-sector liberalization in Ghana (it was harder to see change happen quickly in this context);
v)   the best way to achieve greater expenditure strictness and reflection of major priorities in Ghana's budget (some new spending controls were initiated, but high off-budget spending still remained common as of 1997);
vi) the kinds of taxation reform to emphasize, such as value-added taxes

(the 1995 Ghana VAT experiment proved a political disaster and was postponed, then reintroduced in early 1998);

vii) how best to achieve reduced inflation and stronger monetary policy objectives in Ghana (an area of less policy success);

viii) the importance of poverty alleviation and greater regional equality as goals within Ghana (important achievements were registered on these issues); and

ix) how best to achieve increased investment levels and export gains to raise growth rates towards Southeast Asian standards (higher growth rates were reached, but still well below Asian NIC levels).

In general, both the IMF and the Bank tend to identify Ghana as a (qualified) positive case, even in the broader context of such an extensive agenda. The IMF provided the country with extensive financial support, in six agreements amounting to U.S. $1.301 billion between 1983 and 1988, including three stand-by arrangements, one three-year SAF, one three-year EFF, and one three-year ESAF agreement.[42] Killick's assessment of Ghana's position in the context of these agreements was that there had been a "clear overall improvement," although continuing high inflation rates and low domestic savings and investment rates left Ghana "aid-dependent" with a "mixed" record.[43] The World Bank provided Ghana with further structural assistance lending between 1983 and 1994 of more than U.S.$1 billion, and another $1 billion in project funds.[44] The Bank identified Ghana in its 1994 review as achieving the largest improvement in macroeconomic policies from 1981-86 to 1987-91 of all the 26 Sub-Saharan African adjusting countries it was dealing with, and as the only African country (among the same 26) with an adequate macroeconomic policy as of 1990-91. This finding was based on Ghana having virtually no difference between official and unofficial exchange rates, running a small budget surplus, and keeping expansion of narrow definitions of the money supply low.[45] Real per capita income growth rates were over 2 per cent annually for six of the nine years from 1985 to 1993 (inclusive) and real GDP grew at more than 3 per cent annually for all eleven years from 1985 to 1996 (see Graph 6.2).[46] Taking just the years 1987-91, for which the World Bank had sufficient comparable data, the average annual per capita income growth rate for Ghana was 1.3 per cent, compared to 0.1 per cent for all adjusting Sub-Saharan African countries.[47]

Nevertheless, there were problems associated with some aspects of Ghana's economic performance after the initial phases of structural adjustment change. One was the re-emergence of rising inflation rates, which reached as high as 70 per cent by early 1996 before declining. The reason may reflect macroeconomic policy mistakes, according to the Institute of Economic Affairs: "The inevitable response of the economy to the re-emer-

142   A POLITICAL ECONOMY OF SOUTHERN POVERTY

Graph 6.2: Annual Growth Rate of Real GDP in Ghana, 1985-97

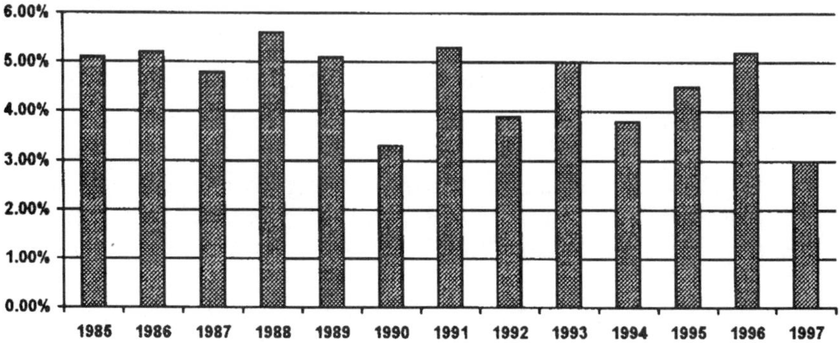

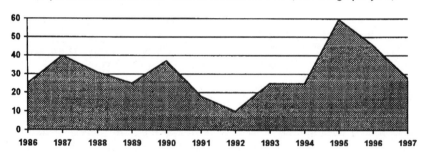

Source: Institute of Economic Affairs, *Economic Review & Outlook*, Dec. 1995; Loxley, *Ghana: The Long Road to Recovery, 1983-90*, p.26. Updated.

Graph 6.3: Annual Inflation Rates in Ghana, 1986-97 (Percentage per year)

Source: Ghana, *The Budget Statement*, 1996, p. 47; Loxley, *Ghana: The Long Road to Recovery*, 1983-90, p.84. Updated.

gence of macro-economic instability following government's failure to control public expenditures in the preceding two fiscal years."[48] (See Graph 6.3, which shows this higher rate of price increases after 1992.)

The Institute of Economic Affairs (IEA), based in Accra, sees the high rate of inflation as reflecting the expansion in the money supply (M2) by some 46 per cent in 1994, instead of the target of 5 per cent — itself a result of positive capital inflows associated with public-sector divestitures, and of use of Bank of Ghana credits to finance public-sector corporations rather than doing so through subventions in the national budget (thus avoiding another budget deficit). As of 1998, in a context of tight IMF-led monetary policy changes, there had been decline in these rates to below the 28 per cent annual level.

The imbalances in infrastructure and opportunities between the Accra-centred region and more distant regions also remain dramatic and work powerfully against an integrated, overall national economy in Ghana. Much of Ghana is considerably poorer and far less positively impacted by structural adjustment than the bustling expansionism from Accra to Tema. There have been reflections of these regional frustrations over limited economic opportunities in the open armed conflict between Dagombas and Konkombas that again erupted in 1995 in Northern Region (though in a more restricted way than in 1994).[49] Ghana has responded to some of the inequalities in the country with PAMSCAD (Program of Action to Mitigate the Social Costs of Adjustment) — an essential-medicine program, employment effort, and regional infrastructure plan with expenditure levels of some U.S.$70 million.[50] Ghana has also stressed decentralization of resources to district assemblies, especially in poorer areas.

The other gap in Ghana's adjustment performance has been in its agricultural development. Ghana Members of Parliament concluded this at a special workshop on budget priorities in 1994 at Sogakofe in Eastern Volta and worked to get the government to accept their view. The strongest message from these MPs, according to finance officials, was that there should be more emphasis on agricultural expenditure; and at least one-third of workshop participants interviewed stressed this point as an area in which they had succeeded in moving the 1995 budget, thanks to "the change in the assertiveness of Committee members," as one MP put it.[51] The World Bank stressed this same need for increased attention to agricultural development in its 1995 Country Assistance Review, noting that the poor are mostly rural and major equity concerns must be addressed in the north through agricultural improvement.[52]

Perhaps the most important point on which to conclude, however, in assessing the IFI role in Ghana, is to stress that a major outcome of the Ghana-IFI relationship has been the marked recovery of social spending and the reinvigoration of social infrastructure in the country. After the social devastation of the economic crisis in Ghana, the increase in state revenue after 1983 permitted all three elements of social welfare expenditure to rise as a share of GDP — from under 1 per cent in the case of both health and social security-housing to close to 2 per cent (of a much higher GDP by 1989.)[53] Capital spending on health and education also rose significantly, primary school enrolment rose by 10 per cent between 1985 and 1989, the malnutrition rate among children was cut in half, and 67 per cent of children under the age of one were immunized in 1989 rather than the 13 per cent of a few years earlier.[54]

This improvement of living standards across the population showed up significantly in the details from two intensive poverty surveys conducted across the country for 1988 and for 1992. As these conclusions have been summarized, "Between 1988 and 1992 the proportion of Ghana's population in poverty fell somewhat, from 37 to 31 percent. Almost all the improvement in incomes came from economic growth; income distribution remained fairly stable. The income gains benefited most regions, especially rural areas, and particularly women there — although poverty increased in Accra. Living standards among the poorest groups remain seriously low. Most of Ghana's poor are food crop and export crop farmers with incomes about one third of the national average."[55]

Local studies have confirmed that these broad national patterns seem to be continuing in the same direction. Examining seven villages in two districts in the relatively poor Volta Region, using the 1988 and 1992 World Bank approach, Brown and Kerr found that the incidence of poverty declined from 56.5 per cent to 51.3 per cent of households between 1993 and 1995; they also found that all of this decline was accounted for by female-headed households, who went from poverty-incidence rates of 63.9 per cent in 1993 to 49.8 per cent in 1995.[56]

b) Costa Rica: The World Bank has called the case of Ghana a "win-win" example, because economic stabilization and adjustment also permitted increased social spending and per capita income gains.[57] Costa Rica involved more difficult trade-offs.

Again, the basic pattern of a massive devaluation, combined with extensive IFI financial support, was repeated. The colon was permitted to fall in 1980-81 from some 12 cents U.S. to a value of 3 cents, then to gradually float lower over the period to 1991, to a level of about 1 cent U.S. At the same time the IMF arranged six agreements over 1980-89, for a total support of some U.S.$700 million (in the form of five stand-by arrangements, and one three-year EFF).[58] There was also a reduction during the 1980s in the Costa Rican budget deficit, with a surplus emerging on current operations, but a small overall deficit still resulting from "modest capital spending."[59] The massive devaluation, combined with IMF support, also seemed to significantly improve the balance of payments account of the country. The value of goods exported increased by 247 per cent over the 1980-95 period, while the value of goods imported increased by only 221 per cent, still leaving the trade balance on goods negative by U.S.$565 million in 1995 — but this was offset by a positive balance on services (mainly tourism) of U.S.$295 million and a positive balance on capital account of U.S.$465 in 1995.[60]

The impact on the capital account and on the related interest and profits account had come less from the IMF structural support and more from the extensive IMF-led debt renegotiation that Costa Rica engaged in during the restructuring period. Among the many reschedulings of debt undertaken, forced by the 34.6 per cent of exports needed to pay interest in

1982-83, was the dramatic U.S.$1.6 billion commercial debt buyback and rescheduling negotiated in 1989 (at a time when total Costa Rican debt was U.S.$4.5 billion). Close to $1 billion in debt and past-due interest was purchased at 16 cents on the dollar, with the rest converted into one of several options involving new, longer-term lower-interest bonds with 18-36-month interest guarantees.[61]

In addition to these broad efforts at stabilization and restructuring in Costa Rica, the IFIs have (as in Ghana) sought more particular goals. Reduced inflation has been one of these, and there was some success in the earlier stages in reducing rates from 90 per cent down to 16 per cent by 1989, in a context of tightened monetary policy. There have also been efforts to liberalize the operation of financial institutions, leading to wider private bank access to the Central Bank's discount facility. And there have been some privatization initiatives, raising the private sector's role in electricity generation and reducing state employment numbers.[62]

The stabilization and adjustment impact of the IFI role does appear to have been successful, as Killick concludes. Although the case does not appear to have been as much of a "win-win" situation as in Ghana. The country has overcome a balance of payment and domestic budget instability but its per capita GDP declined by 5.8 per cent between 1981 and 1990, more than the 3.4 per cent decline for Central America and the Caribbean as a whole. Average real wages in Costa Rica declined by 21.2 per cent between 1980 and 1991 and had not returned to 1980 levels even by 1995.[63] This was of greater significance in Costa Rica as a poverty indicator than it would have been in Ghana, because in Costa Rica landless farmworkers made up a majority of the active population in agriculture (unlike the pattern of peasant agriculture smallholders in Ghana).[64] Thus the Costa Rican government, against some IMF opposition, felt it was important to incorporate explicit antipoverty measures into the adjustment program, including some wage adjustments for low-paid workers, a food-parcels program for 40,000 needy households, and credit subsidies for small-scale farmers and ranchers.[65]

Graph 6.4 shows the recovery of economic expansion in Costa Rica, tracking real per capita GDP changes, while Graph 6.5 shows the average real wage level per year on an indexed basis (1990 = 100), providing an indication of social costs of adjustment and how they changed over time.

Unlike Ghana, as well, there would appear to have been reductions in the share of social welfare expenditure associated with the IFI relationship with Costa Rica. Health spending declined from some 7 per cent of GDP in 1981 and 1982 to levels around 5 per cent in 1987 and 1988. Housing expenditure was centred out by the IMF as an area to be cut and was reduced from 7 per cent of GDP in 1987 and 1988 to less than 5 per cent in 1989. Training and other economic support was reduced from around 5

Graph 6.4: GDP Per Capita Growth Rates, Costa Rica, 1981-97

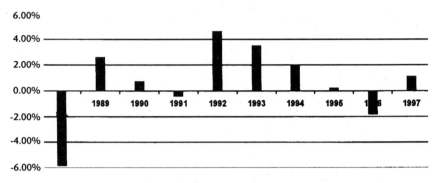

Source: CEPAL, *Notas Sobre la Economía y el Desarollo*, United Nations: Santiago de Chile, Dec., 1995, p.48 – 1981-90 data is cumulative, remaining data on yearly basis

Graph 6.5: Average Real Wage Index in Costa Rica, 1980-95 (1990 = 100)

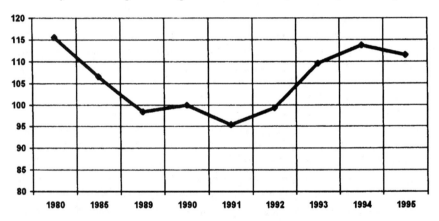

Source: CEPAL, *op. cit.*, p. 51.

per cent of GDP in the 1983-85 period to closer to 3 per cent in 1988 and 1989. This is a variable pattern, but it is far different from the clear increases in social spending in Ghana.[66]

It is possible, then, to conclude that Costa Rica's experience with the IFIs was successful, in that essential financial backing was provided, major devaluation established strong progress towards external stabilization, fundamental debt reduction and rescheduling were achieved, internal macro-economic conditions were significantly improved (including lower budget deficits and less inflation), and the external balance of payments situation was positively restructured. However, there were per capita income decreases from carrying through the adjustment process, rural and urban wage-earners were hurt, and some social spending was reduced. But by 1994 Costa Rica was emerging from the experience with very low urban unemployment rates (4.3 per cent compared to 6.3 per cent in Chile, 9.1 per cent in Uruguay, 8.9 per cent in Colombia, and 11.5 per cent in Argentina), and positive per capita income growth rates (of 1.9 per cent in 1994).[67] Pressures on the poor had been countered by direct governmental policy interventions.

Costa Rica, then, might not have been a "win-win" situation. It was, instead, a case of social costs being absorbed (albeit with an insulation strategy for the poor) in order to achieve macroeconomic restructuring that did reorient the society in a manner that made its economic future more viable in the changed international economy. All this was done in a democratic political context that did, for instance, permit excluded groups to challenge aspects of important environment-related land policy in 1988 and bring about changes that provided more equitable access for peasants to reforestation financing previously limited to larger landowners.[68] As Berry and Stewart conclude, "This must be counted as one of the more successful adjustment performances in the region, in the sense of re-establishing growth without a lengthy period of significantly higher poverty than before."[69]

c) Kenya: The Kenyan case was certainly not a "win-win" situation for most Kenyans, nor was it a success story to which the IFIs could clearly point. The IFI relationship with Kenya did include some areas of achievement, such as movement to a devalued exchange rate (falling from 13 cents U.S. in 1980 to some 4 cents by 1991) that adjusted export and import incentives to reduce illegal currency markets in the country. This more certainly did assist the competitiveness of exports.

However, not only did Kenya fail again and again to implement policies consistent with the IMF and World Bank loans it negotiated (and therefore often later failed to receive payments under those agreements), but insofar as the conditionality arrangements were pursued, they seemed not to improve the performance of the Kenyan economy.

So far as the unimplemented agreements are concerned, Hecox reviews the 1979-85 IMF and World Bank relationship with Kenya to demonstrate this. Between August 1979 and the end of 1984, the IMF negotiated four stand-by agreements with Kenya for U.S.$840 million — yet each of the first three were cancelled because the country quickly exceeded credit ceilings and other conditions. Meanwhile, the World Bank launched a first structural adjustment loan in early 1980 on which a first review recommended that the second tranche not be released; this was only released five months later, after a second review. A second structural adjustment loan

was approved in July 1982 — and this time it took four reviews (all negative) before the second tranche was released, in January 1984.[70] Finally, in
1992, the Bank cancelled the second tranche of yet another loan, because
the Kenyan government was so off-track in macroeconomic terms and had
reimposed grain movement controls despite agreement to the contrary.[71]

In terms of the impact of the IFI relationship, the IMF and the Bank had
aimed at greater domestic fiscal balance, at much reduced ISI manufacturing protection to encourage exports, at an end to favouring the large farm
sector to better boost peasant production, at related reforms in grain marketing, at price decontrols, at privatization and reductions in public-sector
employment, and at financial liberalization — with the main emphasis on
the first three of these points. This was a broad agenda, and it attacked the
sources of power, privilege, and wealth of important social forces in the
tightly structured political economy of Kenya. As Hecox notes, the conflicts
over implementation of IFI goals reflected "the power of entrenched groups
to frustrate, delay and even kill intended structural reforms in a developing
economy. This should not be surprising. But both donor staff and Kenyan
officials supportive of structural reform were apparently caught off
balance."[72]

In the end, the questionable impact of the IFI role in Kenya undoubtedly reflected the confrontational interplay among Kenyan officials, the
IFIs, and these political powerful and privileged social forces. For certainly
there seems no overall consistency to the IFI-Kenyan relationship, but
instead a shifting and often contradictory pattern without continuity. Even
the Bank's own analysis suggests this, pointing out how effects seemed to
change between the first 1981-84 phase and a second 1985-91 phase:
"Much of the stabilization gain of the early 1980s was lost in the late 1980s
— the budget deficit increased almost to the levels of the crisis period, and
high inflation reemerged."[73] Thus the fiscal deficit as a share of GDP
declined by 5.8 percentage points in phase one, and then increased again
by 4.5 percentage points in phase two. Inflation fell by 11.1 percentage
points in phase one, and rose again by 4.7 points in phase two; the current
account deficit as a share of GDP declined by 8.2 percentage points, then
rose again by 4 points; and debt service as a share of average exports rose
from 28 per cent in 1984 to 30 per cent in 1991. Gross investment levels
also fell from 23.8 per cent to 20 per cent of GDP from phase one to phase
two, and manufacturing exports as a share of manufacturing output
decreased from 13.3 per cent to 6.1 per cent. Import liberalization was
slow, as the ISI sector fought hard to maintain its level of protection. Agricultural marketing systems also continued to favour large-scale farmers
rather than small-scale peasants.[74]

The result of Kenya's much less successful relationship with the IFIs
shows up in various ways. First, Graph 6.6 shows the relatively poor growth

Graph 6.6: Annual Real GDP Growth Rates in Kenya, 1990-97

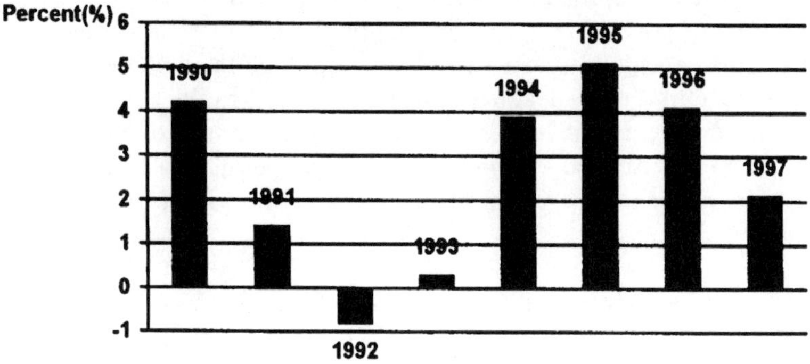

Source: World Bank, *IFC Discussion Paper No. 31*, February 1997. Updated.

performance of the Kenyan economy in the 1991-97 period, compared to Ghana, with only large increases in international coffee and tea prices leading to better performance in 1995-96. Inflation also rose to 46 per cent in 1993, before declining. Second, while Ghana has seen significant reductions in rural poverty in the context of its restructuring program, the situation in Kenya has been very different. According to the World Bank:

About 47 percent of the rural population is estimated to have been below the poverty line in both 1981-82 and 1992, meaning that there was no significant improvement in the incidence of poverty between those two years. About half of the population was, therefore, unable to consume a minimum requirement of food and essential non-food commodities. Further, the shortfall in consumption (the difference between the minimum required consumption and the actual consumption) increased and inequality worsened; the Gini coefficient increased from 0.4 to 0.49. This deepened rural poverty in Kenya fell especially heavily on women [as noted in chapter 4]. In urban areas, the incidence of poverty was 30 percent in 1992. The urban unemployment rate doubled to reach 22 percent in 1992.[75]

Social welfare expenditure in Kenya, especially for health and for education, has declined as a share of GDP, falling from 10 per cent in 1982 to 8 per cent in 1989.[76]

Third, Kenya has also found itself in major and open conflict with the broad international donor community, as well as the IFIs. The authoritarian and erratic actions of President arap Moi, amidst growing Kenyan public protests calling for democratization, ultimately led most donors to suspend international assistance in late 1991. The World Bank's cancellation of the second tranche of its agricultural sector loan added to this pressure, as did postponement of further support under several other loans. Pressure was strong for movement towards more transparent and democratic forms of government, and eventually the president changed his position and accepted multiparty democracy, although the first elections under the new system did not lead to fundamental shifts in the structure or policies of government. The lead-up to 1997 elections was also marked by anti-democratic practices, coercion by presidential authorities, and open violence by various pro-government and antigovernment groups in the country.

d) In Summary: The three cases of Ghana, Costa Rica, and Kenya demonstrate significant differences in how IFIs interacted with nation-states in responses to global economic pressures and consequent domestic adjustment crises. The three cases suggest the importance of political and social factors in helping shape how those IFI relationships work or fail.

Clearly no single pattern of IFI impact can be expected to prevail, even though obvious common IFI perceptions are at work in these three cases. Strong governments with coherent priorities can seek objectives of their own, such as the benefits for the poor and vulnerable that both Ghana and Costa Rica put into effect. Powerful privileged groups working through the state, as in Kenya, can seriously impede the impact of IFI policies that would hurt them (as with budget retrenchment and rapid trade liberalization).

Yet in some circumstances, where an economic crisis has become particularly devastating (as in Ghana, and in Tanzania, Mozambique, Uganda, and some other African cases), IFI involvement in conjunction with a politically effective regime can bring to bear external resources that have such a strong immediate payoff that a "win-win" situation may be possible, where widespread and broad-based consumption and income gains can accompany basic economic restructuring. In other circumstances, of high indebtedness and postponed adjustment (Costa Rica, and Uruguay, South Africa, Zimbabwe, and other Latin American and African cases), IFI co-operation with responsive democratic regimes may bring about fairly broad political acceptance of a period of shared austerity to achieve restructuring objectives. The most difficult cases are inevitably where less legitimate regimes, with economic situations less vulnerable than Ghana's, nevertheless must deal with the impact of adjustment crisis, but in a context dominated by tight-knit powerful and privileged social forces. This is the Kenyan case, and it may also be the case in Nigeria, the Ivory Coast, and Mexico, as well as some other Southern countries. The IFIs push for extensive restructuring strategies, but the diverse forces and conflicting interests that interact in domestic politics make the IFI impact often highly marginal and certainly always unpredictable. The result, if the Kenyan evidence holds for the other situations, may involve significant and continuing worsening of conditions for the poor.

That political economy reality may be why the overall evidence on the IFI role is so divided and unclear. Even the World Bank itself could not make strong claims for its record in Africa in its 1994 assessment, *Adjustment in Africa*. In that study, of the 26 countries involved in adjustment programs, only 6 emerged as significantly positive macroeconomic performers — and only 14 of the 26 improved their per capita growth rates even marginally under the auspices of such programs. Indeed, taking agriculture alone, only 13 of 28 such African countries improved their average annual growth rates in that sector between 1981-86 and 1987-91.[77] For many countries, it may be that the IFIs simply cannot do the job of bringing about economic restructuring, given present realities.

Certainly the evidence from these three cases suggests that significantly different outcomes can emerge from the IFI-country interface in the context of structural adjustment policies. Table 6.1 provides a summary of data from the three examples that points out these differences in outcome from the structural adjustment period. The data show that the two African cases were hurt more by the international economic crisis around the second oil price shock.

But the evidence also emerges in the Ghana case of a significant recovery in growth rates, a marked improvement in currency reserves and export performance, and substantial movement towards domestic macro gains in the national budget balance and domestic investment levels. All these results suggest a good degree of adjustment success, combined with higher social spending (especially on education and social welfare supports), with a much greater income share for poorer citizens than in either of the other cases, and with improved agricultural performance of importance to the majority of the poor.

In contrast, the Kenya data show much less success in achieving macroeconomic goals of domestic and international balance, with marked reductions in growth rates, investment levels, export performance, and international currency reserves. At the same time, social expenditure has been cut back significantly (in health and education), and poor agricultural performance helps explain why poverty has worsened during a time when the poor are already worse off in their share of national income than elsewhere in Africa. Costa Rica shows an intermediate case, where adjustment measures have had fair success in achieving increased exports, improved budget positions, and a recovery of growth, but where costs have occurred in the form of reduced social spending and even slightly lower domestic investment.

State structures with political legitimacy, then, may well be crucial to economic adjustment success. Both Costa Rica and Ghana have been able

Table 6.1: The Impact of Structural Adjustment in Three Countries, 1980-97

Category	Ghana	Costa Rica	Kenya
GDP/capita (1980 vs. 1995)	US$404 – 371	US$2415 – 3078	US$ 427 – 337
PPP/cap as % of U.S. (1987 vs. 95)	7.4% – 7.4%	19.8% – 21.7%	5.7% – 5.1%
GNP/cap. growth rate yrly (85-95)	1.4%	2.8%	0.1%
GDP yrly rate (%) 1980-90 vs. 90-97	3.0% – 4.3%	3.0% – 3.7%	4.2% – 2.0%
Yrly Agric growth 1980-90 vs. 90-97	1.0% – 2.7%	3.1% – 2.9%	3.3% – -0.8%
Yrly Export grow. 1980-90 vs. 90-97	2.5% – 7.1%	6.1% – 8.7%	4.3% – 2.8%
Income pct. (89-92), lowest 40%	19.9%	13.1%	10.1%
Yrly inflation rate 1985-95 average	28.6%	18.4%	13.0%
Govt. deficit/sur. 1980 vs. 1995	-2.9% – -0.9%	-3.5% – -0.4%	2.5% – -0.3%
Social spndg % of GDP (80 vs 95)	4.2% – 8.7%	19.6% – 17.9%	9.1% – 7.4%
Dom. inves. as % of GDP (80 vs 95)	6% – 19%	27% – 25%	29% – 19%
Intl. cur. reserves 1980 vs. 1995	US$million 330 – 804	197 – 1060	539 – 384

Source: Calculated from "Selected Indicators," World Development Report, 1997, 1998, pp.214-45.

to draw on such legitimacy, while Kenya has not. And that general point, in turn, may help explain the moves towards democratization in many Southern countries. That move has come in Ghana, Tanzania, Mozambique, and Uganda as these governments have developed their relationships with the IFIs. They have seen that greater popular involvement helps build a stronger capacity to achieve what is crucial to their society in the IFI relationship. In the same way, states that already have such a democratic basis, or are developing it (such as Costa Rica, Zimbabwe, or South Africa), can interact more effectively with the IFIs and ensure wider benefits from increased access to resources and less concentration of adjustment burdens on the poor. The semi-authoritarian and authoritarian regimes (such as Kenya, Congo-Zaire, or the Ivory Coast) seem to show an inconsistent lack of continuity and coherence, which weakens the potential benefits (and raises the potential costs) of the IFI relationship. Not surprisingly, the poor in these political settings seem to bear these higher costs most heavily.

4: Poverty and the Macroeconomic Crisis

So far this chapter has analysed responses to profound global economy changes, and how those changes brought macroeconomic pressures and IFI interventions to different Southern countries. The analysis has stressed the variety of experiences in the South. But what must not be underemphasized is the broad common impact of the world restructuring taking place. For most non-oil-producing Southern countries, this period of international turbulence and IFI involvement brought on major economic changes that had important implications for poverty conditions.

In countries such as Ghana, where the macroeconomic crisis played itself out over a longer time period without an IFI role and in a situation of especially poor commodity-export earnings, the data on social devastation show a massive and comprehensive downturn in most facets of human life. Similar large declines in social and economic indicators occurred in other countries, such as Tanzania, Uganda, and Mozambique. In these countries IFI external resources and even many of the policy conditions that came with those resources (such as large-scale devaluation, improved budgetary situations, reduced ISI protection, and improved incentives for peasant farmers) have been crucial elements in basic economic revivals that have brought growth, reduced poverty, and begun to re-establish essential social service infrastructure.

But that cannot entirely overshadow the fundamental continuity of poverty from the crisis and resulting downturn experienced by each country. To visit Maputo in Mozambique in 1996, for instance, was to witness much poorer housing, sanitation, and employment conditions than in the early 1980s, despite the economic revival that had come from an end to the long post-independence civil war and from IFI assistance.

The governments of these hard-hit crisis countries have had to argue toughly, too, for IFI approaches that have met what Southern leaders saw as priorities for their people. Ghana and the World Bank have had open disagreements, with Bank economists pushing for faster privatization and Ghana insisting on the need to rebuild certain national institutions felt to be essential for unity.[78] Even more complex disagreements have been fought out publicly in Mozambique, with one IFI (the International Monetary Fund) pushing strongly for much tougher government cutbacks to reduce inflation, and the World Bank and the United Nations Development Programme supporting the government in its battle for more stress on growth and debt cancellations.[79] So far those on the "expansionary" side

have won, with the 1996 Mozambique Consultative Group Meeting providing U.S.$881 million, some $10 million more than the government had
requested.[80]

In another set of countries, the original impact of the crisis was mitigated
to some degree, sometimes by especially buoyant commodity exports and
sometimes by large-scale borrowing. In these cases, such as Costa Rica
(and its Latin American and African counterparts), the impact of the crisis
and the IFI response led to the imposition of some socioeconomic costs,
but also brought longer-term economic adjustment benefits. But how these
costs and benefits were divided would determine whether working through
the crisis would mean more poverty problems or limit effects on the poor.
Costa Rica, the case study showed, stressed measures to insulate the poor
and thereby somewhat limited poverty effects. But this was not the governmental strategy in Brazil, where IFI structural adjustment was marked by
an expansion of poverty. As recent World Bank research there concluded,
"Macroeconomic instability lowered average income for the poor and hurt
the poorest the most. Although income declined over the 1980s for all
income groups, it fell most for those at the bottom — in contrast to the
1970s when those at the bottom and the top shared equally in the gains
from growth."[81] In Zimbabwe, there was much more government emphasis on direct antipoverty actions, including direct shelter and food-provision
programs in the southern cattle-raising parts of the country hard hit by
drought, so that the structural adjustment process there does not seem to
have expanded poverty.[82]

Then too the cases of failed IFI intervention are many, as the evidence
on structural adjustment policies makes clear. Sub-Saharan Africa has been
the crucial test for the World Bank, with the great majority of countries
signing structural adjustment arrangements during the 1980s and 1990s.
Yet, even in their own assessment in 1994, the Bank could identify only one
country (Ghana) out of 28 signing agreements that had "adequate" macroeconomic performance. As for the IMF, Killick's blunt judgement from
1995 was that "Sub-Saharan Africa has undoubtedly been subjected to
more conditionality per capita than any other region — and has achieved
the least adjustment."[83] This ineffectiveness in Africa suggests that both the
Bank and the Fund may have employed overkill with respect to the conditions that both sought to establish in what administratively were often weak
state systems in notably vulnerable economic conditions.

Thus a whole set of countries, tied to French currency levels by the CFA
franc that they used (convertible at a fixed exchange rate into French
francs), found it virtually impossible to carry through successful adjustment strategies because they could not easily employ the major currency
devaluation tool that crisis countries such as Ghana, Mozambique, and
Uganda used by moving to flexible exchange rates. Comparing the 12

African fixed exchange-rate countries against the 16 flexible-rate economies (among the 28 World Bank adjustment cases in Sub-Saharan Africa in the 1980s-90s period), GDP per capita changes fell from an annual average of +0.4 per cent (in 1981-86) to -1.7 per cent (in 1987-91) for the 12 during the policy adjustment period, while the change for the 16 flexible-rate countries was an increase from -1.5 per cent to +0.9 per cent. Real export growth and increases in gross domestic investment as a share of GDP also marked the flexible-rate cases, but not the fixed-exchange rate countries.[84]

This maintenance of a fixed-exchange rate system, at a time when the French franc was appreciating in value internationally (and therefore led to automatic increases in the value of the CFA franc, while massive devaluations were reshaping the competitiveness of many Southern countries), was a major factor in increasing poverty. Export-crop producers, in particular, found their markets squeezed, and output fell. Government expenditure cutbacks had to be very large to achieve some macroeconomic balance, and thousands of urban jobs were lost. In Senegal some 11,000 urban jobs were eliminated, and prices fell by 5 to 10 per cent for cotton and groundnuts, the main source of peasant cash income, leading the World Bank to conclude, "In sum, poverty may have become worse in Senegal in the 1980s."[85] The same conclusion was reached for the Ivory Coast — much higher urban unemployment and severe income declines among export-crop peasants meant "poverty has become more widespread in the country."[86] But the expansion of the poor in Cameroon was perhaps the most dramatic case in Africa, with average per capita income declining by 50 per cent over 1985-93 and a "rapid impoverishment with a very sharp decline in per capita consumption and a marked increase in the incidence of urban poverty. While fewer than 1 percent of households in Yaounde and Douala fell below the poverty line in 1983, more than 20 percent of households in Yaounde and 30 percent in Douala did so in 1993."[87]

The adjustment failures in the fixed-exchange rate regimes, despite extensive IFI help (over the 1981-91 period the Ivory Coast, for instance, received nine World Bank loans for a total of U.S.$1.430 billion, and seven IMF arrangements for SDR1 billion), represented one source of increased poverty. Only with a change in the fixed-rate regime after 1994 did improvements emerge. Other countries, such as Kenya (and some of its African and Latin American counterparts), represented another source of continuing poverty. The political economy realities of these countries have meant that no continuing, coherent IFI-based strategy could really be seen to take shape. Despite IFI involvement, no perceptive analyst could claim that the IFI role resulted in a decisive impact in Congo-Zaire, Nigeria, or Somalia—other powerful political and social forces were simply far too determinant in erratic domestic changes unrelated to any IFI conditionality. These were cases in which the triple impact of economic crisis, powerful and privileged power elites, and consequent inconsistent and conflictual IFI intervention made the expansion of poverty particularly likely. The absence of democratic political mechanisms to be able to challenge these regimes and change policy direction suggested the likelihood of continued government on behalf of the favoured few.

The extremes of poverty that could develop in such situations, with particularly severe consequences for women, are demonstrated in Guatemala and Honduras, where state control by small wealthy minorities has established poverty conditions for the majority, based especially on severe land inequality in rural areas. As the World Bank sums up the situation for Honduras, "Most of the poor live in rural areas and are engaged in agricultural activities or in agriculture-related services. Inequality of land tenure is a major determinant of rural poverty. About 7 percent of the poor live in urban areas. Women, especially in rural areas, are a particularly vulnerable group among the poor." Bank research shows similar realities in Guatemala:

Approximately 75 percent of the population is estimated to live below the poverty line, which is defined as an income that is insufficient to purchase a basic basket of goods and services. Almost 58 percent of the population have incomes below the extreme poverty line, which is defined as the amount needed to purchase a basic basket of food.... More than 90 percent of the indigenous population live on an income that is lower than the poverty line. There is also a high degree of inequality in income, consumption, and, most acutely, land. According to the most recent agricultural census (1979), only 2.5 percent of Guatemala's farms control 65 percent of the agricultural land, while 88 percent of the farms control only 16 percent of the land. The Gini Index for land distribution was calculated to be 85.9. This unequal pattern dates back to the colonial era when the Spanish crown granted large extensions of land to colonizers. All of Guatemala's social indicators reflect this widespread poverty and severe inequality.[88]

These are the extreme cases of massive poverty that debts, downturns, and crisis could perpetuate and promote, as world economic turbulence played itself out through societies run by the few and dominated by the privileged.

5: Conclusion

The profound shocks and discontinuities in the world economy from 1973-82, combined with serious problems in agricultural and industrial policies, brought socioeconomic crisis to most Southern countries. One symptom of that crisis in many countries was the build-up of huge international banking debts. Another symptom was the rapid expansion of IFI intervention in most Southern countries. But the fundamental effect of the crisis, in itself, was above all to choke off economic growth in non-oil-producing Southern countries and to dramatically increase the domestic pressures on people that resulted in deepened poverty. From that conclusion there is simply no escape. In general global economic restructuring has brought macroeconomic crises to many Southern countries, exerting powerful pressure towards deepening and spreading Southern poverty.

The World Bank and the IMF have become important institutions in the process of these crises working their way through individual Southern political economies. But neither the Bank nor the Fund could insulate Southern countries from these powerful pressures. Nor could the IFIs alone prevent such massive world economic changes from worsening poverty conditions in most non-oil-producing Southern countries. But the *interplay* between Southern governments and the IFIs did become a key factor shaping the impact of macroeconomic crises on the poor.

Such a widespread international macroeconomic set of crises (and the IFI ineffectiveness in many responses) did force some change in IFI direction. The World Bank, for instance, developed much more serious and probing programs on Southern poverty in the 1990s, with special new attention being paid to gender equity concerns, and the Bank began to devote a significant share of its to studies to the nature, depth, and dynamics of such poverty and gender inequality in most Southern societies.[89] As knowledge is built, particular projects to respond to aspects of Southern poverty, from China to Mexico to Brazil, have begun to emerge from the Bank. In the IMF, too, there has been a shift since the early 1980s to concern with overexpenditure on the military. Clearly, external criticism — by UN agencies, Southern countries, NGOs, and various Northern country aid agencies — has pushed the World Bank into developing effective ways to measure changing income distribution and poverty conditions, in order to assess how social spending and changes in incentive systems are actually affecting people.

Another question for the IFIs, given these mixed policy results, concerns the pressures to change their form of decision-making. In a world subject to rising movements towards democratization, the dominance of decisions in the IFIs by a small number of Northern countries is increasingly subject to question. At one international seminar in Canada, Ariel Buira from the Bank of Mexico strongly criticized how the United States had come to have a veto over at least 18 areas of IFIs decision-making. Frances Stewart from Oxford University suggested putting the IFIs under the general authority of a UN Economic and Social Security Council (somewhat parallel to the present UN Security Council), which would divide authority for shaping

IFI policy more widely among Northern and Southern countries than is now the case.[90] These views reflect perspectives increasingly expressed in many countries, to which the IFIs will have to respond as economic internationalization advances. An all-party committee of the Canadian House of Commons considered these questions in 1993 and came to unanimous conclusions across party lines, stressing that there should be a fundamental and independent review of IMF and World Bank structures and mandates under the auspices of the G-7 countries, in order to encourage reform of the IFIs.[91]

The poverty impact of the macroeconomic policy challenge depends less on the IFIs and their conditionality alone, though, and more on Southern governments and their interplay with the IFIs and resulting policy decisions. In the end, making fairness part of economic restructuring seems to emerge as a major concern in Southern states that reflect the priorities of its their citizens. It has been the states that have moved to democracy (such as Ghana and Mozambique) and the states that have maintained their democratic basis (such as Costa Rica and Zimbabwe) that have dealt with downturns and crisis in ways that have given priority to reducing poverty or insulating the poor. And it has been erratic, semi-authoritarian states, run for a favoured few (such as Kenya, Congo-Zaire, Cameroon, or Guatemala) that have seen poverty grow and inequalities become more blatant in the context of structural adjustment programs. In the end the process of widening democracy more directly in Southern countries depends not only on the political economy factors that shape state structures, but also on the growth of new community-based social movements speaking directly for the poor and less-advantaged peoples in the making of decisions.

Notes

1 David Plank, "Aid, Debt, and the End of Sovereignty: Mozambique and Its Donors," *Journal of Modern African Studies*, vol.31, no.3 (1993), pp.412-13.

2 See IMF, Policy Development and Review Department Staff Team, *Private Market Financing for Developing Countries* (Washington: International Monetary Fund, 1995), p.61.

3 See Country Operations Division 1, *Republic of Kazakhstan — Transition of the State*, vol. 1, report no. 15353-KZ, World Bank, Washington, July 1996, pp.32-35.

4 See Biplab Dasgupta, "The Changing Role of the Major International Oil Firms," in *Multinational Firms in Africa*, ed. Carl Widstrand (Uppsala: Scandinavian Institute of African Studies, 1975), pp.296-97.

5 All data from Morris Miller, *Coping Is Not Enough: The International Debt Crisis and the Roles of the World Bank and the International Monetary Fund* (Homewood: Dow Jones-Irwin, 1986), pp.34-47.

6 UNDP, *Human Development Report, 1992*, New York, 1992, p.50.
7 See Tony Killick, ed., *Adjustment and Financing in the Developing World* (Washington: International Monetary Fund, 1982), pp.4-8.
8 Tony Killick, *IMF Programmes in Developing Countries: Design and Impact* (London: Routledge, 1995), p.7.
9 See an interesting description of the operations of this process by Francisco Sagasti, in *Development and Global Governance*, ed. Roy Culpeper and Caroline Pestieau (Ottawa: IDRC, 1996), pp.69-70.
10 For more details, see IMF, *Private Market Financing for Developing Countries*, Table A4.
11 Ibid., Tables A13, A10.
12 G.K. Helleiner, "The IMF, the World Bank and Africa's Adjustment and External Debt Problems: An Unofficial View," *World Development*, vol.20, no.6 (1992), p.788.
13 World Bank, *Adjustment in Africa: Reform, Results, and the Road Ahead* (Oxford: Oxford University Press, 1994), pp.214-15.
14 CEPAL, "Preliminary Overview of the Latin American and Caribbean Economy, 1995," *Notas Sobre la Economia y el Desarrollo* (Santiago de Chile: United Nations, 1995), pp.42-43.
15 See IMF, *Private Market Financing*, pp.18, 79. A 1994 South African international bond issue raised over $1.8 billion.
16 United Nations Development Programme, *Human Development Report, 1992*, (Oxford: Oxford University Press, 1992), p.75.
17 See Killick, *IMF Programmes in Developing Countries*, p.16.
18 Helleiner, "The IMF, the World Bank and Africa's Adjustment and External Debt Problems," p.788.
19 World Bank, *Adjustment in Africa*, p.36.
20 Quoted in Patrick Smith, "Aid Conditionality is 'Swamping' Africa," *Africa Recovery*, United Nations, vol.7, no.3 and 4 (March 1994), p.15.
21 Miller, *Coping is Not Enough*, pp.28, 107.
22 See John Loxley, *Ghana: The Long Road to Recovery, 1983-90* (Ottawa: North-South Institute, 1991), pp.4-12.
23 *Ibid.*, p.11.
24 See J. Herbst, *The Politics of Reform in Ghana, 1982-1991* (Berkeley: University of California, 1993), pp.40-41.
25 Noted in Loxley, *Ghana: The Long Road to Recovery, 1983-90*, pp.12-14.
26 See Chad Leechor, "Ghana: Frontrunner in Adjustment," in *Adjustment in Africa: Lessons from Country Case Studies*, ed. I. Hussain and R. Faruqee (Washington: World Bank, (1994), p.156; the second quotation is drawn by Leechor from Chand and Van Til.
27 See IMF Assessment Project, *IMF Conditionality, 1980-91* (Washington: Alexis de Tocqueville Institution, 1992), p.55.
28 Killick, *IMF Programmes in Developing Countries*, p.89.
29 CEPAL, "Preliminary Overview of the Latin American and Caribbean Economy, 1995," pp.66-67.
30 Albert Berry and Frances Stewart, "Market Liberalization and Income Distri-

bution," in *Global Development Fifty Years after Bretton Woods*, ed. R. Culpeper et al. (London: Macmillan Press Ltd., 1997), p.233.

31 See IMF Assessment Project, *IMF Conditionality*, 1980-91, p.113.

32 Comment by Mosley, quoted in Gurushri Swamy, "Kenya: Patchy, Intermittent Commitment," *Adjustment in Africa: Lessons from Country Case Studies*, ed. Hussain and Faruqee, p.193.

33 The data is drawn from T. Killick and M. Thorne, "Problems of an Open Economy: The Balance of Payments in the Nineteen-Seventies," in *Papers on the Kenyan Economy*, ed. T. Killick (Nairobi: Heinemann Educational Books, 1981), pp.60-68.

34 See Swamy, "Kenya: Patchy, Intermittent Commitment," p.199.

35 Michael Chege, "The State and Labour," in *Industrialization in Kenya*, ed. P. Coughlin and G.K. Ikiara (Nairobi: Heinemann Kenya, 1988), p.180.

36 Swamy, "Kenya: Patchy, Intermittent Commitment," p.212.

37 See IMF Assessment Project, *IMF Conditionality, 1980-91*, p.115.

38 See Helleiner, "The IMF, The World Bank and Africa's Adjustment and External Debt Problems," p.785.

39 See Loxley, *Ghana: The Long Road to Recovery*, 1983-90, pp.26-29.

40 See Herbst, *The Politics of Reform in Ghana*, 1982-1991, pp.44-47.

41 See Loxley, *Ghana: The Long Road to Recovery*, 1982-1991, pp.26-29.

42 See IMF Assessment Project, *IMF Conditionality*, 1980-1991, p.60.

43 Killick, *IMF Programmes in Developing Countries*, pp.100-1.

44 See World Bank, Country Assistance Review: Ghana, June 1, 1995, Internet, World Bank Home Page.

45 See World Bank, *Adjustment in Africa*, pp.58, 268-69.

46 Dr. Kwesi Botchwey, *The Budget Statement*, Republic of Ghana, Accra, February 1, 1995, p.37.

47 World Bank, *Adjustment in Africa*, p.138.

48 Institute of Economic Affairs, "1994 Annual Report: Economic Review and Outlook," draft report prepared for CIDA, Accra, Ghana, March 1995, p.11.

49 See, for example, the *Programme of the Workshop on Rehabilitation of Internally Displaced Persons of the Northern Region Ethnic Conflict Area*, Tamale, Ghana, April 11, 1995; this program outlined sessions to discuss agriculture, education, health, housing development, water and sanitation, and income generating activities within the Northern Region.

50 See Loxley, *Ghana: The Long Road to Recovery, 1982-1991*, pp.43-44.

51 This workshop was sponsored by CIDA in October 1994, and brought together members of the Finance and Public Accounts Committees of the Ghana Parliament. Steven Langdon and David Slater worked as the Canadian consultants organizing the workshop; Joe Hyde worked as the Ghanaian consultant.

52 See World Bank, Country Assistance Review: Ghana, June 1, 1995, Internet, World Bank Home Page.

53 See IMF Assessment Project, *IMF Conditionality, 1980-1991*, p.114.

54 Leechor, "Ghana: Forerunner in Adjustment," pp.182-84.

55 See "Ghana: Is Growth Sustainable?" *World Bank—Annual Reviews*, no.99 (December 1995).

56 See Lynn Brown and Joanna Kerr, "Ghana: Structural Adjustment's Star Pupil?" in *The Gender Dimensions of Economic Reforms in Ghana, Mali and Zambia*, ed. L.R. Brown and J. Kerr (Ottawa: The North-South Institute, 1997), pp.40-44; Brown and Kerr, however, also note that the depth of poverty for poor households has increased between 1993 and 1995, and this greater seriousness of poverty is most evident among female-headed houses.

57 World Bank, Country Assistance Review: Ghana, 1995.

58 See IMF Assessment Project, *IMF Conditionality, 1980-1991*, p.55.

59 See Killick, *IMF Programmes in Developing Countries*, pp.100-1.

60 CEPAL, "Preliminary Overview of the Latin American and Caribbean Economy, 1995," pp.55-56, 59-60.

61 See IMF, *Private Market Financing*, pp.62-63.

62 CEPAL, "Preliminary Overview of the Latin American and Caribbean Economy, 1995," pp.24-25.

63 Ibid., p.48, 51.

64 See O. Mehmet, *Economic Planning and Social Justice in Developing Countries* (London: Croom Helm, 1978), p.71.

65 Killick, *IMF Programmes in Developing Countries*, p.103.

66 IMF Assessment Project, *IMF Conditionality, 1980-91*, pp.100, 113.

67 CEPAL, "Preliminary Overview of the Latin American and Caribbean Economy, 1995," pp.6, 11.

68 See Peter Utting, "Social and Political Dimensions of Environmental Protection in Central America," in *Development and Environment*, ed. Ghai, p.253.

69 Berry and Stewart, "Market Liberalization and Income Distribution," p.233.

70 See W. Hecox, "Structural Adjustment and Industrialization in Kenya," in *Industrialization in Kenya*, ed. Coughlin and Ikiara, pp.200-3.

71 See Swamy, "Kenya: Patchy, Intermittent Commitment," p.195.

72 Hecox, "Structural Adjustment and Industrialization in Kenya," p.215.

73 Swamy, "Kenya: Patchy, Intermittent Commitment," p.229.

74 See World Bank, *Poverty Assessments for 1995* (Kenya section).

75 Ibid. (Kenya Section).

76 IMF Assessment Project, *IMF Conditionality, 1980-1991*, p.115.

77 World Bank, *Adjustment in Africa*, p.245.

78 Ken Sigrist, "The World Bank in Ghana," in *Training Seminar for MPs at Sogakope* (Accra: Ministry of Parliamentary Affairs, October 1994).

79 See "Government Call for Debt Relief," *Mozambique Inview*, Maputo, April 15, 1996, p.1.

80 See Katherine Marshall, "Chair's Closing Statement," Mozambique Consultative Group Meeting, Paris, April 17-18, 1996, p.2; "World Bank Meeting in Paris on Mozambique," *Mozambique Inview*, April 15, 1996, p.9.

81 World Bank, *Poverty Assessments for 1995* (Brazil Section).

82 Ibid. (Zimbabwe section).

83 Ibid., p.169.

84 World Bank, *Adjustment in Africa*, pp.144-45.

85 M. Rouis, "Senegal: Stabilization, Partial Adjustment, and Stagnation," in *Adjustment in Africa*, ed. Hussain and Faruqee, pp.346-47.

86 See L. Demery, "Cote d'Ivoire: Fettered Adjustment," in *Adjustment in Africa*,

ed. Hussain and Farugee, pp. 122-23.
87 World Bank, *Poverty Assessments, Financial Year 1995* (Cameroon section), Internet.
88 Ibid. (Honduras section, Guatemala section).
89 See Peter Gibbon, "The World Bank and African Poverty, 1973-91," *Journal of Modern African Studies*, vol.30, no.2 (1992), pp.193-220.
90 See A. Buira, "The Governance of the International Monetary Fund," and F. Stewart, "Global Financial Institutions for the Next Century," in *Development and Global Governance*, ed. Culpeper and Pestieau.
91 *Report of the Sub-Committee on International Financial Institutions of the Standing Committee on Finance* (Ottawa: House of Commons, June 8, 1993), pp.23-25. Chaired by S.W. Langdon.

PART III

Democracy and New Directions

CHAPTER 7

The State and Democratic Change

In the late 1960s an indigenous Swahili mining entrepreneur discovered large deposits of what were then very valuable fluorspar deposits in the Kerio Valley in Kenya. He began to discuss plans to develop these with various large multinational corporations. By late 1970 he was negotiating a project with a consortium of Dutch-Canadian-German firms including AKZO and Alcan. The plan, which would have left managerial control in Kenyan hands, called for linkage investment in a chemical plant in Kenya using fluorspar as an input. But Continental Ore, the huge U.S. mining multinational, refused any deal that left managerial control out of its hands and went directly to state authorities in Kenya, forming a partnership deal with the state's Industrial and Commercial Development Corporation. The Kenyan government intervened to strip the Swahili of his mining claim and awarded it to the new firm.[1]

In Ghana the Agricultural Research Institute has worked closely with government support and with various donor agencies (including CIDA, Canada's aid agency) to develop extension programs to take Green Revolution seed technology to small-scale maize producers throughout the country. Yet peasant producers have nowhere come close to the significant output increases shown on research station test plots — mainly, the director says, because the government decided, as part of budget changes agreed with the World Bank, to cut fertilizer subsidies significantly (despite the key role played by such supports in promoting Green Revolution innovations in Asia).[2] As a result, community-based groups are taking on a larger role in agricultural extension outreach to improve small-scale maize production in Ghana.

In the early 1990s a grim civil war was killing thousands in Mozambique and leaving behind deadly land mines. The United Nations worked out a ceasefire and supervised an election across the country. The government won the vote, but narrowly. In the newly established parliament, an Economic Affairs Commission (headed by an opposition MP) began to

165

develop proposals to take democratic forms of governing to the local level, so that Mozambicans can shape their own district priorities with more attention to immediate community needs. Remarkably, both government and opposition MPs are working co-operatively together to achieve this goal.[3]

These snapshots capture some of the changing dynamics of state institutions in the South amidst the evolving pressures of global poverty. The processes are complex, with variations in different settings, but certain broad patterns are there to be seen, analysed, and understood.

1: A Political Economy of the State

What is the place of state institutions in the broader mix of structures that make up the "instituted process of material want-satisfaction" that Polanyi considered to represent "political economy"? This question has been addressed from a number of different traditions.

Modernization theories have stressed certain functions common to all states: maintaining order, recruiting personnel, and building non-personalistic bureaucratic values, for instance. This overly abstract view has thus avoided considering both the impact of international forces on particular states and the divergences in state priorities because of varying state structures and histories. Classic Marxian views see the economic base as determinant, with a derived political superstructure reflecting the relations of production shaped by that base (an approach surely too narrow in its exclusive tie to economic conditions). Neo-liberal views show strong preferences for market forms of resource allocation and see the great bulk of state activity as "rational action" by state-based actors seeking to maximize personal returns from their positions of power. Again this is a universalistic view, highly simplistic in what James Manor calls a much more "untidy world" full of complexities that subvert such easy solutions.[4] Manor points to state institutions, such as those of India, that play varied and often contradictory roles — with some areas in which the state is a guardian and protector of the status quo, some areas in which it is a "reformist liberator" seeking to eliminate injustices, and some neutral arenas in which social groups in effect renegotiate their relations.

No clear-cut characterization, then, may be possible. But many post-colonial Southern states may have had, broadly, what Alavi and Saul have called an "overdeveloped" character — not in the sense that Leys has criticized, of such states being especially large or strong in bureaucratic terms — but in a more subtle sense related to the state's relations with social groupings.[5] Under colonialism the state exercised political dominance over all indigenous social groupings, with much evidence suggesting that this same basic relationship often continued after independence. As a result, whatever political force or faction (or ethnic group leadership in many cases) captured the state had a relatively powerful position in dealing with other indigenous social groupings, which in turn had little economic strength in dealing with the state, given how their development and entrepreneurial expansion had been blocked and retarded by colonial control. The controlling faction could use its relatively powerful state position to divert economic benefits to itself (using some of the mechanisms of manipulating regulations noted in chapter 6), but within two limits: first, respecting the strength of outside economic forces, which were often very important in providing these benefits; and, second, maintaining stability domestically in the relationship between the capitalist relations of production tied to outside forces and the non-capitalist mode of production that was usually still generating domestic benefits of importance to the financial viability of the state (such as tax revenues from peasant agriculture exports).

Thus, in the case of the Kenyan example noted above, the government had sufficient autonomy and power to move against the local Swahili businessman and shift the benefits of his mining discovery to enrich those involved with the state through the ICDC. But this could be done because the action did not represent any major squeeze on peasant producers and because it also benefited two important groups of multinational corporations already in the country: those from the United States in the form of Continental Ore, and those from Britain with investments in another partner in the enterprise, Associated Portland Cement, whose loading facilities would be used for the fluorspar exports.

Successful, stable, postcolonial states, from this perspective, may have had to keep achieving such a complex ongoing symbiosis involving a number of factors: good relations with external global capitalist pressures; sufficient sharing of economic benefits internally to maintain expansion of the number of insiders being aided by the state; and sufficient sensitivity to peasant or other non-capitalist modes of production so that these sectors would not be destabilized and begin to set off major political discontents in the countryside. This meshing of capitalist and peasant modes of production, furthering of domestic "insider" enrichment, and maintenance of state-multinational corporation symbiosis was a tough challenge and could only succeed where foreign investment was fairly concentrated, peasant export prices remained adequate, and those in power did not get too greedy and kept spreading the benefits of postcolonial enrichment.

Periods of excessive peasant exploitation could break a country apart, as happened in the Pakistan-Bangladesh split. Disruption of the external economic link could shatter the whole symbiosis, as happened in Uganda, when President Idi Amin attacked the local Asian community with its wide international linkages. Exclusion of key regional leaders from enrichment-sharing could set off separation movements, as in the 1966-69 Biafra rebellion in Nigeria. And serious downturns in export prices could also destroy the symbiosis, as happened in Zambia after copper prices collapsed.

This symbiosis model, then, should be seen as a "tightrope challenge." Its perpetuation required not only favourable circumstances but also political skill on the part of the regimes in power. Sometimes a miscalculation could be and was countered by external military intervention, as with French armed initiatives in Western and Central Africa to restore regimes. But more often imbalances in the symbiosis led to coups and countercoups by social groupings (often based in the military) that sought to reorient the sharing of the state-organized enrichment process. The army-led overthrows, from Pakistan to Ethiopia to Lesotho, from Zaire to Nigeria to Liberia to Ghana, from Central America to Brazil to the Latin American Southern Cone, all testified to the military interventionism that could be provoked by the breakdown of the complex state symbioses.

This view of the relative autonomy of many Southern states in the post-colonial, post-World War II world — in which global economic pressures were increasing and the domestic segmentation between modes of production was evident but complicated — was a good reflection of how Marx analysed the French state under Louis Napoleon in the 1850s. Marx saw the "Bonapartist" state, in a context in which French industrialist and commercial social groupings were weak, as "completely independent" of domestic social forces and able to operate in a powerful way to bring industry and trade "to prosper in hothouse fashion under the powerful government" (see chapter 3).

Adrian Leftwich's social science analysis of what has been called the "developmental state" places the same emphasis on the relative autonomy of state institutions, run by a determined development-oriented elite, also quite insulated from oppositional social groupings in the political economy.[6] The essence of this "development state," Leftwich says, is the experience of consistent rapid economic growth, and on this basis eight political economies stand out, with average annual growth between 1965 and 1990 of 4 per cent or better: Botswana (8.4 per cent), South Korea (7.1 per cent), Taiwan (7.0 per cent), Singapore (6.5 per cent), China (5.8 per cent), Indonesia (4.5 per cent), Thailand (4.4 per cent), and Malaysia (4.4 per cent). These states have that determined elite (for instance, in 1984 half of Botswana's 11 ministers were retired civil servants, highly educated, with long careers administering economic strategy first as bureaucrats and then as cabinet ministers). They are relatively autonomous (as marked by the South Korean state's longtime control of banking, for example), they have an insulated bureaucracy (the key Economic Development Board in Singapore, for instance, is not even accountable to Parliament), and they exercise effective control over non-state economic actors (such as trade unions and small business groups).

The record of these so-called "developmental states" suggests that broadly based and widespread development gains can be achieved in some cases of states with "overdeveloped" autonomy in relation to their domestic social groupings. But even the record of these eight consistent growth cases is mixed, when poverty and equality concerns are considered. With malnutrition for under-fives at 35 per cent and under-five mortality rates of 75 per 1,000, for instance, Indonesia compares poorly with the Philippines (30 per cent and 53 per 1,000) at the same average income levels, and even worse with China (16 per cent and 47 per 1,000) at lower average income levels. (See chapter 1.)

At the same time the much larger number of other quite autonomous Southern states dealing with symbiosis challenges clearly faced, on balance, serious problems of maintaining continuing economic growth and stability. The progression of military coups marked that reality. Only a small number of post-World War II Southern regimes maintained a consistent democratic character in dealing with these changing pressures, even considering just their period as postcolonial states. Perhaps the most prominent were India and Sri Lanka in Asia, Senegal in Africa, Barbados, Trinidad, and Jamaica in the Caribbean, and Costa Rica and Colombia in Latin America.

Yet, as the Soviet-U.S. world rivalry ended, and as economic globalization advanced, the South experienced a dramatic change in political institutions. There was a movement towards democracy in most Southern political economies. In Asia, Indonesia became exceptional in its authoritarian style — with even China moving towards democratic elections and governing bodies at the village level. In Eastern and Southern Africa, Somalia, Rwanda, and Burundi resisted the trend. Elsewhere in Africa, Zaire, Nigeria, and the Ivory Coast led a larger group of authoritarian holdouts. In Central America, settlements began to take all countries towards multiparty regimes. In the Caribbean and South America virtually all countries moved towards democracy. Only the Middle East, from Libya to Iran and on to Afghanistan, showed few signs of change.

As the United Nations has described the decade of the 1990s, "Compared with even a few years ago, the world today is a much freer place."[7] In 1974 only 39 countries (one in four in the world) were governed by democratically elected regimes, while in 1997 some 117 countries (two out of every three) were choosing their leaders in open democratic elections.[8] What explains this democratic trend? And what difference does it make to the lives of people?

2: The Dynamics of Democratic Change

Democracy is a broad concept. It includes not just competitive elections — so that voters gain choices in picking those who govern them — but it also involves the widening of access to government information and the freedom to debate political issues both at a personal level and through independent media. Thus the movement of both Tanzania and Ghana to permit vigorous opposition newspapers is just as crucial as the establishment of new multiparty voting systems. Beyond freedoms of speech, association, and competing political parties, it has also become clear that widened activity and political initiatives by independent movements of people contribute to building a democratic *civil society* that encourages participation and ensures equitable capacities for different social groupings to speak out and influence state decisions.

So why have so many Southern states been moving in democratic directions? It is, of course, possible to be cynical and see this emergence of democracy as mainly an external imposition, a result of pressure from "Northern" countries making use of the greater leverage brought about by global economic turbulence and greater Southern economic and political weakness. In some cases, such pressure has clearly played a role, as in Kenya, where the 1992 suspension of external aid and cancellation of a key World Bank loan did precede President Moi's reluctant move to multiparty democracy. But one has also to consider that in Kenya a strong and broadly based domestic opposition movement, cutting across a wide number of class and regional lines, seemed to have pushed the donor community to act. External agencies and internal social forces have also pushed hard for democratic changes in Central America that would end civil wars in that region.

But much more important than these particular institutional interventions were the fundamental changes in the form of the triple development crisis traced in the previous three chapters. Especially for states trying to maintain a careful symbiosis among external relations with the global economy, domestic meshing of capitalist and non-capitalist modes of production, and benefit-sharing among domestic insiders with ties to state institutions, the macroeconomic crisis of the 1980s posed enormous challenges to existing policy strategies. Foreign exchange pressures undercut industrial projects and rural export systems. The intervention of the IMF and World Bank threatened many of the veiled privileges that had made symbiotic relationships acceptable to key groups. The crucial coalitions that kept states operative began to fall apart. The price-change shocks, both internal and external, of the macroeconomic crisis exploded old understandings, and many existing states simply did not have the broad acceptance or legitimacy in the society to carry out significant restructurings.

In a few states, such as Nigeria, the Ivory Coast, and Kenya, strong domestic social groupings had by the 1980s developed the economic and political power, in close relationship with extensive foreign investment sectors, to maintain key elements of the insider-outsider social and economic polarization. So regimes stayed in power, frustrated any major moves towards widespread democratization, and (as seen in the data on poverty in the Ivory Coast and in Kenya) deepened the poverty experienced by the majority.

In some other states the collapse of failed regimes in the context of the macroeconomic crisis led to democratic replacements, often after popular pressures and demonstrations of various sorts: Brazil, Uruguay, Argentina, the Philippines, Bangladesh, Nepal, and Malawi are examples. In other cases authoritarian governments made last efforts at elections and failed to hold on, as in Zambia and Chile. In a few other cases some regimes (such as Tanzania and Mozambique) did make the transition to more democratic institutional settings, in which free elections showed popular support for the governments in power. There were also cases in which governments were overthrown and gradual but genuine moves to democracy took place (such as Ghana and Uganda).[9]

A major thrust in such situations was a strong drive to achieve democratic mandates and thus improve the domestic legitimacy of regimes within the country, because only regimes with domestic legitimacy could carry forward major social and economic restructuring and thereby respond effectively to the extensive shifts in the international economy. Without such a mandate, governments would have little capacity to interact more equally with the IFIs and would find the IFIs able to push their externally based conditions through as the dominant policy priorities, with little country capacity to resist. Regimes with democratic mandates would have more ability to carry forward more independent reforms and thus also considerably more strength in arguing for different reform priorities.

In Ghana, for instance, the old economic strategy of protected industry, peasant cocoa earnings that provided major state financing, and political sharing of benefits among bureaucratic and military elites simply collapsed as the massive oil-price increases destroyed the chances of importing anything else, peasants stopped producing because they could buy nothing, and protected industry had no one to sell to. As health worsened, schools shut, and infrastructure broke down, a young group of radical faculty and junior military officers took over. They sought Soviet help, but the wilting Cold War meant there was no more aid there to provide, so they turned to the IMF and the World Bank, got the economy moving again, began to revive agriculture, fixed their balance of payments problems by a massive reduction in the value of their currency, and then began to build new democratic institutions that would give their intervention popular roots. This increased legitimacy meant they could stress antipoverty measures like PAMSCAD, and insist the IFIs support such initiatives. Democratic institutions were thus introduced in the rural districts through the establishment of local assemblies, and then the Rawlings regime brought Ghanaians into the drafting of a new constitution and eventually revived parliament — and won a democratic national election in 1992. In late 1996 Rawling's National Democratic Congress won again, basing their 53 per cent victory on the outsider regions in the north and east, which had gained from the profound shift of resources to poorer, rural areas, a shift spurred by the new regime.

At least two other routes to democracy have been travelled. One involved countries that had experienced rapid economic expansion based on fairly egalitarian social structures and highly sophisticated technological training for their labour forces. It is difficult to keep such populations productive and creative in economic terms, yet dominated politically, and these sorts of factors combined to expand democratization in countries such as Korea, Thailand, and Taiwan.

In other settings violent confrontations could only be ended through a transition of power by eased and organized democratization. This was the case in South Africa, where one of the most devastating, arbitrary, and comprehensive forms of subjugation since the U.S. Civil War was finally ended. Democratic change in Zimbabwe and Namibia had important effects too, with difficult periods of follow-up, but the socioeconomic transformation in South Africa will be a much more complex process.

Democratization in Southern countries, then, has not been an imposed transition, nor has it simply been the consequence of one worldwide trend. There have been forces of example that have surely had some influence, but the main factors at work, and the contexts shaping change, have differed from country to country. Often important local social forces have played a major role, as in the mobilization of professional groups against President Hastings Kamuzu Banda in Malawi, the demonstrations by civil servants, teachers, and traders in Benin in 1989, and the challenge from the Congress of Trades Unions in Zambia against President Kenneth Kaunda.[10] The result has been more extensive in its impact in some cases than others: Ghana has written a whole new constitution, based on multiparty elections and constraints on executive power; Uganda has tried to keep non-party democracy, leaving the position of the President relatively unchecked. The conflicts have been tougher in some contexts: Mozambique had to settle a civil war via elections; Tanzania only added new party choices. Not surprisingly, the results of democratization have therefore varied.

Given the pressures underlying shifts to democracy, not surprisingly the major result may be the greatly increased leverage that such moves have given some Southern governments in dealing with financial pressures from the international finance institutions. The classic case is how the Mozambique government was able to stand up to the IMF over pressures to cut back its budget and increase interest rates in 1996. Mozambique had just settled a long-running civil war, and the government had won a close election victory in a UN supervised election. Rejecting the IMF position, Mozambique argued instead that more growth had to take place through cancellation of some debts and major financial help from the international donor community. Both the winning and the losing parties in parliament united to agree on this point, and in the end the World Bank supported the government, contradicted the IMF position, and helped see that the government received U.S.$10 million more in assistance than it had requested (including U.S.$314 million in debt relief). The democratization process had given the government strong domestic legitimacy in making its case, especially because both former warring parties in the civil war, now both in parliament, could agree on this position.

Other cases, as we've seen, show the same general point: Democratic governments have been able to place much more stress on responding to poverty in making economic choices in their negotiations with the IFIs. In Costa Rica, for instance, when IMF conditional loans were worked out to help with heavy debt loads, the democratic government was able to insist that special help for the poor be included (such as a food-parcels program for 40,000 poorer families), despite IMF opposition. In Ghana the PAMSCAD program to help displaced public-service workers was put in place and assisted many new micro-enterprises to emerge.

Parliaments established in various countries as part of the democratization push, when they have been elected on a genuine basis and with a sense of true accountability, also seem to play important roles in keeping governments much more tied to local people's perceived needs and hopes. In South Africa, for instance, women MPs from the African National Congress in several state governments have formed special offices at the local level to raise and promote women's concerns, something rare in the past in Africa, but a clear result of the close ties of these women to women-dominated trade union groups and other women's bodies that are part of the liberation movement in South Africa.[11] MPs from Ghana's more rural constituencies have also pushed hard through parliamentary committees and special sessions with the Ministry of Finance to have more focus on the poverty concerns of poorer peasants in Ghana's budget decisions.[12]

The existence of elected and responsive parliaments also means MPs have an important ongoing role in reflecting popular reactions and concerns to governments, even in more authoritarian settings. In Kazakhstan in Central Asia, for instance, by 1996 the parliament's Budget Committee included members from areas with diverse fears and priorities as the country tried to come to terms with major revenue losses of 50 per cent over three years resulting from the break with the Soviet Union. These differences made the Budget Committee a sensitive sounding board against which government could test out different ways of handling the reorganization of priorities.[13] Such committees and elected parliaments can also be direct transmission belts for popular grievances, improving government's ability to make decisions that people will accept and for which there will therefore be fewer implementation costs. Ghana, for instance, had a major

problem implementing a new value-added tax in 1995. When I sat in at a
district assembly meeting with one of the MPs, I could see the depth of
anger and misunderstanding that would eventually lead to the postponement of this tax.[14]

Democratic governance at the centre is important in increasing accountability and popular legitimacy of national decisions. But just as important
in expanding popular participation and widening the access of people to
state choices that can spread development benefits more widely are changes
that involve decentralization of authority and democratic forms of community involvement in such local state institutions. This is an increasing trend
in Southern countries, and it is one that the central government level has
helped to expand. The emphasis is on the establishment of new mechanisms of local accountability and co-operative work by a wider range of
people, which requires democratic forms of choice, discussion, information-sharing, and openness to work effectively. This has become clear even
in China, which has resisted democratic forms at national levels but has
established a vigorous system of village-level elections and decision-making
to pursue local-level objectives. These democratic village governments
appear to have been set up on an ad-hoc bottom-up basis by local people
who were looking for some way to replace the rural commune structures
that had been dissolved. By 1997, 95 per cent of villages held elections —
by secret ballot — to choose committee members for three-year terms.[15]
Provincial and national governments have responded favourably to these
local initiatives to elect small village governments, because it appears that
the vigour of these local institutions is a crucial factor in the widespread
successful and broad-based development that has kept China's very rapid
growth rates consistent with high degrees of poverty alleviation as well.[16]
The same energetic self-help efforts are evident in Ghana through village-
based water and sanitation committees in the poorer northern parts of the
country. The record of district assemblies in Ghana is more mixed, but
there are (again) parts of the poorer north that have benefited from access
to new resources as a result of this local-level democratization.[17]

In general the spread of democracy has encouraged community-based
movements, and other people's groups within the civil society, to emerge,
to move energetically to improve their access to resources they can use, and
to begin having an impact on the wider process of decision-making in the
society.

3: Civil Society, Community Groups, and Movements for Change

In recent years in most Southern countries, a wide range of social movements has significantly increased their activity. These movements have

covered the spectrum of social groupings, from rural-based and local community organizations to women's movements to urban-based "civil society" groups to national trade union entities — and they have been responding to gender inequalities, environmental concerns, the pressures of growing poverty, the objectives of rural water supply and agricultural improvement, urban social infrastructure gaps, and visions of empowerment. These movements have helped propel the shifts towards democracy in many Southern countries, and they have also been encouraged in their own expansion and their momentum by the democratization that has provided the necessary political space for their work.

Particularly significant has been the considerable expansion of women's movements working for social change in many Southern countries. Ghana, for instance, has a long tradition of powerful women's organizations at the local level. Bukh, for instance, describes how the formation of a new women's organization in a Volta Region village drew on pre-independence communal co-operation by women through the institution of the Queen Mother within the tribal structure.[18] The Bureau of Integrated Rural Development in Kumasi has also undertaken research into the deep community roots of women's groups in the Techiman area of Brong-Ahafo.[19]

The widespread expansion of women's movements has been related to the deepening economic crises. As the UN Research Institute for Social Development concluded, "In Latin America, poor women's organizations emerged massively during the period of economic crisis and democratic transition in the late 1970s and 1980s." As the UNRISD study shows, some of these community-based initiatives — such as the communal kitchens that women set up with government support in many parts of Lima, Peru — were needs-based and had few connections with each other or with a wider struggle for empowerment and change. But some organizational efforts had wider effects. "Other research concludes more positively, although cautiously, about the potential of women's organizations to influence policy agendas and negotiate power in their local communities — through interactions with neighborhood associations and/or co-operatives, political parties, municipalities, religious institutions and NGOs."[20]

Some parts of Asia have seen similar movements towards empowerment by poorer women. Perhaps the most dramatic case has been in Bangladesh, where extreme rural poverty has pushed the poorest of women out of household seclusion and into active work in services, industrial production, and farming — often after men have deserted their families under the pressure of poverty conditions. Aminur Rahman, summarizing this process from her field research in Bangladesh, pointed out how crucial it was for such women to form social groupings to provide mutual reinforcement and a sense of solidarity because of the strong cultural norms against women playing such public roles in an Islamic society. BRAC (the Bangladesh

Rural Advancement Committee) became an extremely important indigenous organization, pulling 700,000 of the poorest people in the country into 13,000 community organizations, and the Grameen Bank became a crucial source of credit for the poor, with some 92 per cent of its borrowers being women.[21]

Women's groups have not been the only driving force for empowerment of the poor. In certain situations groups expanded under harshly repressive governments and found a means of acting by developing an independence from any formal political links, articulating a concept of "civil society" separate from the state and avoiding overt opposition to that authoritarian state. Schuurmann has traced how the repression of political parties after the overthrow of democracy in Chile led to the emergence of such new social actors. Unable to challenge through elections for political power, these actors formed new social movements to provide basic self-help services to the poor and to work for human rights, as well as to advance the equality of women. These local-level social movements came to make up civil society in Chile.[22] Over time, this broad range of civil society institutions became the basis for the defeat of the Pinochet government in the referendum of 1988, thus setting off the transition back to democracy in Chile — just as civil society movements (especially the trade unions and civic associations providing basic community services in black townships) gave a boost to the transformation of South Africa to majority rule[23] — and independent civil society organizations (including the churches) led the battle for democratic change in Eastern Europe.

With the strong trend to the decentralization of powers and responsibilities to local levels in many Southern countries, such community-based people's organizations have gained a heightened importance in many settings. As Patricia McCarney stresses, after reviewing the serious problems in Southern cities in providing sanitation, transportation, education, and health services: "In response to state incapacity to address these local problems, organizations in civil society have flourished. There are now organizations for squatter communities, tenants' associations, savings and credit associations, area development committees, security committees, women's associations, and even independent research and management advisory bodies."[24] These civil society groups, McCarney says, are providing the bulk of most housing and transportation in Southern cities now and are creating themselves as an important power bloc in urban centres. Indeed, she argues, the ability of such groups to bring about real devolution of power *and* financial resources to local levels will determine whether poorly served urban governance will improve in the foreseeable future.

Community-based organizations are equally important in rural areas. Kothari has stressed this point in analysing strategies for action against rural poverty in India.[25] In the Philippines, a rural coalition (CPAR — the

People's Agrarian Reform Code) has pushed for land reform, taken over idle lands, and reforested coastal mangrove areas.[26] Clear evidence also exists in the water development experience in Northern Ghana. The selection of water and sanitation committee members has included local residents involved in community-based organizations; and where this was done only to a very limited extent (for example, Zabzugu in Northern Region and Lawra in Upper West Region) the village Watsan committees were not very successful in raising community funds to assist the financing of the new clean water sources. As well, in the four cases (out of fourteen selected priority villages for water development) in which fundraising and community commitment had been especially successful over the 1992-94 period, all four villages had by far the largest percentage of their residents in each region already holding membership in at least one community organization. In those four villages as a whole an average of 60.5 per cent of the residents belonged to at least one community-based organization, while the other ten villages ran at an average of 43.9 per cent.[27]

The community-based organization of fishing families in the Solomon Islands, led by women, shows similar capacity in rural common-property resource cases of civil-society initiatives to protect the longer-term environmental viability of the local economy (see chapter 4).

But does the changing state truly offer the chance for community-based movements to bring about changes that benefit the poor, or are groups limited to defensive local self-help efforts? It is certainly necessary to remain objective and questioning on this point. The establishment of multiparty democracy in Kenya did not lead to a change in government, and the opposition MPs elected have privately stressed their beliefs that little has changed regarding controls on the press, human rights abuses, and blocks on freedom of speech in that country.[28] Analysts of the Southern Cone countries in Latin America also stress that the military remains strong in Chile, Argentina, and Uruguay and that what is taking place is a "transition to democracy" rather than the establishment of fully democratic conditions.[29]

Ponna Wignaraja, however, suggests that a long-term perspective may be appropriate: "Social change does not necessarily mean 'big bang', once-for-all revolution and a unidirectional movement. The long revolution can proceed slowly or faster, and even in a zigzag fashion, depending on a number of unforeseeable factors." Thus to start the process of empowerment of the poor and overcoming poverty, Wignaraja says, "In most countries, whatever the current social formation, economic and political space exists or can be found for this kind of systematic change to occur. The historical conditions also exist for the sowing of seeds of change."[30]

This potential for bringing about change in a democratic context becomes clear in the activities of the environmental movement in India.

Maadhave Gadgil and Ramachandra Guha show how activists there have emerged from some communities, connected up with others, and have taken three broad directions forward.[31] Some groups have formed around particular struggles, where they have sought to stop particular ecological threats. They have blocked several dam projects that threatened important ecological or agricultural resources. As well, major struggles have been played out internationally over the Sardar Sarovar dam, with tens of thousands of people mobilized to make a difference. The protests grew so effective that the World Bank eventually withdrew its financial support from the project, although the Indian government did proceed within some changed new emphases on compensation.[32]

Secondly, other groups in India have stressed popular education on environmental concerns. Some have promoted a strong environmental message through the media and using other means such as walking tours and eco-development camps. One especially effective group, the Kerala Sastra Sahitya Parishad (KSSP), a popular science movement in Kerala state, used plays and folk songs throughout their state to develop opinion against deforestation and pollution. To promote environmental concerns some groups have used the Gandhian technique of the 'padayatra' or walking tour. One such action, for instance, the Save the Western Ghats March of 1987-88, took seven months to prepare, involved over 150 voluntary groups, and covered over 4,000 kilometres of hill terrain, reaching 600 villages along the route.

A third approach has stressed programs of ecological restoration. The Dashauli Gram Swarjya Mandal group (DGSM) set off the successful Chipko "tree-huggers" movement that blocked forest exploitation in the Himalayan Mountains. Then the DGSM moved into direct reconstruction work at the grassroots, a move (led by women particularly) to expand afforestation efforts in heavily eroded areas of the Himalayan valleys. Activists have also organized several local self-help irrigation projects to counter drought and consequent land degradation.

Indian environment groups have certainly had successes, as with their international campaign to get the World Bank out of the Sardar Sarovar project, but other efforts have had more mixed results. Few major dam projects have actually been stopped, and the restoration efforts have been marginal in the huge and complex context of the Indian political economy. There are also difficulties in a system of representative democracy for a broad community of tribal peoples (like those of the Jharkhand region) to express themselves in effective defence of their common resource base and in favour of a community-based pattern of development built on communal use of that base.[33] Nevertheless, the new movements for "ecology with justice" in India are vibrant signs of the openings provided by democracy for poorer people to seek empowerment and change.

There has also been a significant spread of African environmental groups in Ghana in recent years. One example is the Green Earth Organization, begun in 1983 by a group of students concerned to respond creatively to the drought in Ghana that year. It has gradually built up an educational role on environmental issues and now works on a community-based level in six of Ghana's regions. Its major areas of concern have been the rapid pace of tree-cutting and export from Ghana, the neglect of sanitation infrastructure in the capital city of Accra, and the importance of integrating local people's priorities with national park development in Ghana.[34] The organization was one of seven Ghanaian environment-oriented non-governmental organizations that met with the new Resident Representative of the World Bank when he took over the Ghana position in 1995. The Green Earth has also played a leading role in co-ordinating the communication among the wider movement of some 135 non-governmental organizations now active on a range of issues in Ghana.

Besides new environmental movements, Brazilians, for example, formed a broad range of social groupings in their increasingly democratic context. As Leilah Landim reports, Brazil came to have 196 women's groups, 447 entities that saw themselves as popular groups and movements, 565 that struggled over questions of black identity, and 402 environmental organizations.[35] Landim stresses, "The balance of the past two decades has been positive and original, above all in the area of building popular organizations and associations of all kinds." However, despite these successes, extreme inequalities remain in Brazil, as well as what Landim calls "short-circuits" in communication with the broad mass of the population in the country. "We have many walls to topple and many bridges to build," she concludes. "In Brazil — and in Latin America — the rising tide of democratization brings new hopes."[36]

Trade unions have also been important organizational forces for change in some cases — such as South Africa, where the organized labour movement was "the de facto leader of the internal democratic opposition,"[37] before the white-run government finally began to surrender. The labour movement also worked for more egalitarian policies in such Caribbean cases as Jamaica and Trinidad. Peasant co-operatives supported by the national union movement have been active in the forestry sector in Honduras.[38]

The spread of democracy has encouraged and backed the emergence and expansion of new social movements as well as in many cases reflecting the pressures from civil society organizations. This social transformation taking place at the community level is a crucial step towards changes that empower the poor and begin to counter the spread of Southern poverty. But this is just one step. The development and achievement of different policy priorities, at both the community and the national levels, represent the next difficult challenge.

4: Conclusion

On a superficial level, the changes in Southern political economies in the last 10 to 15 years have been dramatic and entirely contrary to what might have been anticipated. Faced by fundamental external economic shocks, confronted by major industrial policy failures, and squeezed by growing rural inequality and environmental pressures, the logical expectation might well have been that Southern states would increase repression, suppress any threats to their survival brought on by democratic moves, and seek to tie themselves more tightly to external political and military forces that would help the beleaguered Southern political leadership to maintain power.

This course was indeed followed by some Southern governments. Congo-Zaire was a classic example, and so too was Indonesia. But most Southern governments found their structures of political economy severely shaken. The post-World War II patterns of three-way symbiosis simply could not survive. The meshing of modes of production in rural areas, which marked the structural segmentation of most Southern states (in which large-scale land redistribution had not taken place), came under massive pressure in most cases — from expanding cattle-rearing in parts of Latin America, for instance, and collapsing peasant export-crop prices in Africa and parts of Asia. The symbiosis with foreign investment was undercut deeply by the disintegration of ISI manufacturing in the face of foreign-exchange crises; and the increased sharing of benefits among insiders was broken by these severe economic problems and by IFI efforts to rationalize state allocations in tackling macroeconomic imbalances. Some few states, led by more autonomous, development-oriented bureaucracies, had made the shift to export-oriented industrialization and mostly continued to experience high growth rates based on skills training, rural egalitarianism, and interventionist investment strategies. This was the case in South Korea, Taiwan, and Singapore.

But most Southern states, with their political economies' balancing act destroyed, and growing economic distress spreading, either collapsed and directly set off a transition to democracy — or found that they could restructure their failed strategy only by gaining new domestic legitimacy for their governmental institutions through movements towards democracy. Fundamentally, then, the developmental crisis of the 1980s found a major response, remarkably, in the massive shift to democracy in the South.

This shift had a profound impact on the lives of millions of poorer people in Southern countries. The shift gave a greater leverage to newly democratized regimes to bargain on a more equal basis with the IMF and the World Bank. Democratic institutions led those regimes to give more weight to the concerns of the poor, which led in turn to more efforts in the context of structural adjustment programs to safeguard the interests of the poor. Still, not enough was done to significantly reduce poverty. Some policy moves (such as cutting maize fertilizer subsidies in Ghana) were made that hurt the peasantry. But policy moves aimed at poverty concerns were being taken with IFI support, as in Ghana with PAMSCAD and Costa Rica with food support.

Another impact of the shift was the emergence of democratic parliaments in many Southern countries, with MPs in many cases actively taking community concerns forward to governments and pushing for local priorities. This change provides a much more substantive, well-rooted texture to central government decision-making, especially with respect to economic policy. As well, extensive decentralization of decisions and resource allocation is taking place from the centre to more flexible and responsive local governments and community institutions in many Southern countries. By and large, the impulses towards democratic participation and governance are much stronger at this local level — so much so that even a regime such as China began striking local initiatives to establish democratic village-governing committees.

The movement towards democratic institutions has also greatly increased the political space for new popular movements and community-based independent organizations to work energetically for empowerment of the poor, gender equity, environmental improvements, and better-distributed urban services. Civil society remains a separate sphere from state institutions and political parties, but it has become an increasingly crucial source of the energy and dynamism driving ahead changes in those Southern countries in which democracies have been defining themselves.

The process of democratization in Southern countries, then, is well underway. Some countries, such as Nigeria or Indonesia, are only now being touched by this broad set of institutional changes. Some countries, such as China, have been cautious about the levels at which they accept democratic structures. Some countries that have adopted democratic structures, such as Kenya, have limitations on wider democratic freedoms that make the changes less significant. But it is the broad process of change that is most important, and the dynamics of that process are clearly making poverty concerns and related gender-equity issues into growing preoccupations in many Southern countries. The major forces behind that increasing focus are the expanding social movements and community-based organizations that are placing the empowerment of the poor on the Southern policy agenda.

Notes

1 For more details, see S.W. Langdon, *Multinational Corporations in the Political Economy of Kenya* (London: Macmillan Press, 1981), pp. 178-82.

2 Interview, Agricultural Research Institute, Kumasi, Ghana, May, 1996.
3 Parliamentary Workshop, Mozambique-Canada, Maputo, Mozambique, May, 1996.
4 See James Manor, "Politics and the Neo-liberals," in *States or Markets?* ed. C. Colclough & J. Manor (Oxford: Clarendon Press, 1991), pp.306-20.
5 For material on this debate, see H. Alavi, "The State in Post-Colonial Societies — Pakistan and Bangladesh," *New Left Review*, vol. 74 (1972); J. Saul, "The State in Post-Colonial Societies — Tanzania," *Socialist Register 1974*, 1974; C. Leys, "The 'Overdeveloped' Post-Colonial State: A Re-evaluation," *Review of African Political Economy*, vol. 5 (1976).
6 See Adrian Leftwich, "Bringing Politics Back In: Towards a Model of the Developmental State," *Journal of Development Studies*, vol. 31, no. 3 (1995), pp.400-27.
7 UNDP, *Human Development Report 1992*, p.26.
8 World Bank, *World Development Report, 1997*, Washington, 1997, p. 111.
9 See Rosalind Boyd, "Monitoring and Observation of the Constituent Assembly Elections in Uganda," *Centre for Developing-Area Studies*, McGill University, Discussion Paper 81, 1994.
10 See E. Gyimah-Boadi, "Civil Society in Africa," Working Paper, Institute of Economic Affairs, Ghana, July 1997.
11 Personal discussions at Parliamentary workshop, Mbatho, South Africa, June 1995.
12 Personal Interviews with Members of Parliament and Ministry of Finance officials, Accra, Ghana, May 1995.
13 Personal assessment, World Bank Parliamentary workshop with Budget Committee, Almaty, Kazakhstan, November 1996.
14 Personal observation, Sub-district Assembly Meeting, Kumasi, Ghana, May 1995.
15 "China's Grassroots Democracy," *The Economist*, Nov. 2, 1996, p. 33.
16 See "A Framework for International Donor Assistance to Chinese Village Self-Governance," report to CIDA et al. by a project formulation mission to China, March-April 1996, p.4: "The village committee is the cornerstone of a larger grassroots self-government initiative which serves to introduce democratic elections, democratic management, democratic policy-making, and democratic supervision. ... Chinese research has shown that the village self-government system contributes significantly to economic growth, implementation of government policy, and social stability at the grassroots level. Regular elections have contributed to a greater sense of accountability in village management inasmuch as committee members recognize that the most important criterion for re-election is their economic performance in raising village income."
17 See Ellen Bortei-Doku Aryeetey et al., "Review of District Assembly Capacity for Decentralization and Development Initiatives," report to CIDA, Accra, Ghana, December 1994.
18 See Bukh, *The Village Women in Ghana*, pp. 91-93.
19 Interview with Tina Peprah, Research Fellow, Bureau of Integrated Rural Development, University of Science and Technology, Kumasi, Ghana, May 1996.

20 See United Nations Research Institute for Social Development, "Women's Organizations in Comparative Perspective," UNRISD Internet Home Page: Geneva, 1996.

21 See A. Rahman, "Women, Cultural Ideology and Change in Rural Bangladesh," *Canadian Journal of Development Studies*, vol. XV, no. 3 (1994), pp. 429-44.

22 See Schuurman, ed., *Beyond the Impasse*, pp.193-95.

23 See Glenn Adler and Eddie Webster, "Challenging Transition Theory: The Labor Movement, Radical Reform, and Transition to Democracy in South Africa," *Politics and Society*, vol. 23, no. 1 (1995), pp.75-106.

24 See P.L. McCarney, ed., *The Changing Nature of Local Government in Developing Countries* (Toronto: Centre for Urban and Community Studies, 1996), p.11.

25 Kothari, *Poverty*, pp.126-27.

26 See G.J. Schmitz and D. Gillies, *The Challenge of Democratic Development: Sustaining Democratization in Developing Societies* (Ottawa: North-South Institute, 1992), p.63.

27 See "Case Study of the GWSC Assistance Project from 1990 to 1994," pp.19-21, 88-89.

28 Personal interview with leading Kenya Opposition MP, Ottawa.

29 Schuurman, ed., *Beyond the Impasse*, pp. 192-95.

30 Wignaraja, ed., *New Social Movements in the South*, pp. 23-25.

31 See Maadhave Gadgil and Ramachandra Guha, "Ecological Conflicts and the Environmental Movement in India," in *Development and Environment*, ed. Ghai, pp.101-36.

32 See Sardar Sarovar, "Report of the Independent Review." Undertaken for the World Bank (Ottawa: Resource Futures International Inc., 1992).

33 See Smitu Kothari and Pramod Parajuli, "No Nature with Social Justice: A Plea for Cultural and Ecological Pluralism in India," in *Global Ecology: A New Arena of Political Conflict*, ed. Wolfgang Sachs (London: Zed Books, 1993), pp.234-39.

34 Interview with George Ahadzie, Executive Director of Green Earth Organization, Accra, May, 1996. See also issues of *The Green Dove*, No. 4, 7, 8, 1995, that show the focus on these three areas of environmental concern.

35 Leilah Landim, "Brazilian Crossroads: People's Groups, Walls and Bridges," in Wignaraja, ed., *New Social Movements in the South*, p.223.

36 Ibid., pp.226-29.

37 Adler and Webster, "Challenging Transition Theory," p.92.

38 P. Utting, "Social and Political Dimensions of Environmental Protection in Central America," in *Development and Environment*, ed. Ghai, pp.252-57.

CHAPTER 8

Reorienting Policy Priorities

The democratic changes taking place in most Southern societies revolve around both a new responsiveness and accountability from state structures and broad new openings for community-based, civil society movements that give poorer people more leverage in improving their situations. The macroeconomic context in many Southern countries has improved somewhat (although this will continue to be a major policy preoccupation), but new, more fundamental reorientations of broad policy priorities are emerging in some nations that reflect the democratic shifts.

In Ghana in 1997, when new parliamentary committees on finance and public accounts gathered for wide-ranging workshop discussions about their roles and policy priorities over the next four years, the strong conclusion was to place more stress on support for smallholder peasant farming. As part of their discussions they heard a tough critique of Ghana's existing agricultural research and support services. Those programs, it was said, were too tied into international farming research efforts that ignored key crops grown for food purposes in Ghana and were not responding effectively to environmental problems in the country.[1]

In China a 1994 policy statement stressed, "China is convinced that the key to achieving sexual equality is to enable women to take part in development as the equals of men." Other official statements recognized that the "the road toward emancipation and progress for Chinese women has not reached its end."[2] One aspect of these gender inequalities involved how the "one-child policy" in urban areas had led to some half-million abandoned baby girls in over 800 orphanages across the country. Policy-makers in Beijing conceded that care for those children was at "a very low standard," and must be improved.[3]

With other Asian women suffering from even greater inequalities, policy reorientation is shifting more attention to their difficulties. In Bangladesh, as we have seen, questions of gender equity and rural improvement have been intertwined through the work of the Bangladesh Rural Advancement

185

Committee (BRAC) and the Grameen Bank. Both work at empowering rural women and have had considerable success in targeting credit to small groups of women for purposes of economic improvement, in turn improving the leverage of hundreds of thousands of poor women in their relations with men.[4] In Zimbabwe a 1996 project also stressed credit, but in that case for smaller, urban-based enterprises, so they can better benefit from major trade policy changes aimed at reshaping incentives towards export markets. Some U.S.$110 million was to be provided to encourage indigenous Zimbabwean firms to expand their economic role and employ more people.[5]

These portraits all underline a broad package of reorientation towards an antipoverty strategy based on a central role for gender equity, for spreading agricultural gains, and for supporting small-enterprise expansion (especially in the informal sector). Crucial to this process is improved resource access by the poor (to land, education, and credit) as well as an end to the ISI privileges that large (usually foreign-owned) industries have had in trade and other policies. For many years development experts have stressed the need to tackle poverty problems directly, but two strands in the experience of recent years give new force to the antipoverty analysis. The fundamental issue of gender equity has become a genuine priority. It is now widely recognized that it is "particularly women, for whom escape from poverty is especially difficult," as a World Bank report puts it. "Formidable legal and cultural barriers can hinder the entry of women into the labor market. After entry they are often segregated into casual or dead-end, low-paying jobs. At home the psychological burden of culturally induced low self-esteem, added to the physical burden of domestic chores, inhibit their mobility and block opportunities for gaining better work."[6]

The second strand is the importance of Southern country issues of environmental degradation, which are now also seen as a key part of any successful strategy. There is, the World Bank notes, "much more awareness today of the two-way relationship that exists between poverty and environmental degradation. The daily livelihood of the poor, particularly in rural areas, depends vitally on the local environmental resources—forests, irrigation water, and fisheries. The local commons also provide elementary insurance for poor peasants — a fallback source of food and fodder in bad years. With the erosion of grazing lands, the decimation of forests, and the silting and increasing toxicity of rivers, the life of the rural poor, particularly in many parts of Africa and South Asia, has become even more insecure and impoverished."[7]

A new vision is thus being defined in many Southern countries. Unlike the elite-run, centralized, male-dominated, large-scale industrial vision of the "modernization" advocates, this new vision is gender-conscious, bottom-up, small-scale, decentralized, rural-oriented, and "green."

What does such a vision mean, in greater detail?

Because great variation exists in country and even community consider-ations, and because the emphasis of the new approach is on poorer people defining directions for themselves at a community level, no comprehensive policy prescription can be presented. Still, certain broad points can be made about policy reorientation.

1: New Rural Directions

Perhaps the strongest conclusion from the past record of small-scale peasant agriculture is that smallholders have a high capability in utilizing their land resources and are quickly responsive to new input options and economic opportunities. But wide rural inequalities and environmental insecurities enforce much risk-minimizing behaviour.

From the rapid adoption of new rice-seed technology in irrigated parts of South and East Asia to the effective cultivation of cocoa in West Africa, from the introduction of new forest cover to help regenerate land in Ghana to the successful smallholder Green Revolution in maize in Zimbabwe and output gains on small plots after land reform in Chile, the record is exten-sive in revealing potential dynamism among rural Southern smallholders. Yet, as we have also seen (chapter 4), certain broad failures in agricultural development policies have in many cases, blocked this dynamism and help explain the widening prevalence of rural poverty in many Southern coun-tries.

Thus the most profound reorientation involved in making poverty reduction the fundamental national priority is to stress and to reshape rural development strategy in most Southern countries, emphasizing antipoverty goals as well as output-increase goals. This will mean different particular policy emphases in different circumstances, because the situations facing the agricultural world vary so much both by country and by area within each country. But one over-riding characteristic will have to mark each change in policy thrust, if serious reforms to reduce rural poverty are being sought. The strongest single emphasis of an antipoverty agricultural strat-egy must be its basis in listening to and interacting intensively with local communities of poorer agriculturalists.

This must mean an end to extensive discrimination against rural women. As Speciosa Wandira Kazibwe, vice-president of Uganda, told the 1995 International Food Policy Research Institute meeting on world food planning, "Unless you invest in women farmers you are wasting your time. Women are going to be the engines of change." She stressed that in Uganda 80 per cent of food production was in the hands of women and that women did 60 per cent of the planting, 70 per cent of the weeding, 60 per cent of the harvesting, and 90 per cent of the food processing. "Women must be helped to own land. Until they do we cannot expect them to improve productivity. They need credit, and they will repay it. We have discovered that in one typical project 88 per cent of the women had repaid their loan while not more than 40 of the men had done so."[8]

This emphasis on gender equity must be combined with more stress on environmental challenges. Again and again, Southern governments (and Northern aid donors) have ignored the issue of environmental sustainability of smallholder livelihoods in manipulating access to and control of Southern country natural resources. The Honduras case of eight large foreign shrimp companies dominating shrimp development and wiping out indigenous coastal artisanal fisheries is one example. The way in which timber concessions granted in Sarawak undercut sustainable peasant farm communities and polluted local rivers is another. Rainfall declines to Manya Krobo peasant farms in Ghana, caused by the elimination of tree breaks against dry Sahara winds as a result of flooding brought on by the construction of the huge Volta River Dam, represent another example. Environmental destruction of the fragile ecology of Amazonian rain forests by Brazilian slash-and-burn agriculture has been a particularly tragic mistake.[9] The major inadequacies in relocating Indian families affected by flooding from the Sardar Sarovar Dam on the Narmada River are another classic example of environmental damage to many poor households. They were grave enough that they eventually led the World Bank to exit from the project.[10]

The absence of control by women over land resources has had major detrimental environmental effects in Kenya and Zimbabwe, for instance (see chapter 4). The inability of southern Zimbabwe women to sell cattle when drought conditions required it was seen to have cost households thousands of cattle and millions of dollars in assets; and the blockage of Embu women in Kenya by men when it came to tree-planting prevented efforts at land reclamation and fuelwood replenishment there. The case of Solomon Islands women who were able to use their control over fishing rights to insist on preservation measures that protected the whole fishery shows how greater gender equity can contribute to environmental sustainability.[11]

Complex debates are taking place about how best to understand the nature of gender inequalities. Shahrashoub Razavi and Carol Miller, for instance, contrast approaches that focus especially on the separate economic role of women, as distinct from approaches underlining the complex connections of men and women interacting in co-operative and competitive ways within the mutually interdependent household.[12] But there is no question that national policy-makers in most Southern countries have neglected questions of women's land tenure rights in agriculture, instead orienting agricultural extension services towards male farmers, and have skewed rural credit highly against women in peasant production. These failures have often created or perpetuated the environmental discrimination experienced by women and in particular cases have led to rural development project failures because of lack of attention to the realities of male-female farm relations.

Fundamental reorientations are needed in both gender-equity priorities and environmental concerns and in the relationship between these two elements of revised antipoverty agricultural strategy. Rural environmental degradation is often the major ongoing threat to long-term agricultural viability, especially for the poor. Richer farmers may have the capacity to escape for longer periods of time from growing environmental pressures, by shifting to more exotic (and capital-intensive) crops for export (such as specialist fruits) and by increasing their use of high-priced inputs of fertilizers. But poor farmers, particularly women, will face the downward spiral of overused, lower productivity land seen in Sarawak, Embu (Kenya), or southern Honduras. The deforestation evident in Ghana, Ethiopia, and Brazil will hurt their livelihoods. An activist and well-supported rural environmental strategy, comprising components such as tree-planting, protection from negative competitive resource use, and safeguarding of water resources, should be implemented with major peasant input. There also needs to be a special focus on gender-equity goals. These reorientations underline the importance of the South African efforts to highlight women's concerns through the special women's offices with parliaments and legislatures, in which female ANC and other legislators are organizing together to see that liberation also means working for gender equity. It is also why the women's organizations in Northern Ghana are such a major positive sign of change in the way they are working hard within the water and sanitation committees.

Both gender equity and environmental considerations also need to be key concerns in future rural development policy in the context of the Green Revolution. The 1995 IFPRI Conference on Future Food Supplies noted that waterlogging and nutrient imbalances were becoming a Green Revolution problem in some parts of Asia, but scientists from Cornell University and the Hunan Hybrid Rice Research Centre in China described research that could achieve 15 to 20 per cent increases in rice yields, despite this.[13] Women, however, have become the main producers in agriculture in China, but land division based on the lower points they received in the past on commune work teams, as well as loss of land rights in traditional marriage relations, reduces returns and incentives for them from the agricultural sector.[14]

The main additional challenges in Green Revolution policies lie in the differentiated impact of the new seeds and in reliance on higher fertilizer inputs. In the case of wheat, irrigation has clearly been a crucial basis of improvement, and the reliance on tubewells and other relatively expensive irrigation sources has skewed wheat benefits heavily in favour of wealthier farmers. Small producers were seen to have gained much less in India, and the dominance of large farmers led to investment in machinery to handle the larger crops that badly cut employment opportunities for landless labourers. The wheat Green Revolution in India, Pakistan, and Mexico has deepened rural poverty for many people already on the margins economically. The maize Green Revolution in Zimbabwe and Ghana also failed to help overcome poverty. Maize production among African smallholders in Zimbabwe concentrated its gains among a small minority of three Shona parts of the country, while most peasants in the drier areas gained little. In Ghana crop outputs did increase more widely among smallholders, but marketing structures were not in place to reward producers for the marked production increases, and government policy had not stressed local storage facilities; price increases for fertilizers also hurt maize expansion efforts. Even in the case of rice, where micro-studies showed local community and regional results that tended to benefit all levels of society, including the poor, the bias of rice gains at a broader level towards areas of irrigated agriculture (where fertilizer could be best used) meant that many poorer producers in drier rain-fed areas and in monsoon flood plains continued to experience rural poverty — whether in Bangladesh, in many parts of India, or in more remote, upland parts of China. This is even more so the case in situations in which the crops stressed by local farmers are items such as yams (in Ghana) or tef (in Ethiopia), in which international research programs for new seeds have not been stressed — or in which intercropping makes sense in the local environmental context between crops that benefit from fertilizer inputs (like high-yield maize) and other crops that are hurt by such inputs (like cassava).

This is not to suggest that the Green Revolution, with its large overall food production gains, is on balance a development policy failure. But there are rural poverty-policy failures within the implementation pattern of the new seed/high input technology that should be corrected. As Kothari puts it in the context of India, "The Green Revolution may have provided a major breakthrough for nations wanting to achieve self-sufficiency as well as for raising the status of agriculture in national priorities, [but] there is need to adopt these practices with conscious care and to adapt them to fulfil social goals. They must substantially raise employment and the incomes of the poor, not just aggregate output."[15]

A policy priority should be to root Green Revolution technology in the local context. Interaction between local communities and national agricultural research institutions and their extension personnel will draw on developed Green Revolution knowledge and adapt it locally. But as stressed by Amanor in the context of Ghana, the overriding goal should be to develop farm extension expertise that can work with farmers, draw on their insights, and help broaden the knowledge that farmers themselves are developing so that wider numbers of farm producers can make use of this knowledge faster.[16] This represents a more farmer-centred method of drawing on innovative ideas, both local and imported. Amanor makes the point for the areas he is studying that women own or lease almost as much farmland as men and that the national extension service must therefore respond to them too.[17]

Perhaps the fundamental Green Revolution antipoverty goal in many Southern countries, though, is to take on land redistribution. There is a wide scope for major land reform in Latin America, many parts of Asia, and some important areas in Africa. Earlier (chapter 4) we have noted the particularly inequitable cases — such as the 2.5 per cent of Guatemala's farms controlling 65 per cent of all agricultural land, leaving 75 per cent of the population below the poverty line, the 6,500 white settlers who farm half the good agricultural land in Zimbabwe, or the 87 per cent of the best agricultural land in South Africa owned by a mainly white 10 per cent of the population — as well as the marked success of the land redistributions in Korea and in China in reducing the prevalence of rural poverty. Certain states in India, such as Kerala, have also been successful in improving nutritional standards and living conditions across the whole population through a land reform that created 1.5 million new small landowners (out of a population of 27 million).[18]

Appropriate policies will vary by country, and even by region within countries. But the evidence is strong that land redistribution is crucial to significant antipoverty efforts in many circumstances when combined with Green Revolution innovations, and that such tenure changes can bring about important social and economic gains, with wide benefits beyond the rural poor.

Such redistribution policies in many countries should also focus on rural infrastructure, in a reversal of past priority given to urban (and/or industrial and export-crop) areas. This problem remains especially severe in Africa. It is only possible to reach many villages in Ghana, for instance, by footpaths. In Tanzania the rich Ulanga farming area remained cut off by impassable rivers and mud-blocked roads for a third of the year. In Mozambique and Angola, low colonial expenditures and subsequent civil wars meant only very loose links within the country. In Latin America many villages in the Andes and in the Amazon area are isolated. Meanwhile, four-lane freeways carry drivers from international airports to capital cities, and roads to export-crop cocoa areas in West Africa and tea and coffee areas in East Africa remain good. Poor infrastructure often extends to storage facilities, supply sources for seed and fertilizer inputs, and limited health and education resources to support rural households.

The results of poor transportation and communication access worsen what are often already major national policy biases against non-cash crop exports. Sometimes, as in Kenya, this bias involves bans against food-crop movement from one district to another, to maintain insider monopolies that keep prices low to food farmers by preventing any competition. Sometimes, as in Ghana, competition is simply missing, because it is so difficult to reach food-crop farmers that any middleman who does penetrate remote areas can sell inputs at high prices and buy outputs at low prices, because nobody else is likely to show up as a counter-bidder. Getting access to rural credit in such circumstances is also especially difficult for the rural small-holder (which is why the successes in getting rural credit to women in rural Bangladesh have been so important). These particular problems tend to be part of a larger bias shown by many Southern countries, whereby they establish national pricing policies for crops in attempts to keep the prices of food crops low to maintain political stability in urban areas and try to tax away a significant portion of cash-crop export revenues in order to finance other state expenditures. Add to these factors the ISI privileges that commonly raised basic consumer goods prices, while rural farm prices were being squeezed, and the fundamental inequities of much past Southern agricultural policy appear clear.

Rajni Kothari stresses that an antipoverty approach does not always have to be pursued through broad national policies, since many states may run up against strong social forces that make universal implementation difficult. He outlines "a whole series of small and localized efforts that question macro thinking" and points out that these "open up spaces and create hope" in India.[19]

But policy change cannot just occur at the local level if the rural poor are really to improve their positions. That is why he also stresses rural industrialization, high priority for environmental improvements for marginal agriculture, and improving education for the rural poor (especially young girls) to establish a greater sense of dignity and challenge to those in power. These points are all part of changing priorities by supporting smallholders, stressing the environment, and working towards gender equity to overcome poverty.

The education focus deserves special emphasis. Poverty analyses of 15 Southern countries by the World Bank in 1995 indicated that rural poverty was far more serious than urban poverty in 80 per cent of the cases studied, and that women or women-headed households were particularly disadvantaged by rural poverty conditions. The report identified serious rural education gaps for the poor (either in terms of lower enrolment levels, decreasing education expenditures, or poorer quality facilities compared to urban schools). These countries included such large Latin American nations as Brazil and Argentina, such African cases as Kenya, Zambia, Senegal, and

Ghana, and such Asian examples as Sri Lanka.[20] That is why Canadian development assistance, for instance, is placing special support on projects to improve the access of girl children to education.

2: New Industrial Directions

In a rural-centred strategy, it might be expected that the main policy implication for the industrial sector would be to reduce its size, eliminate its state privileges, and reorient credit and infrastructure provision in the direction of the countryside.

Taking that course, though, would ignore the existence of complementarities between industrial and agricultural expansion, such as the provision of lower-cost basic consumer goods and farm implements that encourage rural development. Also, with a greater emphasis placed on national food-crop production and less on export crops in agriculture, a more dynamic export performance by small Southern industrial enterprises can help meet the goals of maintaining macroeconomic balance. Despite the importance of rural poverty concerns in many Southern countries, the dramatic expansion of people in Southern cities (from less than 300 million in 1950 to 1.2 billion in 1990) means that employment issues associated with small enterprises are often important antipoverty policy considerations.[21]

Gender equity issues require special attention in urban areas, where women experience major poverty concerns, especially in the informal sector. As Joekes concludes (see chapter 5), women in the informal sector in Southern countries have incomes and working conditions that are significantly worse than elsewhere in the urban economy, and yet the great majority of women work in that sector (despite the attention that Joekes devotes to EPZs, where women workers have been expanding their presence).

Some of the major policy directions taken by Southern countries in industrial strategy need to be subjected to basic questioning. In particular, many Southern governments erected high and growing trade barriers to encourage the establishment of (usually) large-scale ISI enterprises. The problems with this approach have been well documented: with uncompetitive cost patterns persisting for the protected manufacturing process (preventing any ongoing export success and raising local consumer prices); and with consequent selection of highly capital-intensive production technology (with low job spin-offs) being made in this highly protected context. Special help in the form of state financing often added to this encouragement of high-priced, capital-intensive equipment.

This pattern usually added significantly to adverse poverty trends by raising prices for basic consumer items for the poor, limiting urban formal-sector job opportunities, and encouraging state support to the ISI sector rather than to the poorer rural parts of the country. The large-scale ISI strategy was also strongly biased against women workers. An examinination of the data from various perspectives (such as Boserup's more market-oriented view or Saffioti's structuralist/dependency framework) came to the same conclusion: that ISI industrialization "led to the systematic exclusion of women from the industrial labour force."[22]

A second choice, usually intertwined with this large-scale ISI strategy, was to rely on foreign multinational corporations to lead the ISI process. A strategic drive carried MNCs into many Southern countries to try to win dominant positions in local markets by setting up producing subsidiaries, and their advantages of control over technology and access to capital (and marketing expertise) gave them a powerful leverage in winning privileges from Southern governments. The benefits of these privileges could then be shared with local "insiders" in the political economy (see chapter 7), while the state provided import protection, state loans, and regulatory support to the MNCs.[23]

This MNC reliance could have even more negative effects on the poor, as MNC industry undercut small-scale, labour-intensive local competitors through heavy advertising and state manipulation of tax measures. This adverse MNC impact on small-scale soap and shoes enterprises in Kenya was clear, even though the small firms were providing more jobs per unit of output, were located more in rural areas, had more local linkage spinoffs, and were providing low-cost basic consumer items important to the poor.[24]

This detrimental MNC effect could be even more devastating, however, where parent companies neglected basic social commitments, as in the Bhopal case in India. In Bhopal, the U.S. multinational Union Carbide built a huge pesticide complex, employing thousands of people. In 1984 the plant developed a toxic leak that eventually covered a 25-square-mile area, killed some 2,500 people, and injured at least 70,000 more. Most of these people were in the poor shantytown around the plant. The evidence seems clear that Union Carbide knew of safety problems at the plant, failed to act on them (despite having acted on similar problems in its U.S. plants), owned over 50 per cent of the plant capital, controlled key management decisions at the plant, and yet was able to escape any liability for the disaster in the U.S. court system.[25]

A third key decision for many Southern countries has been to use Export Processing Zones as a major mechanism for trade policy shifts to export-oriented manufacturing — from the Maquiladora system in Mexico to the EPZs that now mark most Asian economies. Just as ISI represented the isolating out of particular single manufacturing processes to try to carry on locally, so the logic of the EPZ is to draw in materials and technology from all over the world and try to shape particular single manufacturing processes to carry on using local labour. The distorting impact on the internal economy of the Southern country is not as great as with the ISI "hothouse" cultivation (as Lipton put it), but the dynamic relationship with the rest of the economy and the spread effects to poor people not employed in the EPZs are likely to be truncated, just as much ISI was. It is also common to have unregulated air and water pollution problems associated with EPZ enterprise, as the laissez-faire trade philosophy of the zones is matched by governmental neglect of environmental rules. These zones tend to rely heavily on women employees, unlike the ISI industrialization model, but this seems to be tied particularly to the much lower wages that can be paid to women than to men who have already had more experience with wage-bargaining in the ISI sectors.[26] There has been little sign over time that these large wage differentials between men and women in Southern industrial sectors have declined much, even as the EPZs have expanded.

Overall, what has been taking place is a basic decision by the "insiders" dominating many Southern countries and their powerful corporate and political allies in the North that an advanced-technology, large-scale industrial sector, tied increasingly by export links to the global industrial system, would be transferred to the South. That basic choice relies on some inputs from the poor, particularly for less-skilled labour (especially from women) in the EPZs, but it excludes the great majority of those in poverty in the South. Those who are marginalized in this way in the urban areas become the members of the diverse, insecure, and rapidly expanding informal sector.

The crucial question then becomes whether an alternate policy path exists — or is the alternative simply to dismantle ISI and its formal-sector privileges and choose a neo-liberal course that lets the market correct past inequities?

Certainly there are those who argue that the informal sector is no source of urban economic dynamism, but a residual low-productivity sector that "does not provide the comprehensive solution to the difficulty in attaining accelerated growth in Ghana and many other African economies."[27] But other analysts, such as Macharia in Kenya, see more potential for creative informal-sector expansion, given changes in the Kenyan industrial policies that have promoted larger-scale ISI through harassment of informal-sector enterprises. As we have also seen (chapter 5), a United Nations analysis indicated that independent small-scale women's enterprises in the informal sector make a vital contribution to national economies and to widening women's economic opportunities. Economic development policy in Botswana (with its consistently high per capita growth rates) has even aimed at cross-the-board credit support for indigenous small-scale enterprise, with the expectation that small firms meeting objective criteria to obtain loans would achieve job expansion benefiting the poor.

In practice, such uncritical support for the informal sector has proved questionable. Kaplinsky provides a detailed analysis of this non-target-based Botswana approach, revealing it to be a major failure. Within five years only half of the small-scale enterprises could even be found. His conclusion is that without careful attention to technology choice questions and to marketing strategies, the new small enterprises could not achieve their objectives — and those key points were what the neo-liberal Botswana approach neglected.[28]

For Kaplinsky, then, the heart of an alternative industrial policy is a strategy of appropriate technology choice and of significant governmental support for such choices. His work shows how small-scale choices, with greater local employment effects, more linkages to the local economy, and more positive environmental impacts, are often available — as with the cases of bread production in Kenya, small-scale cement manufacturing in China, and small-scale sugar refining in India. Advanced-technology alternatives from the industrial countries exist in these cases and will provide market dominance to large-scale firms that can pre-empt production. Yet the small-scale alternative is not just more appropriate in social and antipoverty terms but also carries important economic advantages in efficiency of production and lower-cost provision of basic needs to the poor. In India, for instance, the country could be producing its sugar requirements from 2,682 small plants with 836,784 workers, or from 327 large plants with 284,490 workers and 41 per cent greater capital investment. In Kenya, 81 small-scale plants employing 25,920 could be providing national sugar needs, as opposed to 2.6 large plants with 4,420 workers and 3.7 times more capital investment.[29] The same choice exists between decentralized jobs versus centralized capital investment in the case of bread production in Kenya.

Kaplinsky stresses that movement in the direction of such appropriate technology is going to involve more than just dismantling past ISI privileges. Arguing for an "AT-enabling state," he points out that activist efforts will be needed to assist entrepreneurs in the search for smaller-scale technologies, to shift incentives against powerful foreign-oriented, larger-scale enterprise units, to encourage greater indigenous technological capacity by stressing technology transfer in disembodied terms that favour absorption and adaptation (such as purchase of know-how through arms-length contracts), and to discourage product choice that forces highly capital-intensive, large-scale production techniques.[30]

Beyond these areas of emphasizing appropriate technology, two other policy areas of concern stand out. First, just as with smallholder agriculture, access to credit appears to be a major blockage. There are, after all, massive differences in interest rates facing small-scale versus large-scale enterprises. Micro-enterprises from Asia, Africa, and Latin America have all identified this imbalance as a crucial impediment, a point that makes the case for special lending efforts to small enterprise, though this would have to be undertaken in the reviewed way that seems to have been successful with PAMSCAD in Ghana, rather than the laissez-faire vacuum that failed so badly in Botswana. This is also one of the areas in which strong legal regulations are needed to ensure equitable opportunities for women. Wage discrimination and unequal job access have both been identified, too, as problems for women in the industrial sector. Such inequalities persist even in China, where women's labour-force participation is particularly high.[31]

Finally, Aryeetey makes the point that encouraging and building stronger connections between informal-sector enterprises and larger commercial enterprises could improve the wider impact of small firms in the economy. The gap that exists here, he suggests, is part of the reason that informal sector enterprises have not been able to achieve export successes — and stronger indigenous commercial firms with international links could provide that connection.[32] If there is to emerge an alternative to EPZs that can be more effectively tied to widening economic benefits for the poor in Southern countries, the success of informal-sector enterprises in moving in this direction may be an essential goal.

3: A Strategy for Radical Change

The elements of a fundamental reorientation of direction in many Southern countries, as sketched here, are radical, in that they represent a profound shift of priorities from the old, centralized, elite-based vision of modernization for the small minority — which has brought mass poverty, slow growth, and wide inequalities to many Southern societies. The vision that democratization opens up is a gender-balanced, rural-centred, green, bottom-up spread of broad-based opportunities and action against poverty.

But is such a vision a political possibility? Is there a political economy process of change that could bring about such a reorientation? The answers to these questions bring together the two broad themes outlined earlier: the dynamics of democratic change in most Southern countries, and the emergence of civil society movements in the political and social space opened up by democratization.

As Albert Hirschman put it in his book *A Bias for Hope*, "The fundamental bent of my writings has been to widen the limits of what is or is perceived to be possible. ... One important way of rekindling perception and imagination and of developing an alertness to dialectical, as opposed to purely cumulative, social processes is to pay attention to the unintended consequences of human actions."[33] Indeed, entirely contrary to what might have been expected, the external economic shocks of the 1980s, the agricultural and industrial policy failures that these shocks revealed, and the need to respond more effectively to the autonomy-threatening interventions of the IFIs led many Southern countries to democratize their governmental structures. The rise of new community-based movements outside the state both spurred on and reflected this democratic change, in the process providing significant new social actors in Southern political economies: popular groups based in rural communities, women's organizations working for gender equity, environmental movements, and urban associations pulling together those in the informal sector.

The basic strategy for radical reorientation, then, becomes a continuing process involving the cumulative interaction between national-level democratization and community-based efforts for change by these civil society movements, aiming at different aspects of poverty reduction. The community-based efforts become not only learning experiences at the micro-level, helping to identify specific policies and tactics that are more effective in countering poverty, gender inequalities, and environmental degradation, but also political initiatives highlighting the importance of these concerns on the national policy agenda of the society. Links among these community-based and civil society groups also develop, helping to work through differences in the priorities and understandings of the dynamics of the political economy. Alliances may even be built among community-based organizing groups, involving joint approaches to participatory impact assessment to ensure that efforts aimed at fighting poverty at that level are actually having their desired effects.[34]

Democratic institutions such as parliaments can play an important role in helping community-based organizations make the transition of broad reorientation of priorities from the local to the national level. ANC Members of Parliament in South Africa, for instance, have close ties with particular civil society organizations (such as individual trade unions, farm organizations, or women's groups); part of their role is to connect government into the ongoing dialogue within these groups and in turn to channel insights from local work into broader governmental decision-making. Members of Parliament in Lebanon are also involved in continuing policy dialogue with social policy movements in that country. Ghanaian MPs on the parliamentary finance committee are discussing outreach meetings with various rural community organizing groups in that country.[35] Parliaments are made up of elected representatives who often have close personal contacts with civil society movements at the local level as part of their democratic role (unlike bureaucrats or centrally chosen presidents and government leaders). This contact gives parliaments the potential intermediary role of connecting government to a growing, dynamic drive for reorientation that is achieving bottom-up momentum.

The challenge at the national level nevertheless is still to achieve the formation of a successful political force that represents a continuing coalition for radical change, interacting with the community-based and civil society movements working for reorientation. Such a reformist political movement faces fundamental challenges. It will have to gain autonomy from the powerful social and economic forces that have benefited from the insider-based, centralized, large-scale urban privileges of past policies. Otherwise, as in the Kenyan case (see chapter 6), policy changes may be announced, but the old powerful social forces at the top effectively block them, and poverty persists or worsens.

Above all, the reformist political coalition must build a constituency in those rural areas in which successful reorientation will mean most in overcoming poverty. If reformist forces are not able to capture strong support in the countryside, in a democratic context a fundamental reorientation will not proceed. Yet the democratic context is crucial to making the basic reorientation a political economy possibility. Capturing that rural constituency becomes essential to significant change.

Building a rural-based constituency for broad change over a sustained period of time is far from easy. As Herbst notes in discussing Ghana, historic political loyalties persist (built on past urban-rural splits involving high taxes on export-crop producers), and these may undercut efforts to build a poverty-oriented rural base less tied to that export-crop pattern.[36] In other places particularistic loyalties in rural areas (of religion, caste, or local ethnic language) may make it especially difficult to capture a comprehensive rural base. In addition, social differentiation remains important in many rural communities, and it can lead to patron-client relations that inhibit poor smallholders from voting with their own socioeconomic interests in mind.

Nevertheless, this framework of political economy analysis does suggest a viable basis for successfully achieving fundamental reorientation. Some cases may even emerge that suggest that what is feasible in theory is also practical. South Africa is clearly an example of how a national political force can come to govern with antipoverty policies in close interaction with community-based civil society movements that sustain and further those political reorientations.[37] In India community-based organizations for rural change and civil society movements have made strong continuing efforts to challenge the status quo. In 1996-97 this campaign led to a radical reform coalition briefly taking power in New Delhi (albeit with Congress Party support), and some of the state-level efforts in Kerala and West Bengal (and elsewhere) towards land reform, more environmental concern, and support for the poor became reflected at the national level. In Ghana, too, the success of the National Democratic Congress government in winning major support in rural areas (including some parts of formerly opposition-loyal Ashanti region) in the 1996 elections confirmed the pro-rural infrastructure strategy that has reduced poverty significantly in the country, especially in rural areas (see chapter 6).

All of this analysis, of course, assumes that the governmental structure in most Southern countries retains an ability to implement a fundamental reorientation in priorities, given continuing global economic pressures and external IFI leverage. As the 1997 World Bank's World Development Report stresses, a growing pessimism has mounted in recent years about the role of the state and state policy in Southern countries in providing leadership that would reshape development directions. "The pendulum had swung ... to the minimalist state," the Bank notes. Yet the Bank has argued that this new orthodoxy went too far. "As often happens with such radical shifts in perspectives, countries sometimes tended to overshoot the mark," resulting in "neglect of the state's vital functions, threatening social welfare and eroding the foundations for market development.

"The consequences of an overzealous rejection of government have shifted attention from the sterile debate of state versus market to a more fundamental crisis in state effectiveness. ... Development without an effective state is impossible."[38]

Building a more effective state is a difficult challenge, especially when development strategy aims at poverty reduction, social equity, and long-term environmentally sustainable growth, not just at short-run increases in GNP. This "governance challenge" is partly a matter of not neglecting crucial policy concerns (such as how to maintain macroeconomic balance), partly a question of restructuring governmental institutions (especially involving decentralization of state functions), and partly an issue of changing how governmental institutions work (particularly to make them more transparent and responsive to people in their operations).

The impact of macroeconomic crises can be devastating for Southern countries. Balance of payments gaps can block off key import needs and undercut rural producers. High and continuing national budget deficits, financed by internal monetary expansion, can set off spirals of hyperinflation, which hit the poor especially hard. Long-term and high levels of foreign borrowing as a response to foreign currency needs can set off a heavy reliance on external investors and cause periodic economic downturns (as in Mexico and parts of Asia) that devastate the living standards of small-scale rural and urban households. All of these imbalances can draw in IFIs on very tough terms that limit national autonomy, and they can enforce major social expenditure reductions that set back poverty, gender equity, and environmental priorities.

Training workshops for parliamentarians on macroeconomic concerns, professional upgrading of skills in finance departments, and strong roles for analytically skilled central banks are important steps towards building macroeconomic effectiveness. So too are the development of strong macroeconomic policy units within governments — and the expansion of independent economic research institutions within Southern societies. Such macroeconomic policy-depth can convert the IFI dialogue within countries from a threat based on external financial leverage to a valuable mechanism for professional interchange and macropolicy improvement.

Restructuring state institutions for greater effectiveness can also include the streamlining of central government ministries and functions to concentrate the work of an improved, better-paid, higher-morale bureaucracy on a narrower range of especially critical tasks. In addition to achieving macroeconomic balance, the crucial tasks for Southern country states include:

- establishing a foundation of law that is consistently and independently applied;
- investing in key public goods such as education, health, and collective transportation and communication infrastructure; and
- protecting the vulnerable through social assistance and collective security measures.[39]

An effective state will focus on the most important priorities within each of these functional areas to ensure that antipoverty objectives are achieved, rather than carrying forward a vast range of activities in other functional areas or spreading efforts in these functional areas across a wide range of particulars.

Perhaps the major focus of restructuring the state for improved effectiveness is represented by decentralization which is an increasing trend in many Southern countries. In Ghana, for instance, a strong push has been underway to strengthen 104 rural-based district assemblies via a common fund from national revenues to draw on for local development plans. In South Africa, perhaps the most fundamental step yet taken to respond to the inherited inequalities of apartheid is the meshing together of former white and black municipalities into single new local government entities. In Mozambique, decentralization of economic development is seen increasingly as a potential mechanism to boost a rural economy badly damaged by civil war and infrastructure destruction. In Asia too, decentralization to local levels of government has been at the heart of the "people power" change in governance in the Philippines and has also been stressed in Indonesia. Indeed, of the 75 developing countries with populations of over five million, all but 12 have undertaken power shifts to local governments in recent years.[40] But increasing financial pressures, debt problems, and often growing poverty have made this move towards decentralized democracy a complex and challenging process everywhere. New forms of popular participation have emerged in response, and local civil society groupings have come to emphasize new gender and environmental concerns.

The potential direction and dynamism of interaction between these community-based NGOs and economically strengthened decentralized govern-

Diagram 8.1: Northern Ghana and Community-Based Organizations, 1998

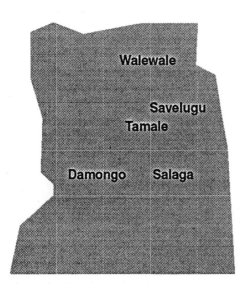

Organization, Goals and Area:

1. JIDA (Juxtapose integrated Development Association), rural intervention planning, Salaga

2. CODEC (Community Devt. Centre) - wildlife/environ-ment work, stress women, Damongo

3. Amasachina - rural devt. health improvements, base is in Tamale, work in many areas

4. SBDU - improve rural plans & infrastructure, NGO & Assembly training, Savel-ugu-Nanton et al.

5. Neighbours in Need - rural impact analysis & planning, Walewale area

ments are apparent in the Northern Region of Ghana. As of early 1998, district assemblies in this poorer part of Ghana were receiving more financial support from the national common fund to undertake local development efforts, and they were beginning to work closely with emerging community-based co-ordinating NGOs in choosing priorities and deciding how best to plan their growing activities. Diagram 8.1 shows a map of the area and some key local NGO co-ordinating groups and where they are active; these groups are co-operating closely together so there is a regional focus to development thinking as well as good contact with the regional minister.[41]

Finally, developing a more effective state is about increasing the democratic accountability of government structures so that people feel a much greater sense of access and responsiveness with respect to state institutions. Gyimah-Boadi notes that an increased transparency of African state operations is provided through timely auditor general's reports, the work of key public watchdog agencies, and the vigour of the independent press in some countries — but that excessive secrecy remains at top levels of government.[42] Kothari points to similar problems of lack of openness and restricted information in India as an impediment to ongoing community-based action against poverty.[43]

Again, the emerging democratic parliaments in many Southern countries may play a crucial role in strengthening the transparency of state institutions, in building accountability and responsiveness of governing authorities to people, and in establishing a greater capacity for outsider social groups to achieve policy reorientations by the government. Strong representatives from disadvantaged regions and poorer social groups can make use of the committee systems of parliaments to probe and highlight their concerns, to articulate the importance of accountability, to dig out key information needed by community-based groups, to act as watchdogs on government ministers and bureaucracies, and to link actions in their constituencies with similar movements for accountability and responsiveness in other parts of a country. In the case of Ghana's Northern Region, for instance, newly elected MP John Mohammed has developed close ties with community-based groups and is able to work effectively in co-operation with them.

In general, Members of Parliament in most Southern legislatures do not experience the same heavy-handed central control from party managers in leaders' offices that characterizes politics in Canada, and so Southern MPs are often much better able to play this creative role in search of greater government responsiveness and information-sharing. They are also more often able to work somewhat independently for the concerns of their constituencies. Thus one finds both government and opposition party members of the Economic Affairs Commission in Mozambique coming together to fight for decentralization of policy-making, which they believe will make the state more effective for the people they represent. Similarly, NDC and opposition NPP members of the public accounts committee in Ghana, gathering in one discussion group, all stressed that they represented rural constituencies and all agreed strongly on policy reorientation to help poorer rural smallholders.

4: Conclusion

Given the deepening poverty and the developmental crisis that most poorer nations experienced from 1980 into the 1990s, a reorientation of priorities in Southern countries is a crucial step in the push to overcome poverty.

A new vision has been emerging from the democratization of much of the South. In place of the failed pattern of top-down, large-scale ISI bene-fiting a privileged minority, this new vision is bottom-up, gender-conscious, small-scale, and green. Dominated by antipoverty goals, the new strategy stresses the role of smallholders and the landless in rural areas and sees small-scale appropriate technology enterprises in the urban informal sector as supplementing this rural emphasis.

In rural areas land reform is often a crucial part of this change pattern, in conjunction with Green Revolution seed innovations that are much more responsive to peasant needs and farming knowledge and in concert with gender equity and environmental goals that bring sustainable agricultural improvements for the whole community. Improved small-scale rural credit, especially for women, and more investment in rural public infrastructure are major parts of the strategy. Continuing support for education is crucial. In urban areas the shift away from foreign MNC reliance and rejection of large-scale ISI puts the emphasis on credit and new marketing linkages for the informal sector, using appropriate technology and more opportunities for women.

This reorientation vision is now not just an idle dream. The interaction of national democratization and community-based civil society movements could make it real in some Southern countries — especially with the reform of state institutions to make them more effective, decentralized, and responsive. The democratic parliaments emerging in many Southern coun-tries could make a significant contribution to the achievement of such a fundamental change. But just as Southern societies have been influenced from the outside for centuries, so too the reorientation of Southern priori-ties is not likely to be an insulated process, secure from outside forces, espe-cially from the North. Canadians will be a part of this interaction, but what sort of role can they play? Will our role be a problem that people working for egalitarian change in the South will have to cope with? Or will Canadi-ans be allies in the effort to realize the new antipoverty vision being pro-moted by Southern democratization?

Notes

1 Kojo Amanor, "Abstract: Future Funding Priorities for the Agricultural Sector," prepared for Ghana Parliamentary Finance Committee, Policy Work-shop, Elmina, Ghana, March 1997.

2 Quoted in Linda Hershkovitz, *China Gender Equity Strategy*. Prepared for CIDA, China Program, May 1995, p.26.

3 Personal interview, Ministry of Civil Affairs, Beijing, China, March 1997.

4 See A. Rahman, "Women, Cultural Ideology, and Change in Rural Bangladesh," *Canadian Journal of Development Studies*, vol. XV, no.3 (1994), pp.438-40.

5 World Bank, "Zimbabwe-Enterprise Development Project," December 1995.

6 Ibid., paragraph 3.

7 "Distribution and Growth: Complements, not Compromises," *World Bank Policy Research Bulletin*, vol. 6, no. 3 (May-July 1995).

8 Quoted in report on meeting, "Forecasting the Future," Internet, People and the Planet Home Page, 1995.

9 See Landim, "Brazilian Crossroads," on the assassination of ecologist and union leader Chico Mendes, p.225.

10 See Sardar Sarovar, *Report of the Independent Review* (Ottawa: Resources Futures International, 1992), esp. pp.180-98.

11 See the cases, as discussed in detail in *Development and Environment*, ed. Ghai, chapter 4.

12 See Shahrashoub Razavi and Carol Miller, "From WID to GAD: Conceptual Shifts in the Women and Development Discourse," Occasional Paper no.1, UN Fourth World Conference on Women, United Nations Research Institute for Social Development (UNRISD), Geneva, February 1995.

13 "Forecasting the Future," Internet, People and the Planet Home Page, 1995.

14 Hershkovitz, "China Gender Equity Strategy," pp.23-24.

15 Kothari, *Poverty*, p.129.

16 Amanor, *The New Frontier*, chapter 7.

17 Ibid., pp.96-99.

18 See Barbara Chasin and Richard Franke, *Kerala: Radical Reform as Development in an Indian State* (California: Institute for Food and Development Policy, 1994), pp.54-56.

19 Kothari, *Poverty*, pp.127-28.

20 World Bank, "Poverty Reduction: the Most Urgent Task."

21 The population figures are from Rakesh Mohan, "Urbanization and the Economy," in *Urban Research in the Developing World*, vol.4, *Perspectives on the City* ed. Richard Stren (Toronto: Centre for Urban and Community Studies, 1995), p.145.

22 Ruth Pearson, "Gender Issues in Industrialization," in *Industrialization and Development*, ed. T. Hewitt et al. (Oxford: Oxford University Press, 1991), p.229.

23 For detailed examples of this process, see D. Gachuki and P. Coughlin, "Structure and Safeguards for Negotiations with Foreign Investors: Lessons from Kenya," in *Industrialization in Kenya*, ed. P. Coughlin and G.K. Ikiara (Nairobi: Heinemann Kenya, 1988), pp.91-111.

24 For details, see Langdon, *Multinational Corporations in the Political Economy of Kenya*, chap.4.

25 Details drawn from Alana Mullaly, "MNC Accountability: A Case Study of the Bhopal Disaster," paper for CD200 course, Trent University, 1997. Based on such sources as Thomas Gladwin, "Environment, Development and Multi-national Enterprise," in *Multinational Corporations, Environment and the Third World*, ed. C.S. Pearson (Durham: Duke University Press, 1987), pp.3-31.

26 See Pearson, ed., *Multinational Corporations, Environment and the Third World*, p. 231.

27 Ernest Aryeetey, "The Potential for Expanded Economic Activity in the Infor-

mal Sector," occasional papers, no.1, Institute of Economic Affairs, Accra, Ghana, March 1996, p.2.

28 Kaplinsky, *The Economics of Small*, pp.177-80.

29 Ibid., pp.113, 118.

30 For an excellent discussion, see Ibid., pp.206-20.

31 Hershkovitz, *China Gender Equity Strategy*, pp.24-25.

32 Aryeetey, "The Potential for Expanded Economic Activity in the Informal Sector," pp.8-10.

33 A.O. Hirschman, *A Bias for Hope* (New Haven: Yale University Press, 1971), pp.28, 34.

34 See E.T. Jackson, "Participatory Impact Assessment for Poverty Alleviation," paper for International Evaluation Conference, Vancouver, November 1995, pp.9-10.

35 Personal discussions with Members of Parliament at Parliamentary Workshop sessions in South Africa (1995), in Ghana (1997), and in Ottawa for those from Lebanon (1997).

36 Herbst, *The Politics of Reform in Ghana*, 1982-1991, pp.86-93.

37 See G. Adler and E. Webster, "Challenging Transition Theory: The Labour Movement, Radical Reform, and Transition to Democracy in South Africa," *Politics and Society*, vol.23, no.1 (1995), pp.75-106.

38 World Bank, *World Development Report 1997: The State in a Changing World*, pp.24-25.

39 Ibid., chapter 3.

40 Patricia McCarney, *Cities and Governance* (Toronto: University of Toronto Press, 1996).

41 This information is drawn from field observation of meetings between local district assembly chief executives and community-based NGOs in Tamale, January 1998.

42 E. Gyimah-Boadi, "Democracy and Governance in Africa: A Preliminary Status Report," *Legislative Alert*, vol.3, no.6 (1996), p.2.

43 Kothari, *Poverty*, p.164.

CHAPTER 9

A New Vision, South and North

I n Indonesia the first half of 1997 saw the climax of the bizarre saga of the rich Bre-X gold mine that never was, leaving behind a bitter spectacle of Canadian corporations in open financial bidding for political influence, each seeking key Indonesian partners able to shape government mine-licensing decisions. A more classic case of foreign corporate-government elite symbiosis to share supposed superprofits could not have been imagined.

Meeting in Northern Ghana in 1995 with local leaders in the poorest part of the country, as they tried to deal with the aftermath of open ethnic killings over control of land and agricultural potential, I heard strong complaints about another new aspect of Canada's North-South role. The Canadian government's aid agency CIDA had provided financial support for a major integrated rural development project covering large areas of the poor region but had then cancelled the project, over the bitter objections of local Ghanaians who had seen hope for the future in what was taking place.

Meanwhile, in a case of what was supposed to have been a Canadian humanitarian effort, the United Nations role in Somalia to try to provide food for the starving and safeguard a ceasefire, personnel in the Canadian military ended up being convicted of torturing and murdering young Somalis rather than building the credibility of the country in a polarizing North-South world.

These three examples suggest that Canada should be seen as part of the global poverty problem for those in the South, not as part of the solution. At the same time though, democratization and the drive for community-based change are bringing more serious efforts to overcome poverty to various Southern countries. Canadians could work with these efforts and strengthen them — or we could tie our country more into global economic forces that have been encouraging much of that poverty and helping it to persist.

Canadians are engaged in a wide range of interactions with Southern countries, and the reality of these ventures is complex. Various Canadian institutions have had a mixed interplay with the Southern change process. There is today a fundamental struggle over the values and visions to be adopted across the world, and this struggle cuts across national boundaries. In practice many Southern social groups and individuals and many Canadians are valued allies in a difficult global battle over basic social and economic priorities.

1: The Canadian Interface with Southern Change

Past Canadian ties with the realities of Southern poverty have revolved around five major direct sorts of connections. Important Canadian direct business investment has gone to various Southern countries. Trade links have been significant in certain cases. Traditional foreign aid projects have taken Canadian contractors and suppliers into conventional roles, setting up new factories and building expensive infrastructure or providing surplus Canadian food supplies in emergency situations. Young people have gone overseas to teach and fill skill gaps through non-governmental organizations such as CUSO (Canadian University Service Overseas) or WUSC (World University Services Canada), and Canadian church missions have promoted the double roles of saving souls and providing schools and health.

Many of these past roles remain important in the Canadian-Southern interface. Huge Canadian resource corporations, such as Noranda, are still operating new mines in countries such as Chile. The shelves of Canadian department stores are dominated by clothing made in Bangladesh, China, and Sri Lanka. A meeting in Ghana with ADRA (the Adventist Development and Relief Agency) finds that its work with small-scale farmers is financed by its church base in Oshawa, Ontario.[1] CUSO, though now limping along with less CIDA financial support, is still sending Canadians to work in Southern countries. But some fundamental changes are evident, and they are increasingly reshaping Canadian-Southern interaction.

One shifting factor in the Canadian North-South mix has been what must be termed a massive reduction in international assistance from CIDA to Southern countries. The legacy of prime ministers Mike Pearson and Pierre Trudeau, who had increased Canada's support for substantial and consistent development aid to Southern countries, was trashed by Liberal and Conservative governments in budget cuts throughout the 1990s. The federal government's "Program Review" in the 1995 Annual Budget cut $1.3 billion dollars from the international assistance allocation over the next three years, taking Canadian aid from what had been just over .5 per cent of our national income in 1976 to .29 per cent of that income in 1997-

98. In absolute terms this meant a yearly drop of support from $2.6 billion in 1994-95 to $2.06 billion in 1997-98.[2] The period 1998-99, would bring a further cut to the international assistance envelope in the Canadian budget, taking the level of Canadian aid to 0.26 per cent of national income, the lowest level in 30 years.[3] As Andrew Clark concludes, "No other major federal program (more than $1 billion per year) has been cut proportionately as much as foreign aid since 1994-95."[4]

Perhaps the most important factor in the new patterns of Canadian North-South connection comes from the explosive growth of Southern-run NGOs and civil society movements. These NGOs, especially in Africa, have increasingly been taking the lead in locally based projects to try to overcome poverty. In Mali, for example, a local NGO became the key organizing link between a users' committee of small-scale farmers and the national agricultural research institute to improve the responsiveness of research to farmers' needs. In Madagascar, local NGOs are working in special participant appraisal reviews of World Bank projects in the country. In Namibia, NGOs played a key role in developing small-scale co-operatives to give African farmers a say in new rural co-operative approaches, rather than leaving all decisions in the hands of four large white-run co-ops. NGOs have also played key roles in co-operative improvements in Uganda and Cameroon.[5] A challenge has therefore emerged for Canadian NGOs to develop viable and equitable partnerships with these important new institutions in Southern countries.

This development of true "partnership" has proved a complex issue for Northern NGOs dealing with the many emerging Southern NGOs, concludes Carmen Malena of the NGO Unit of the World Bank.[6] She identifies six key indicators to assess the viability of such partnerships, such as agreement on mutual goals and values, reciprocal trust, transparency of information between partners, reciprocal accountability in financial terms, understanding of each other's political economy contexts and constraints, and long-term commitment to work together. Based especially on the role of the traditional Canadian and British non-governmental development organizations (NGDOs) she reviewed in Africa, Malena's harsh assessment is, "There are numerous organizational, attitudinal, political and practical factors, both within and outside the NGDO sector, which prevent NGDOs from achieving genuine partnership."[7] Greater financial power in Northern NGO hands, less progressive views than Southern counterparts of how fundamental changes in the South must be, distrust of what Southern NGOs will spend money doing, and home-based pressures for simple, tangible project results all push many traditional Northern NGOs to adopt conventional top-down attitudes in dealing with the new Southern NGOs, Malena says.

Northern NGO failures have also often been conceptual, according to

Jessica Vivian, based on her analysis of NGO work in Zimbabwe. She sees evidence there of a lack of understanding by NGOs of the complexity of environmental problems, of too much emphasis on finding simple "magic bullet" answers to difficult rural development situations, and of too great a reliance on better-off local respondents rather than the poorer members of communities.[8]

Thus another dynamic in the Canadian interaction with Southern countries has been reduced CIDA support for longer-established traditional NGOs and a move to explore other potential institutions for linkages to Southern countries. The traditional NGOs have no longer been seen as working at the creative edge of new thinking about international development questions. Rather, Southern NGOs and civil society institutions themselves have been seen as increasingly important voices to listen to, and new Canadian participant institutions in Southern linkages have emerged as partners able to work with Southern counterparts as genuine partners right from the start, without having to overcome any past baggage of former top-down power relations.[9]

The result has been a shift in CIDA to diversify to include additional new partners to carry forward relations with Southern institutions and civil society movements in the context of changing realities in the South. Although these Canadian organizations often lack longer-term experience in developing countries, they approach their work in Southern countries with open attitudes, with few pre-conceived notions of how things should be run, and consequently with creativity and a willingness to work in an interactive, non-dominating way in projects. Table 9.1 provides an outline of some of the non-traditional participants in development projects in Southern countries in recent years, including illustrations of projects of which they have become part. Virtually all of these institutions have entered the context of North-South interconnections only in very recent years, and all of them have begun to stress an action-research or co-operation-based orientation (from different perspectives) that has given them (and other similar Canadian institutions) a partnership viewpoint on their ties with Southern counterparts. CIDA has undoubtedly drawn such Canadian organizations into their activities to broaden the constituency for the aid program in Canada at a time of budget cutbacks. The result has been a much wider range of mainstream national institutions involved in North-South interaction, rather than mainly specialist development NGOs. This mix enriches and deepens the Canadian interface with Southern countries. The sample of institutions reviewed in this table is involved in a large number of countries (from India to Niger to Brazil in the projects listed in the table, and in many others in projects not noted here). The non-traditional orientation of projects can be seen in the emphasis of many on civil

Table 9-1: Canadian Institutions and Examples of North-South Ties

Name of Institution	Main Activities	Key Southern Ties?	Project Examples
Canadian Urban Institute, Toronto	Urban Research, Planning	1. Philippines	Planning Regional Devt.
		2. Cuba	Reclaiming Havana Parks
Federation of Canadian Municipalities, Ottawa	Urban Liaison, Lobbying	1. South Africa	Governing with NGOs
		2. China	Open Cities trade training
Institute of Public Admin. of Canada (IPAC,) Toronto	Information exchange, discussing public service	1. Uganda	Both cases – Programs on Decentralization
		2. Indonesia	
Villes et Developpement, Montreal	Consortium of 4 university and govt. research groups	1. Niger	Governance issues
		2. Caribbean Basin area	Urban Development
Int'l Cntr. for Human Rgts. & Dem. Devt., Montreal	Promotes Democracy & Human Rights actions	1. Burma	Main areas for human rights work in Asia
		2. Thailand	
North-South Institute, Ottawa	Research & evaluation on Canada's aid policies	Kenya, Sri Lanka, Peru	Assess NGO role in strengthening civil society
Conference Board of Canada, Ottawa	Economic forecasting and international business aid	1. India	Electricity demand study
		2. China	Applied econ. research
Institute on Governance, Ottawa	Government management and consultation systems	1. Philippines	Local government system
		2. Vietnam	Govt. structure reform
Parliamentary Centre, Ottawa	Work with parliamentary committees, training MP's	1. South Africa	Help prov-parl committees
		2. Vietnam	Training parl. committees
Centre for Human Settlement, Vancouver	Research & writing on urban/environment issues	1. China	Urban problems/ environ.
		2. Sri Lanka	Decentralization & govt.
Canadian Labour Mkt. & Productivity Ctr., Ottawa	Building co-operation for Cdn. labour & business	1. Chile	Helping 6 country project on labour-mgmt. links
		2. Argentina	
Ctr. for Community & Urban Studies, Toronto	Research on urbanization, relation to civil society	1. Brazil	How promote participation
		2. South Africa	Governing with NGOs

Source: Interviews with institutions, 1996-97.

society and Southern NGO participation and on decentralization and other governance concerns.

The thrust of many of the projects being undertaken by these non-traditional development institutions reveals a further dynamic in the interface between Canada and Southern countries. CIDA, too, has shifted the focus of a significant portion of its activities. No longer do large dams, railway locomotives, and top-down infrastructure projects dominate CIDA's projects in most Southern countries. While CIDA has less money to spend, and more of its budget has been allocated to business promotion, the agency also now provides active support for human rights improvements and strengthening of democratic institutions through bilateral projects — emphases that were not there in the past. The aid agency has prepared an explicit document to guide its work on human rights, democratization, and good governance, and seeks through projects and other activities to strengthen "democratic institutions in order to develop and sustain responsible government," aiming to "increase popular participation in decision-making."[10] This new orientation within CIDA is strongly consistent with the movement towards democracy in most Southern countries and has led the agency to provide good support for improving the effectiveness of democratic parliaments — one of the institutions playing a pivotal role in connecting community-based civil society movements for change and national trends towards democratization and reorientation of priorities to counter poverty. Financial support for the International Centre for Human Rights and Democratic Development, based in Montreal and active in fighting abusive regimes in Asia, Latin America, and Africa, is also a remarkable Canadian contribution to the wider momentum towards democratization. The International Development Research Centre (IDRC), with its mandate to reinforce Southern institutions that can build up the basis for greater technological capacity in Southern countries, is another extraordinary organization for a Northern country to have kept supporting since the early 1970s, even if financial support for that body has also been reduced recently.

Beyond these official institutional ties, the links of Canadian groups and individuals to the Southern process of reorientation are equally important. Some connections are personal and include immigrant family remissions to relatives abroad. Some are organizational. The Canadian labour movement, for instance, played an important linkage role through representatives based in Southern Africa in supporting the overthrow of apartheid in South Africa. Support groups for the people of East Timor are widespread and active in Canada. Links over the years have developed between various Canadian universities and Southern countries. The University of Saskatchewan in Saskatoon, for instance, worked closely with the National University of Lesotho to improve milk marketing policy and associated training of African researchers. Trent University has programs for its under-graduate students to work with Southern NGOs in Ecuador, Thailand, and Ghana as part of an academic year abroad. Aboriginal groups interconnect across the globe, women's organizations make connections back and forth (through Ottawa-based "Match International," for example), and environ-mental alliances have been made internationally (to fight World Bank financing of the Sardar Sarovar Dam, for instance). Even children's rights linkages have developed as young Canadians have responded to the death of Asian children fighting the long hours and coercive servitude of carpet-making in the unregulated capitalism of Pakistan and India.

Business links, too, continue to grow. Some have had human rights ben-efits that they have ultimately accentuated — as with how the Canadian government eventually used Canadian-owned subsidiaries in South Africa to promote a "Corporate Code of Conduct" that undercut many of the unjust rules and inequities of apartheid in the labour market. But other economic ties have represented less easy challenges to establish. Trade agreements with Southern countries that help stabilize the international terms of trade for raw material exports would assist in countering poverty. So would competition laws that prevented foreign corporations from imposing conditions on their subsidiaries (such as tie-in clauses for pur-chase of inputs, restrictions on freedom to export, and technology require-ments to use imported parent company machinery). Ending special trade import restraints against poorer Southern countries (on their clothing exports, for instance) would help overcome poverty, too. So too would debt relief that extended to loans from the IMF and the World Bank in cases of heavy repayment burdens.

But Canadians are not going to achieve such changes by themselves. And these days U.S. policies are especially inward-looking and unrespon-sive to such long-term global interests. In the end, then, the Canadian-Southern interface may ultimately focus around three other strands of interconnection, each intertwined with these penetrating powers of global markets that are also tying the globe together. One strand is simply the power of transnational communication, as linkages of all kinds, from radios in remote villages to the versatility of the Internet, increasingly bring common images and similar themes into all parts of the world. A second strand is environmental pressures transcending national boundaries, from the potential impact of ozone degradation to the sweep of Chernobyl's poisons across all of Europe. And a third strand is the gradual global response to these overriding pressures. This last strand represents the values that cut across the North-South divide and mean that, in the end, the response to global poverty must be a new global vision of international justice.

The immediate process of change in Southern countries is likely to be mainly internal and aimed at reorientation of national policies. This long-term process of change at the world level is likely to be difficult and to require a confrontation of values and vision that is basic and fundamental. That is the confrontation that lies ahead, both South and North. The multifaceted complexities of the Canadian-Southern relationship will present Canadians with an important role in understanding and participating in that global clash of perspectives.

2: Conflicting Visions, South and North

The decade of the 1990s has been a time of contrasting pain and promise for the dispossessed of the world. As the UNICEF *Report on Child Poverty* noted, poverty prevails among the young in almost all the larger countries of South Asia and Africa and has been growing in the larger countries of Latin America. Mass refugee movements and starvation have marked Central Africa, Somalia, the Balkans, and much of Central America. Environmental pressures, huge land ownership imbalances, and gender inequalities have expanded rural poverty in many Southern countries.

Yet some fundamental social and political improvements have taken place in the world. The overthrow of white racist supremacy in South Africa, with relatively limited bloodshed and a movement to democracy, has been a staggering historical transition. The dramatic expansion of democratic institutions throughout most Southern countries, combined with the new dynamism of civil society movements, should be seen as the prelude to basic policy reorientations that will help overcome mass Southern poverty in many areas. The new emphasis on gender equity and environmental security in many Southern nations is helping strengthen global changes in attitude.

But what this combination of pain and promise also points to is severe divisions in the broad visions of different social groupings in the world. Just as Rajni Kothari analyses "Two Indias" — the privileged who shape decisions in their own interests and the "outsiders" with little share and no real say in their society's future — so too are there increasingly "Two Worlds," with two different visions and sets of values in our global society.

One is the privileged world of high consumption, large-scale global economic business activity, and access to political power and its parallel media clout. That is a world in which a corporate-financed think tank like the right-wing Fraser Institute announces to wide media coverage that Canada has fallen to fourteenth in the World Economic Freedom Index, based on "factors which measure infringements of basic economic freedoms, such as the freedom of exchange, the freedom to keep one's earnings, and the freedom to own private property and use it for personal and commercial purposes."[11] First place is held by Hong Kong, which has not ever had the right to elect its own government. Second is Singapore, where opposition candidates are systematically harassed to prevent any counter party from emerging in elections, and it is illegal to chew gum; rising to fifth place in 1997 is Mauritius, where the election of a new government with increased ties to Islamic fundamentalism has led to the flight of the owner of the main opposition newspaper into exile in Canada, after his printing presses were destroyed.[12] "Freedom," in this world, is the ability of a narrow notion of "economic man" (or woman) to make and keep as much material wealth as possible secure from state regulation or interference. This concept of "freedom" is part of the same vision that saw former British Prime Minister Margaret Thatcher declare there is no such thing as "society" — there are just individuals. Economic freedom for these individuals, the neo-liberal vision proclaims, will lead to prosperity. Thus the Fraser Institute argues, "Countries that have striven for increases in economic freedom — and maintained such policies (especially in the Lesser Developed Countries) — have measured positive growth rates in real GDP over the period measured."[13]

This narrow economic vision of individualism as supreme explains why neo-liberal political thinking so distrusts the state, because neo-liberal analysts cannot conceive of anyone in a state-based position behaving in terms of "public duty" or "community responsibility." Public servants or political representatives (from this perspective) can do nothing else but act as individuals trying to maximize their own personal well-being or status. Within the marketplace economy, such behaviour is fine, this vision suggests, because competition from other economic actors constantly acts as a check on personal goals, with such competition enforcing marketplace efficiency and encouraging innovation and investment as outlets for personal advancement — which in turn will have broad benefits for everyone in the rest of the market system. But such behaviour among bureaucrats in the state is inefficient there (the viewpoint insists), because no competitive checks exist — which therefore requires a dramatic reduction of the state role.

In the microeconomic textbooks, this vision has an inherent logic to it. It fits together with consistency, and it can even be extended to macroeconomic analysis for the overall economy by suggesting that the crucial broad context required for such market efficiency and encouragement of innovation is a macro-situation in which there are the fewest possible uncertainties in the system to upset entrepreneurs and investors. Hence, it makes most sense to keep things completely predictable by avoiding budget deficits, by keeping the expansion of the money supply relatively low and under the control of an independent central banking authority uninfluenced by social or political concerns, and by avoiding balance of payments shifts by running a stable foreign exchange rate. Increasingly, this vision has drawn the conclusion that you can only achieve this "steady-state" form of macro-stabilization by maintaining a fairly high rate of unemployment. This contingency prevents excessive demand for goods and services from the higher wages which fuller employment might bring on, and thereby avoids the inflationary pressures that such consumer demand increases might set off.

As Manor's review of this neo-liberal vision notes, the fundamental flaw in the theoretical perspective is that the real world is much more complex and "messy" than this stylized textbook model. In particular, the model soon breaks down badly when discrimination and inequality are built into the system from the beginning — as happens with gender inequalities and widespread poverty imbalances. The existence of these factors will mean that market demands in the economy do not in any sense reflect people's social needs, but instead reflect the effective demand of a small minority of quite wealthy people. The result (to put the outcome in stark terms) can be a society in which beautifully constructed jewellery for the rich is widely produced, and no decent housing or low-cost transportation or health services are provided by the market for the poor. In such circumstances, the poor majority in urban slums will suffer epidemics that kill the rich as well, until the day the poor revolt ...

Similar contradictions result from factors that simply cannot be priced in the marketplace, such as environmental effects, or the social consensus that supports the rule of law. These are public goods, with an impact that cuts across society regardless of what individuals may do in the marketplace. It is not possible to respond fully to environmental concerns simply through market-place pricing variations, even though some use of such economic incentives may make sense to assist regulatory efforts in certain cases. And once the social underpinnings of the rule of law are destroyed, men with guns will dominate, and personal security will disappear, as in Somalia, parts of Colombia, and many U.S. inner cities.

The individualistic, narrowly economic neo-liberal vision sketched here may seem overdone and exaggerated. But the reality is that minimizing the role of the state in general and downplaying community social concerns are at the heart of the concerted effort to make the world safe for individual economic enterprise that motivates conservative philosophers, neo-liberal politicians, and powerful corporations at the end of the twentieth century. This is a goal that was achieved before, at the end of the nineteenth century, and there is no reason why social forces with such easily popularized ideas so supportive of privileged interests should not aim to re-establish their dominance. Success, ironically, as the World Bank has now pointed out, would ultimately lead to the undercutting of economic markets, as ineffective states prove unable to ensure the rule of law and the continuance of competition on which successful market efficiency depends. Globalized capitalism has also shown its basic instability in 1997-98. An avoidance of dealing with the gross inequalities of spreading poverty and the discrimination at the heart of gender inequity threaten the long-term market role. But unsophisticated narrow arguments to dismantle the over-bearing state are unlikely to be countered by tough realities like this.

It is therefore crucial to outline a vision of the future different from this neo-liberalism of social demolition. The rearguard, status-quo defence of the social welfare state which has so far countered the neo-liberals in advanced industrial societies seems a losing strategy.

A new vision with strong social values is emerging in some of the democ-ratizing countries of the South, and that vision may be what is needed. The new vision is community-based, decentralist, democratic, and egalitarian. It rests on six basic propositions that emerge from a fundamental reorien-tation seen in many Southern countries — views that are making changes happen.

A) Mass poverty is no longer acceptable, and therefore social and economic policy must make rapid poverty reduction, especially among children, the fundamental priority concern. In Southern coun-tries this has meant new attention to land redistribution, dismantling many ISI privileges, and emphasis on new infrastructure and credit/marketing support for small-scale farmers and tenants. On land reform, South Africa is taking a particular lead, as are various states in India. Grass-roots build-ing of smaller farmer-run co-ops in Uganda and Namibia have been part of the same shift, as has ending ISI trade protection and building rural feeder roads in Ghana.

B) A crucial antipoverty element is gender equity; this is a priority not just to counter the discrimination that prevents contributions from women and men from being fairly recognized in society; but the effort against poverty, especially child poverty, requires a major focus on the inequality that women experience. Particularly strong efforts to promote education for young girls are crucial to this goal. So are changes in rural extension institutions and land tenure to recognize the key role of rural women. South Africa, again, has been especially energetic in stressing this perspective, with its various women's bureaus in government. Bangladesh has been another leader with its stress on credit for rural women through BRAC and the Grameen Bank.

C) A third basic element in the new vision is that environmental con-cerns, with long-term effects on the sustainability of local communi-ties and the viability of national societies, must be brought fully into

the political economy decision-making process. Environmental considerations are immensely important in Southern countries, from how timber concessions in Malaysia have disrupted local peasant economies and destabilized gender balances, to the process by which Solomon Islands women led reform moves that safeguarded communal fisheries, to the land monopolization that cattle- and shrimp-raising in Honduras led that increased child malnutrition for most rural families. Some Southern countries have shown that community-based environmental priorities can be made predominant in a democratic context — such as Costa Rica, in which local peasant forces have been able to reshape forestation plans so as to open tree-planting incentives to smaller as well as larger landowners[14] — or such Indian states as Kerala.

D) People should be able to participate vibrantly in shaping what is happening to their communities and their opportunities in those communities. Community-based civil society movements have grown explosively in many Southern countries. They have been encouraged by governments and have found greater capacity to influence their context because of a decentralization of government powers from the centre to local districts and regions. Thus growing community-based groups have made use of regional decentralization in the Philippines, since democracy was established, to shape local priorities.[15] Community-based groups have worked to develop the region on a decentralized basis in Northern Ghana. Local farmer user committees in Mali have been able to bring the national agricultural research effort to respond much more specifically and appropriately to particular farm needs in different areas.

E) Democratic choice in political institutions is essential to safeguarding the rights of community-based movements, giving citizens the chance to shape the direction of their society and providing accountability that keeps political leadership more honest and committed to the country. This availability of choice depends not just on free elections, but on media independence, clear constitutional rules, and a democratic political culture of free speech, free assembly, and the rule of law. There has been, as we've seen, a remarkable upsurge of democratic institutions in most Southern countries, but particularly dramatic cases illustrate the shifts that have taken place and the results for societies — such as Mozambique, where two parties that were fighting a civil war just short years ago now combine in parliament to strengthen the country in bargaining for international debt relief and infrastructure loans to restart a battered economy. Central America is another important case in which repression and revolution are being replaced by governments aimed at reconciliation.

F) A final and fundamental strand in the vision has been achieving the economic space and policy leverage in the global economy to establish national social priorities that reflect national goals and priorities. Achieving such independent space and greater policy leverage has required a realistic appraisal of global economic pressures, resistance to high external debt burdens, greater orientation to export opportunities to cover import needs, and more attention to indigenous technological capacity to encourage more appropriate technology choices and reduce dependence on foreign multinationals. Such goals have also required strategic macroeconomic policy, making full use of flexible exchange rates and interacting effectively with the World Bank and IMF. Excluding the IFIs would rank as unrealistic, and a country such as Ghana has shown it is possible to deal with them, stress antipoverty initiatives (like PAMSCAD), and increase significantly the funding for health and education social priorities essential to its future development. Zimbabwe has also made an increased commitment to key social priorities in a context of macrostabilization.

The emerging Southern vision, then, is a direct contradiction of the neoliberal emphasis on narrow economic individualism and a deconstructed state. The vision stresses democratic, community-based action to overcome poverty, working through a participatory state, that is activist on gender and environmental concerns and stresses social priorities in a framework of realistic macroeconomic balance. An *effective state* is crucial to realizing such a vision. An *activist and responsive parliament* will be a critical instrument in connecting local and national levels of communication and change. A growing sense of *decentralized national unity* will be essential to building the sense of social solidarity within Southern countries that make such profound reorientations succeed.

How widespread is this sort of vision among Southern countries? It is not possible to provide a comprehensive "count," because the nature of an emerging vision is its diffuse breadth and differing pattern of emphases. The particular manifestations that appear in different countries also reflect the many different social and economic conditions faced by specific Southern nations. But it is possible to stress that community-based movements against rural poverty are emerging widely. The trends towards democratization have been seen in the great majority of Southern countries, decentralization has taken place in most, the drive towards both macroeconomic balance, including more educational-health spending efforts, is widespread, and environmental policy concerns are also a major focus in very many countries. Gender equity is the focus of women's groups in the great majority of Southern countries, too, although there is still more open wage and job access discrimination than in advanced industrial countries. Nevertheless, this emerging democratic, "outsider" vision clearly has powerful strands reflected in many Southern countries, and its various dynamics will undoubtedly come together as an integrated perspective as the movements to build alliances for change move forward.

But should this be solely a Southern vision? For many Canadians, these six elements of a different vision of the future connect powerfully to unease and opposition with respect to the impact of the neo-liberal vision in our own country.

In 1990, all of Canada's Members of Parliament, from all parties, voted for a resolution that aimed to end child poverty by the year 2000. By 1998, though, the extent of that poverty was greater than it was in 1990; and years of high national unemployment had made the depth of such poverty greater, as real disposable incomes for most Canadians continued to decline throughout the decade. So a vision that starts from a priority focus on reducing poverty, especially for children, speaks directly to Canadians, too. So too does the emphasis on a vibrant participation by Canadians in decisions that affect them. Many Canadians clearly feel left out of meaningful roles in our Ottawa-centred system, as shown in the upsurge in anti-Ottawa movements in Quebec (the Bloc Québécois) and in the West (the Reform Party). One party wants to destroy the federal government, the other wants to reduce its role to marginal, because "somebody else" runs things in Ottawa. Yet civil society movements in Canada are commonly dismissed by the main political parties as "special interests" — rather than as the contributors to social and community life described in Southern countries.

At the same time, Canadian democracy is seen as increasingly narrowed by the similarity of national party views, the monopolization of the media by several huge corporate empires (the Bassetts and Baton Broadcasting, the Thomson chain, the Conrad Black chain), and the weakening of the CBC. A revitalization of democracy and of Parliament in Canada could give Canada more dynamism and help energize communication between local and national levels. Environmental concerns and gender equity issues are also areas in which policy momentum has lagged in Canada in recent years, as a result of the narrow economic individualism encouraged by neo-liberalism.

Finally, the country's recent ultracautious macroeconomic strategy has had profoundly negative effects on social priorities. The federal government's reductions of some $7 billion in transfers to the provinces for health and educational expenditure[16] have led to extensive pressure on the quality of medical care and of education in Canada, representing an approach to macroeconomic policy balance that has been far more regressive than in many Southern countries. The Liberal federal government set tough but realistic goals of reducing the level of the federal deficit to 3 per cent of national income, which would have begun to reduce debt significantly as a share of national income. But the government then set out to overachieve this target in a massive way, so that the federal deficit would be eliminated entirely by the 1997-98 fiscal year; and a large surplus of at least $3 billion was projected for the 1998-99 fiscal year. That approach represented such a major imbalance in strategy, between the stress on tough economic targets to reassure the investment community and the neglect of social commitments of great significance to the vast majority of non-wealthy Canadians that by early 1998 unattended Canadian patients were dying in the clogged hallways of hospital emergency rooms while unemployment levels remained close to 9 per cent.

The Southern vision, then, of a democratic antipoverty strategy, community-based and using a participatory state, relying on a balanced macroeconomic policy to maintain social priorities, aimed at environmental and gender concerns, represents a counterview that also speaks to Canadians. The vision may seem more crucial in the Southern countries, where more than a billion live in serious rural and urban poverty. But the nature of the international economy is what helps maintain this poverty, and a change in vision in the North, in countries like Canada, would contribute to changing that global structure, too.

3: Conclusion

The human tragedies of global poverty are real. They have names and faces and fears and hopes.

In this book I have collected together some of their experiences and situations, from the sparse life of fishing families in isolated reed houses in remote parts of Zambia to the abandoned baby girls in underfinanced orphanages in poorer regions of China to the Mexico City women forced to endure pollution and low incomes as they try to maintain their families in Xochimilcho. I have also suggested certain major reasons for the inequalities they represent. In rural areas and urban centres, powerlessness has been at the heart of their poverty. And democracy, interacting with community-based group initiatives, has begun to change that basic reality. That is the most fundamental finding of this book.

Democracy is not a wonder-drug, some miracle cure for a social cancer. It is a complex, institution-based process of growing community participation in decisions that also makes governments listen more to people and account to them for what takes place. Real democracy depends on access to information, on honest media, on fair rules to give different viewpoints an equitable chance to be heard, on independent judicial rulings, and on open interaction between political representatives and the people who elect them. Democracy does not work fast, and it can be undercut by powerful private power groups. But democracy also opens the introduction of options that most societies in human history have never experienced, making choices real that can achieve change.

Policies matter, of course, in such democratic choices. Personalities matter, too. But perhaps more than anything else, visions make the difference in the broad directions that democratic societies choose. One could argue that it is the failure of vision in Canada that has left so many choices gravitating towards neo-liberal state demolition, or towards Quebec sovereignty. Both of these political movements offer visions, while other choices offer management of the status quo.

In many Southern countries, another vision is emerging — bottom-up, gender-conscious, democratic, "green," and stressing social priorities and macroeconomic balance. That vision is aimed above all at widening opportunities to overcome poverty.

How should a vision be judged? Perhaps the key questions to ask are, does it respond to the most important realities that mark the global context, and does it do so with a sense of energy and potential to achieve meaningful change? On that basis, the new Southern vision seems to represent a powerful force. It offers hope towards which people can work ... both South and North.

Notes

1 Personal Interview with G. Kwesi Baiden, ARDA Ghana Director, Accra, May 1996.
2 See Department of Finance, Canada, Budget 1995, Ottawa, 1995; also C. Sanger, "A New Era Breaks for South as Aid Budgets are Chopped," *Review: A Newsletter of the North-South Institute*, Spring 1995, p.1.
3 Andrew Clark, "Problems Ahead?" *Review: The North-South Institute Newsletter*, vol.1, no.1 (1997), pp.1-2. This paragraph reflects further revisions in the 1998 federal budget.
4 Ibid., p.2.
5 See Elaine Beaudoux, Andre Bourque, Marie-Helene Collion, Jean Delion, Dominique Gentil, Charles Kabuga, Jurgen Schwettman, Ashih Shah, "Farmer Empowerment in Africa through Farmer Organizations: Best Practices," *AFTES Working Paper*, no.14 (1994), Agricultural Policy and Production, Technical Department, Africa Region, World Bank, Washington, D.C.
6 C. Malena, "Relations between Northern and Southern Non-Governmental Development Organizations," *Canadian Journal of Development Studies*, vol.XVI, no.1 (1995), pp.11-16.
7 Ibid., p.21.
8 See Jessica Vivian, "NGOs and Sustainable Development in Zimbabwe: No Magic Bullets," in *Development and Environment*, ed. Ghai, pp.167-93.
9 See Malena, "Relations between Northern and Southern Non-Governmental Development Organizations," pp.21-22, on power relations between Northern

and Southern NGOs. "Traditionally, (Northern NGOs') control over financial resources has allowed them to exercise their influence over (Southern NGOs) — controlling Southern organizations' activities and dictating the development agenda.... Partnership primarily and unavoidably implies a transfer of power from (North to South). Until a more equitable balance of power between (Northern and Southern NGOs) is realized, it is unlikely that partnership will be transformed from rhetoric into reality."

10 *Government of Canada Policy for CIDA Concerning Human Rights, Democratization and Good Governance* (Ottawa: CIDA, December 1995), p.4.
11 Press release, "Canada Drops to 14th in World Economic Freedom Ranking," The Fraser Institute, Vancouver, May 27, 1997, p.2.
12 See "Crusading Editor Takes a Breather in Canada," *The Ottawa Citizen*, May 28, 1997, p.A4.
13 Fraser Institute, "Canada Drops to 14th in World Economic Freedom Ranking," p.3.
14 Utting, "Social and Political Dimensions of Environmental Protection in Central America," p.253.
15 See Canadian Urban Institute, *Canada-Philippines Co-operative Program in Economic Development and Environmental Protection: Guimaras Experience in Community-Based Planning,* Toronto, 1996.
16 Department of Finance, *Budget 1995*, Ottawa, February 1995, section on "The Canada Social Transfer."

Index

food crisis (1972-73) 79
foreign aid 149, 208, 211
foreign investment 32, 34, 106, 110, 131, 208. *See also* capital investment flows; equity investment
forestation 218. *See also* afforestation; deforestation; reforestation
formal sector 111, 112-15, 116. *See also* informal sector
"Four Tigers" 102
France 32, 105
Fraser Institute 214-15
free trade (Canada) 24-25
Furtado, Celso 22, 53

Gabon 28, 121
gender equity 219; movement towards 16; and industrialization 108-11; and informal sector 115-16; in Bangladesh 185-86; as antipoverty strategy 186; need for strategy reorientation 189; in urban areas 193; as crucial antipoverty element 217
gender inequalities 5; and poverty 13, 74-79, 93; in industrial sector 123; debates on 188-89
Germany 32
Ghana, social problems 3; African success story 3; poverty and inequality 7; child-related poverty data 10; regional disparities 15; peasant cash-crop production 28, 30; Agricultural Bank loans 69; cocoa export prices 70-71; community development efforts 73; peasant women's labour 74; "double day" 74; women's poverty 75; women and cocoa production 75; deforestation 78; community-based initiatives 78-79; maize production 81, 84, 181, 190; Canadian water projects 94; schooling (1976-77) 108; migration levels 108-9; informal sector 111, 112; small enterprises 113-14; formal sector 114-15; reduction of poverty levels 123; economic shocks (1973-82) 132-35; response to economic crisis

138-39; IFI intervention 140-44, 150-52; growth and inflation rates 142; effects of structural adjustment 153; disagreements with World Bank policies 153; as IFI success 154; agriculture project 165; press freedom 170; move to democratization 171-72, 173-74; PAMSCAD program 173; rural politics 173; women's organizations 175, 189; rural community-based organizations 177; environmental groups 179; shifting policy priorities 185; rice production 190; rural infrastructure 191, 192; role of MPs 198; rural-based politics 199-200; decentralization 201, 218; interaction between community-based organizations and government 201-2, 203; building infrastructure 217; and IFIs 219
Gill, Stephen 20-22
Gini index 7, 8, 9, 156
Girvan, Norman 53
globalization 20
global poverty 4-5
government, decentralization of 201, 219
Grameen Bank (Bangladesh) 176, 186, 217
Gramsci, Antonio 20
Great Britain. *See* Britain
Green Earth Organization (Ghana) 179
Green Revolution 67; impact of 79-85; in Mexico 87; dynamism needed 92; countering poverty 93-94; and rural development policy 189-91; responsive to peasant needs 204. *See also* irrigation; seed technology
Guatemala, poverty and inequality 7; child-related poverty data 10; land inequalities 86; poverty extremes 156; land ownership 191

Haiti 10, 11
"Harambee" movement (Kenya) 73
Hart, Keith 112

If you have enjoyed reading this book, you will be interested in the following recently published Garamond Press titles:

Pat and Hugh Armstrong et al
MEDICAL ALERT: New Work Organizations in Health Care

William K. Carroll ed.
ORGANIZING DISSENT: Contemporary Social Movements in Theory and Practice, (second, revised edt.)

Catherine Cavanaugh and Jeremy Mouat, eds.
MAKING WESTERN CANADA: Historical Essays

Patricia Cormack, ed.
MANIFESTOS AND DECLARATIONS OF THE 20TH CENTURY

Tania Das Gupta
RACISM AND PAID WORK

Robert Hackett and Yuezhi Zhao
SUSTAINING DEMOCRACY? Journalism and the Politics of Objectivity

David W. Livingstone and J. Marshall Mangan
RECAST DREAMS: Class and Gender Consciousness in Steeltown

David W. Livingstone
THE EDUCATION-JOBS GAP

John McMurty
UNEQUAL FREEDOMS
The Global Market as an Ethical System

Sylvia O'Meara and Doug West, eds.
FROM OUR EYES: Learning from Indigenous Peoples

Chris Schenk and John Anderson, eds.
RE-SHAPING WORK: Union Responses to Technological Change

Please contact us if you would like to receive a catalogue or more information:

Garamond Press, 67 Mowat Ave., Suite 144, Toronto, On. M6K 3E3
Phone 416-516-2709, fax 416-516-0571, e-mail garamond@web.net
http://www.garamond.ca/garamond/

AGMV
MARQUIS
Québec, Canada
1999